Douglas Brooke Wheelton Sladen

A Japanese marriage

Douglas Brooke Wheelton Sladen

A Japanese marriage

ISBN/EAN: 9783742876416

Manufactured in Europe, USA, Canada, Australia, Japa

Cover: Foto ©Thomas Meinert / pixelio.de

Manufactured and distributed by brebook publishing software
(www.brebook.com)

Douglas Brooke Wheelton Sladen

A Japanese marriage

PANESE MARRIAGE

BY

DOUGLAS SLADEN

LONDON

GEORGE BELL AND SONS
AND BOMBAY

1895

PREFACE

THE fact of the most unpleasant personage in this story being a clergyman of the Church of England renders it necessary, I think, for me to mention that I have not the slightest wish to make any attack on The Church. I only attack the particular type which is pharisaic to human happiness.

Bryn Avon went further. Because of the misbehaviour of one particular specimen of that type, she argued that The Church in general was unworthy of the sacrifice she was making for it, and abandoned the principle she had at stake.

Bryn's argument was wrong, but what she did, I think, was right. For the increase of human happiness is the highest end of existence, and Bryn's sacrifice had been decidedly against it.

The rights of the individual in the case of human happiness, as in the case of Society, must not interfere with the comfort of the community of which he is a unit. But, subject to this limitation, the increase of human happiness should take precedence of everything. The desire for a more rational share of it was a great purpose of the New Woman Movement, and, I am thankful to think, has been largely achieved.

Any age is golden in which women are as freed as men.

DOUGLAS SLADEN.

AUTHORS' CLUB,
LONDON.

Note.—'A JAPANESE MARRIAGE' is an attempt to present the life of the English in Japan, as *The Japs at Home* attempted to present the life of the Japanese themselves. There has, I think, been but one widely-read novel on the subject, and that dealt with the old Japan of Samurai days. Of the Japanese this book touches only the lower class, as they were in the Japan before the war, which has proved Dai Nippon, 'Great Japan,' a first-class Power. It is said that the Japanese gave their islands the name of Great Japan, because they felt that their nation would be the Great Britain of the Far East. It is.

A JAPANESE MARRIAGE

BOOK I

CHAPTER I

THE Yokohama United Club is an oasis in a green
land where you are hardly ever out of sight of water
—an intellectual oasis, for in its snug library you
are surrounded by all the old familiar books and all
the newest, by the thousand. Men as a rule only
go there when they are homesick. The three who
have the responsibility of opening this story were
not in the library, but under the verandah staring
out on the narrow, dusty *Bund* with its straggling
avenue of half-fledged fir trees, douched by the spray
every time the wind gets up. They were not looking at the road, or the men-of-war, or the merchant
steamers of half a dozen nations, or the blue hills of
Kanozan, for one of the troupes of performers which
haunt the Club and the two big hotels on the *Bund*
was in full swing amidst a ring of admiring *riksha*
boys and tiny girls carrying the next baby in the
haori on their backs.

A JAPANESE MARRIAGE

This time the performers were trained monkeys—monkey mendicants, two-sworded monkey *Samurai* and monkey *samisen* players. It was a delicious day, blue sky and softest breeze.

'Are Japanese Aprils always as lovely as this?' asked the man in the light tweed suit of two others in immaculate flannels with crimson sashes round their waists and puggarees folded in cunning plaits round their broad Terai hats.

'Except when they aren't,' said Charley Dacres, whose riding and tennis were ahead of his conversational powers, a short, dark, wiry man, with a clear eye and fresh 'about the gills.' His face, on which he wore only a moustache clipped short enough to show a good mouth with very white and even teeth, struck you as being good-looking because it was so well-bred, though his nose had been broken and one eyebrow distorted by a pony treading on him as a conclusion to his first glorious spill in the hunting-field. He was good form, and could do anything a 'Johnnie' ought to do ; but these were his limitations.

'It sometimes rains, you know,' explained Robert Mathdine, whose clothes (sent out from England) fitted him so well that you felt sure he must be a stupid man. He was a tall, loosely-made man, decidedly handsome with his bright blue eyes, florid cheeks, and fair hair elaborately parted behind, because there was not enough to part on the top. The short *retroussé* nose and crisp fair moustache made his face very English.

'I see,' said their questioner. But Mr. Mathdine saw that he didn't, for he added :

'It rains like the very devil when it does begin here.'

Philip Sandys didn't see yet.

'Oh, it always rains here in the summer, you know.'

'Oh—I understand now.'

'Aren't you tired of watching those monkeys yet, Sandys?'

'No, I never saw them before.'

'I think these shows are so dull,' said Mathdine; 'I rather like the little chaps that go about in red flannel and cock's feathers, and tumble, though they don't do it a bit well—but these monkeys and jugglers, I can't stand them at any price.'

Philip was not listening to him—he exclaimed suddenly:

'Look at that jolly little girl who's tumming the *samisen* and changing the monkey's togs. How *blasée* she is, she does the whole thing as if it were such an awful bore; she's very handsome too with her scarlet lips and wild dark eyes.'

Presently Mr. Mathdine said:

'Let's go up to the Avons now.'

Charley Dacres moved off with alacrity, but the new-comer made no sign.

'Aren't you coming up, Sandys?'

'No, I don't know them.'

'Not know the Avons! Oh, that isn't the least consequence, it's open house there, and the jolliest house in Japan. They've crowds of coolies in smart liveries, and the curios in the house would be a fortune.'

Philip pricked his ears.

'Curios? I should like Mr. Avon, I've a mania for curio-hunting.'

'Curio-hunting! God bless your soul, old Avon doesn't go curio-hunting; don't believe he knows one from another. It's *Wan Hing*, his compradore, who buys all these things for him. Haven't you discovered what useful things these Chinese compradores are yet?'

'Oh, well, I couldn't get on without my compradore; of course he does all my business with the Japs. I should be cheated all round if I tried to do it myself; but I don't make him buy my curios for me.'

'Old Avon does, and he gets the very best new things that come into the market.'

'I don't care for new things. I don't think I should like a man who collected his curios in that fashion.'

'But you should see his daughter; she's the best thing in all Dai-Nippon.'

'What is she like?'

'Oh, I can't describe her—she's beautiful.'

'Has he only one daughter?'

'No, he has another. Man, you must see Bryn Avon; she's stunning.'

'Are you sure they won't mind?'

'Mind? No! they won't mind. They're glad to see anybody that's decent; and as manager of your Governor's Line of steamers, you're worth cultivating by a merchant who doesn't charter his own ships.'

'Well, if you'll take the responsibility.'

'Oh, come along,' said Charley Dacres. '*Rikshas —Kuruma-ya!*'

Hardly were the words out of his mouth when there was a race of all the *riksha* boys on the stand,

They chose the three with the cleanest *rikshas* and the smartest white topees, which, however, the boys took off before they commenced running, and hung on the shafts. In less than half a minute they were flying along the *Bund* behind their swarthy charioteers in dark blue mediæval-looking tunics and hose, past the hotels and the deserted French *hatoba*, and over the little wooden bridge, spanning the creek; which divides the 'Settlement' where Europeans work, from the 'Bluff' where every European lives as soon as he has enough money.

There was another competition at the foot of the Bluff to see which of the bare-legged coolies hanging about with coils of rope upon their arms should push the *rikshas* behind as they crawled up the steep incline. They passed a little row of curio-shops.

'There, Sandys,' said Mr. Mathdine, 'you'd better try those—No, not now—' he added anxiously, as he saw him preparing to pull up, 'they won't stick you much there; their customers are the people who live on the Bluff, and know the value of the trash too well; it's off the beat of globe-trotters. They never go up the Bluff except to feed with the residents, and that after dark.

'Here we are,' he said presently, after they had turned off the main road for a while and rattled along a narrow lane between high banks topped with English shrubs, and looking for all the world like an outskirt of Tunbridge Wells. They drew up momentarily outside an ancient Japanese gate over-shadowed by a heavy roof, with turned-up toes of the orthodox Far East fashion, the whole elaborately carved and painted red.

A JAPANESE MARRIAGE

'Another of the compradore's bargains,' said Mr. Mathdine under his breath ; ' he got it for ten dollars, and it's said to be ten hundred years old.'

The gate was open. The Avons' gate was never closed until the last guest had sped at night. A smiling Japanese, in a dark blue cotton *kimono* with a Cambridge-blue worm squirming over his back, knew them and said, ' Ohayo, Mathdine San, Ohayo, Daker San.'

Mr. Mathdine said that Mr. Avon liked to shed an Oriental air over his establishment and entertainments, and instructed his servants to intermix plenty of Japanese in their conversation with his guests. All his dining-room servants spoke some English. He further added that the Cambridge-blue worm was the Japanese symbol for water, which some savant had told Mr. Avon to be the meaning of his name.

' *Ohayo*, sir,' the servant said to Sandys, who was a stranger, and whose name he did not know.

' *Ohayo*,' said Philip, who had been studying his vocabulary, and knew it meant good morning. It was 4 P.M. by the clock on the Bluff Assembly Rooms. From the Temple doorway to the house it was not far, and the interval was roofed over like the approach to a temple. The house was what rich Melbourne people would call a cottage—a cottage with a ball-room, a billiard-room and a score of bedrooms, covering a good slice of an acre. Having only one story constitutes a cottage in Melbourne. Its lowness made no difference to the view, for it stood on the very summit of the Bluff, one of the queer crumpled hills so typical of Japan that they have been immortalised on the willow pattern plate.

A JAPANESE MARRIAGE

Distance and height are no object when you have every usable kind of conveyance from a carriage and pair to a *jinriksha*. There are not many carriages and pairs in Japan ; the proud possessor almost ranks with an ambassador.

'We won't go into the house, Sandys,' said Mr. Mathdine, leading the way out sideways (Japanese covered ways have no side walls) into a garden that recalled to Philip, but certainly not to Mr. Mathdine or Mr. Dacres, the original meaning of the word paradise. Very likely they had never noticed the clumps of palmettos, the coppices of bamboo, the avenue of flowering fruit trees, and the hundred architectural devices of that paragon of taste, the Japanese landscape gardener. Probably the sole comment they had ever made on the garden was 'the only decent tennis court in Yokohama.'

It was the landscape gardening that riveted Philip's attention ; he hardly noticed the brilliantly-attired players on the several courts, and the swarm of coolies fielding the balls or scuffing along to bring relays of refreshment.

Suddenly out of one of the sets a girl emerged, escorted by a tall auburn-haired young Englishman of the aristocratic type, and the grave, brave face so often immortalised by Lady Butler.

'I'm so glad you've come, Mr. Mathdine and Mr. Dacres ; you know Lord Romney, I think.'

They exchanged greetings in the rather effusive way you contract when over 10,000 miles from home.

'We've brought Mr. Sandys with us, Miss Bryn.'

Bryn took him in at a glance with her quick eye,

7

without appearing to look at him. A well-knit man
of medium height with a straw-coloured beard, and
rather severe features, softened by kindly gray eyes,
and at rare intervals by a smile which lit up the
whole face. Not very well dressed, hardly above the
average in form, probably tiresomely in earnest. She
did not ask, nor did his friends vouchsafe, any explanation as to who he was. They promptly got up
a new game of tennis, from which he was left out,
standing like the last lamp-post in an unfinished
street. Mr. Mathdine and Bryn were to play Lord
Romney and Mr. Dacres. The people who had
been playing with Bryn when the last comers
arrived simply drifted away; they were evidently
not astonished at being left in this unceremonious
fashion.

CHAPTER II

EARLIER in the afternoon there had been a breeze
at Netheravon, as the merchant had called his seat,
without seeing any inappropriateness in the name
for the highest ground in Yokohama. There had
been two little breezes in fact.

'Bryn,' said her sister, 'I do wish you'd see if the
boys (as they call servants in Japan) have got all the
refreshments right. I am tired out with bustling
round Lane and Crawford's, the French Store and
Mei-Di-Ya's, trying to get a change—we always
seem to have the same thing.'

'Oh, Mary, you must do it. I'm resting before the people come.'

'But you haven't done anything all the morning.'

'But I'm going to play tennis all the afternoon; and you can go and lie down when the people come.'

Hardly had she composed herself again to her novel when there was a knock at the door, and her father came in, a liberty that indulgent and *laissez-faire* parent had not ventured to take for several years.

Bryn smelt battle, and jumping up went to the looking-glass and began smoothing her glorious sun-coloured hair, infinitesimally disarranged by lying back as she read. There was pride in every line of features that might have been taken from an old Greek coin, of a figure that would have done for the divine Huntress of the old Greek mythology. There was breed in every point, from her dainty head to her dainty feet.

Arranging her hair put the onus of commencing the conversation on her father; she could go on *ad infinitum* fiddling with hair-pins or brushing the glossy coils no one had ever seen disordered. Mr. Avon felt very nervous; he stood in complete awe of his beautiful daughter; she had a way of looking at him with her calm blue eyes that made him analyse a subject, which would ill bear analysis. This afternoon for some reason or other he had determined to pull himself together; and having ventured into the lioness's den, he thought he might just as well put his head into the animal's mouth.

'What are you going to say to Lord Romney when he comes here this afternoon, Bryn?'

'I'm sure I don't know; it depends on what he says to me. His conversational powers don't as a rule make much demand on one's intelligence.'

'But don't you know what he will say to you this afternoon, Bryn?'

'Mighty little, I should say, judging by his previous efforts.'

'It's no use equivocating; you know he'll ask you to marry him either this afternoon or in the next day or two.'

'Well, I shall say to him what I've said to all the rest, that, so far, marriage has never offered me a greater prospect of complete happiness than I at present enjoy.'

'But just think of Lord Romney! his estates are unpauperised and he is certainly *distingué*-looking; most people would call him very handsome——'

'Oh!'

'——Red hair and freckled face suit his style, and you can't help admitting that he looks what he is.'

'Well, in any case, I should never marry a man whose looks——'

'Well, think what else he has to offer; title, an ancient and unimpeachable name, youth, popularity, and quite a fair share of brains.'

'I could never marry Romney, father, I couldn't love him.'

'It's too bad of you, Bryn. You have had offer after offer from the very best people who come out to Japan. You would not accept Captain Graceby, the world-famed cricketer, with his splendid mill property in Lancashire, or Clement Smith the M.P., who is sure of an Under-Secretaryship when his party get back into power after the general election ; you refused the Marquis of Dorset point blank ; you wouldn't listen to Mr. Bogardus, the handsome young Boston millionaire who has acclimatised the sporting *régime* of England in New England ; and, to come nearer home, you have never allowed Mr. Mathdine or Mr. Dacres to broach the subject to you, though their fathers are heads of the two principal firms in Japan, one of them a baronet, and it is notorious you could have either of them to-morrow. I could mention a dozen others—good enough matches for an earl's daughter every one of them—you have either prevented from coming to the point or unceremoniously rejected.'

'But, father, why do you want me to marry so particularly ? I am only twenty, and I am so happy in my home that I regard with absolute repulsion the idea of surrendering myself to the desires and caprices of a man. You may think me a butterfly. I own that amusement is the central fact of my existence, and that my demeanour to men must seem heartless ; but I have feelings which amount to something like convictions, on this point. Father,' she added, suddenly presenting her red, haughty lips for a kiss, 'why do you want me to leave my home, that is such a paradise to me ?'

The handsome, pretentious Dundreary-whiskered face of Latimer Avon winced ; but he recovered his guard with a little stereotyped speech in the voice of superiority that sounds as if it came from a mouth full of sawdust.

'Well, you know, er-er, I might die any time,

you know, er-er; and your poor sister is not a marrying girl, and I should like to see one of you settled in life, don't you know, er-er, so as to give the other the status of a home. I should like you to contemplate an early marriage, and if Lord Romney could be the man I should not be displeased. Think of that, Brynhild, my love. I don't think we ought to call you Bryn any longer now—it was only a baby abbreviation. Think over what I've said, don't you know. There's a good girl, er-er.'

Bryn, christened Brynhild, sighed, and, noticing that the guests were arriving, stepped across the grass with the elastic grace which was so conspicuous a charm in her, showing her lovely white teeth in the laugh that was half welcome and half *insouciance*.

CHAPTER III

PHILIP stood where the quartette left him, riveted by Bryn's charms. He saw at a glance that Mr. Mathdine and Mr. Dacres felt quite at home in the household, and were both captives to her proud beauty and splendid physique. And envy smote him.

He hardly expected her to make much of a show at tennis. Her dress, which was in the latest London fashion, fitted her so clingingly, and she was so perfectly corseted that activity seemed out of the question.

And yet, as the game went on she displayed an
activity and dexterity which few girls achieve, and
this without her childish fairness flushing to anything deeper than a becoming rose, without a lock
straying from her glossy coils. He was relieved to
notice that she was too absorbed in the game to
allow either Mr. Mathdine or Mr. Dacres or the Peer
any attention beyond the recognition of a brilliant
stroke. But he argued ill of her approachability ;
a woman who does not turn a hair with violent
exercise is not apt to relax her reserve. As the
game progressed it grew obvious that her partner
and she were overmatched. After his weeks on
board ship Lord Romney could not be expected to
be in much practice, but cricket and racquets had
quickened his eye, and when one of his slashing
volleys chanced to come to Bryn, there was nothing
for her to do but to cover her collapse with a half-
beseeching smile to her partner that made her infinitely girlish and attractive. To Philip it seemed
as if the stars in their courses were fighting for Mr.
Mathdine. For the more that Bryn was unamazoned
by Lord Romney's slashes, the more superbly he
rose to the occasion. Time after time her white
teeth shone as he served off the game, or her blue
eyes flashed over his heavy cutting returns. Mr.
Mathdine, though not a person of intellect, was level-
headed enough to appraise these blandishments at
their real value—compliments to his play ; but
Philip, who had never seen her before that afternoon,
felt as if he would have given a year's income to be
Robert Mathdine—the most fortunate man on the
earth we inhabit, the acceptable lover to this woman

A JAPANESE MARRIAGE

How queenly the curved mouth was, with its hauteur in repose, its rare resistless smile; what wonderful blue eyes they were, the clear violet-coloured American eyes, dewy but unconquerable; what gold there was in the hair; what a touch there was in that quiet measured voice of the Amazon deaf to love but worth a kingdom to conquer into love!

Philip Sandys's heart went out to this imperial woman; he stood on and on, watching every motion of the lithe body, the proud repose habitual to the face. Had he known her full name of Brynhild its aptness would have rejoiced him.

While he stood gazing at her physical perfections he heard a soft, almost timid-sounding voice, which said nothing more sentimental than:

'Won't you come and have a cup of tea?' pointing to a little summer-house on the other side of the lawn, copied from the solemn tea-drinking chamber of a temple in Kyoto. There was a whole army of boys; queer spindle-legged, monkey-faced dwarfs of men, looking in their tight doublets and hose for all the world like so many retainers from one of Pinturicchio's pictures, or varlets from the Elizabethan stage, only instead of gay silks these picturesque garments were made of indigo-coloured Bombay cotton, adorned in the middle of the back, like the porter's, with that monstrous Cambridge-blue worm; and their feet were cloven into sandals instead of elongated in preposterous slippers. They were carrying on costly old Japanese dishes all the luxuries procurable in Yokohama, and a good many specially imported by Mr. Avon himself; but Philip hardly

14

deigned these a glance. He was not a gourmet and was far more interested in the native delicacies, in and out of season, oranges scarcely bigger than cherries and destitute of pips ; *persimmons* long past their time, and *biwas* (called by the Australians loquats, and by the Yokohama colony Japanese medlars) not yet in. There were even little cups of the straw-coloured Japanese tea, which the ordinary Briton in Japan despises, but which Mr. Avon liked to have handed round at his parties with choice *saké*, costly seaweeds, and all manner of Japanese confectionery, because he thought this little touch of the Oriental might prove an extra attraction to the globe-trotting big-wigs whom it was part of his system to entice to his house while they were in Yokohama.

Philip Sandys made his selection from the trays offered him by at least five or six kow-towing boys, while he was taking in the personality of Bryn's sister.

After Mr. Mathdine's innuendo he owned to himself a certain agreeable surprise. She had not Bryn's style, but then she had never been a queen. with kneeling crowds of faithful subjects. Her slender figure had not the exquisite rounding of Bryn's, but then it was slender, and her hair, though it was brown instead of golden, had a distinct auburn tint in it. Nothing could have been more perfect than the shape and set of her head. But her features, though perhaps as regular as Bryn's, lacked their uniqueness, and her eyes were only bluey gray, sadly stinted in blue. She was in brief a little, colourless, and rather meagre edition of Bryn. She had a good deal of quiet grace ; but, after her sister's glorious combination of dash and glow, one could not look at the wan clear-cheeked face without contracting the idea that Bryn's wonderful vitality had in some way nourished itself on her sister's, as the young pelicans in mythology fed upon their mother's blood.

Mary Avon's one object in life seemed to be to avoid doing anything that might grate on Bryn's rather aggressive sensibilities.

The Avon establishment was conducted for two ends—Bryn's gratification, and entertaining the best people: the little magnates of the little settlement of Europeans in Japan, and the big magnates who had left home to see the world in three months, a week of which they spent in the Grand Hotel at Yokohama.

When he had finished tea they drifted into a walk round the garden. He couldn't help confessing to himself what a poor creature she looked beside Bryn. Then an idea struck him.

' You're looking very tired ! '

' I'm feeling very tired,' she replied, but did not add why.

' Perhaps you'd rather sit down ? '

' Oh, presently, when we find a shady place.'

Mary Avon was one of those people with whom you feel you can be inquisitive. He could not resist hazarding :

' Your sister seems to like Mr. Mathdine very much ? '

' Bryn doesn't like anybody very much.'

' Except, of course, your father and yourself.

' I don't know.'

He began to feel sorry for the girl,

'If it isn't a very rude question to ask, how old are you, Miss Avon?'

'Only twenty-two.'

Why only? She certainly did not look more; did she mean to imply that she felt an old maid already?

'Would you like to see our Chinese garden?'

'Oh yes; I love anything typically Oriental.'

'Don't you have them in England?'

'No; I don't think I exactly know what they are. Why, haven't you ever been to England?'

'No; neither of us has ever been out of Japan, except down to the China ports. Papa is a merchant, you know, and is haunted by the idea that something would happen to his business if he left it and went so far as England.'

'Were you born in Japan, then?'

'Oh yes, here in Yokohama, both of us.'

She led the way to where a depression on the hill top, perhaps a crater once, had been formed into a tiny lake studded with islands, connected by toy bridges and decorated with votive lanterns, pagodas, and shrines—all of stone. There were carefully trimmed maples, green, pink, copper, white, and variegated, and fir trees trained in the fantastic Japanese fashion round its shores, excepting at the north end, where there was a mass of the fantastic rock-work so prized in Japan and China; and on one island there was a fir tree clipped and tortured into the shape of a peacock with its tail spread, which had been transferred, as it stood, from the garden of a *daimio's* palace, at a huge cost. It was from the garden in question that Mr. Avon's had been imitated,

A JAPANESE MARRIAGE

Philip was lost in admiration, and she was evidently very much gratified with his enthusiastic exclamations, though her replies were not very adequate. She had not much experience of enthusiasm, and, if the truth was told, she would probably have found it more difficult to picture their home without Oriental adjuncts than with.

' Will these little bridges bear ? '

' Oh yes.'

' I'd like to go over all the islands—shall we ? '

' Certainly.'

' But you're tired.'

' No ; I'm better now.'

He interested her ; Mary Avon was not often interested. Perhaps people did not often try to interest her.

' Why — the goldfish have three or four tails each.'

' Six, some of them ; don't they everywhere ? '

' I never saw a goldfish with more than one tail before.'

' How funny,' she said.

' How do you manage that little stream and waterfall at the end of the lake ; is it natural ? '

' I don't know.' Then she broke away from her monosyllables, and added : ' Just there is my favourite place in the garden, where the wistaria's out. You see that wistaria arbour over the water like a tea-house. When it is in full bloom it has bunches of flowers three or four feet long, and they trail over the balcony and dip their ends in the water. Do you have wistaria in England ? '

' Yes ; but not with blossoms four feet long.'

18

'I wonder why? We won't sit there to-day.
I don't like it till all the blossoms are out. I'll
take you to see our Fuji, and then we'll go and sit
in the Dragon's Den.'

'That rock-work place?'

'Yes. It's copied from the Mandarin Garden at
Shanghai. Papa sent Japanese architects over to
China to get the idea.'

The artificial Fujiyama was no more than a tall
mound, with a path winding round it, like the famous
pasteboard Fujiyama in the grounds of Asakusa
Temple. It had a few trees on the top for shade,
and a stone seat for people to rest on while they
took in the view of the matchless snow-mantled
shoulders of the real Fuji, towering 13,000 feet into
the air, a dozen leagues away, and the blue Hakone
Mountains, and the junk-dotted gulf of Tokyo with
the million-peopled city at its head. They rested
a little.

'Now let's go into the Dragon's Den and sit down.'

She led the way into a labyrinth of caves, and
winding stairways, and fretted stone gratings. They
wound in and out, and, when at the end, found a
seat in a Chinese summer-house, with carved black
wood couches and chairs and tables.

Philip felt some misgivings about sitting down.
It was one thing to wander round sight-seeing with
Mary Avon, but it was another to sit down with her
for a long spell. She had not proved overpower-
ingly interesting, although her gentleness and yield-
ingness had something captivating about it. She
had been snuffed out morally, mentally, and phy-
sically by her superb sister, now wholly devoted to

pleasure, though she had in spite of her disinclination
for work been quite the ornament in brains of the
poor little Ladies' College in Japan.

They began by talking, but soon declined into
such gentle exercise as stroking a moustache and
drawing patterns in the dust with a parasol.

Presently they heard voices.   Another couple
had followed them into the Dragon's Den, and the
conversation they overheard was evidently only intended for one listener.   But they were at the
inside end ; they could not get out without passing
the others, and so, after a hurried whispered consulta-
tion, they decided to sit still and hear as little as
possible.

The words they caught were—' Of course, I don't
want to allude to my title, or my wealth, or my
estates, Miss Avon, except in so far as they evidence
that my social position is the kind fitted for you to
shine in.   Won't you reconsider your decision,
Bryn ? '

.   ' Impossible, Romney.   I don't mind calling you
Romney to show you how impossible.   In the first
place, I couldn't marry at all ; in the second, I
couldn't possibly tie myself down for life to a man I
had only known for a week or two.   Men don't
seem to have any idea of the seriousness of marriage.
I'm asked about once a week to exchange a state I
have found a paradise on earth for a lottery with
more blanks than the Manilla sweep.   No, Lord
Romney, I'm not vain enough to suppose that you
will feel my refusal, except for the snub which I
can't help it implying.   If you should, I'd be sorry,
for you're a good fellow, and I can appreciate the

compliment of having a coronet offered for my hand, though it might be misery to accept it. It would be a very remarkable man who could win my consent to marry him.'

'But, Bryn,' he said in a pleading voice, 'you must———'

Just at that moment they came into the summer-house where Philip and Mary were sitting. Bryn with her racquet still in her hand and her cheeks aflame. Lord Romney dignified and *distingué* in spite of his pleading airs. He looked born to command rather than to plead.

There was an awkward pause when Lord Romney broke off his sentence on seeing that they were not alone. Philip was the first to recover his presence of mind.

'We heard enough,' he said. And both the chief actors knew what he meant.

Lord Romney naturally felt annoyed, but he took it so well and with such dignity that he might have gone very near succeeding if he had been inspired to tackle Bryn again in the sympathetic and almost admiring mood with which his humiliation and his tact inspired her.

Outwardly she showed nothing, except a little burning spot on each cheek; but when Philip and Mary retired stammering apologies for what wasn't their fault, he had the bad generalship to arrange the terms of surrender instead of returning to the charge. 'Miss Avon, I asked and obtained your father's consent before I came to you. Shall I———'

'Well, it might be rather awkward for you to

go and explain that it wasn't wanted. I think you'd better let me do it,' she answered with a smile flitting round the corners of her mouth, which showed that the humour of the situation was gradually running away with her. She had played in the old stock comedy of *A Refusal of Marriage* so often, and the hitch in this afternoon's performance had made it none the less diverting. Besides, she was almost afraid to keep serious ; she did not feel so sure of herself as usual. She knew that she did not want to marry, but she was not sure if she could refuse him again just at present. For once in her life she felt rather guilty. She had known that he wanted to propose to her, and she had known that she did not wish to marry him, and yet she had, with her eyes open, been unable to resist giving him the opportunity of proposing by consenting to go into the Dragon's Den with him.

' May I still go with your party to the dancing-girls to-morrow, as was arranged ? '

' Why not ? '

' You won't make any difference to me ? '

' You can be as much with me as ever you like, if you'll promise not to recur to the subject.'. Bryn had quite recovered herself by this time.

' Very well,' he said sadly.

The iron was hot just now, fool !

That night Bryn found herself by no means as glib as she had expected. Her father seemed so thoroughly perturbed by her refusal of Lord Romney, and would hark back to his wish to see one or other of his daughters (which could only mean one) with a fine home of her own before he died, though there did not seem any reason why a hale, young-looking man of fifty should die in such a hurry.

'I suppose you've forbidden him to come to-morrow, Bryn?' he asked of his imperious daughter.

'On the contrary, I distinctly told him that he could.'

'Umph!' said her father to himself, 'worse than I thought.'

He did not understand her as well as usual. In the afternoon, when she and Lord Romney went back to rejoin the tennis party, she had gone up to Philip for a talk. She told herself that she owed it to him; the fact being that he had impressed her; she liked a man who could say or do the right thing at a pinch. A look in the girl's eyes quenched any allusion to what he had involuntarily witnessed.

'Are you a globe-trotter or a recent importation?' she asked.

'A recent importation.'

'Agent for a dozen more insurance companies?'

'No; only for the Sandys Line of steamers.'

'Oh, your name is Sandys, isn't it?'

He nodded.

'A relation?'

'He is my father.'

'I wonder how long it will take you to become a vegetable like the rest?'

'What do you mean?' he asked, doubting if he ought not to be offended.

'Oh, you look like a man of intellect. Every European with any intellect becomes a vegetable after a certain time in Japan. It takes some longer than others, but they can't stop it.'

'But why only the intellectual people?'

'Nothing except money makes any difference to the average man in an office. Life for him is made up of the struggle to get out of bed in the morning, the office, meals, doing the spiciest thing that he can to fool away the time after office hours—and bed when there's no one left to sit up with.'

'You're rather severe on him.'

'Oh, I forgot one thing.'

'What is that?'

'Drinks in between everything.'

'You have also forgotten changing his clothes.'

'Oh—that's his one redeeming feature. A man who takes enough interest in his clothes to change them often wears spotless linen.'

'You've a sharp tongue, Miss Avon.'

'Have I? I can't be sorry, it's the only thing that keeps one from stagnating in this lazy land.'

'You don't look very lazy. I should have thought you danced and played tennis with the energy of a steam-engine. I never saw a girl play tennis so well.'

'Not in England?' she asked with a sudden eagerness.

'Really not.'

Bryn looked quite pleased. She harked back. 'But tennis and dancing don't prevent you stagnating; I feel as if I'd lived behind the door. Japan is all very well as a peepshow for globe-trotters, but it's a poor sort of place to be your whole world—that's to say if you're a European; but I suppose I ought to consider myself an Asiatic—which am I?'

'If you're an Asiatic, Europe no longer leads.'

'Well, I am a most ignorant Asiatic. I positively

don't know anything about anything, beyond what I read with imperfect comprehension in the English society papers.'

'O Lord!' blurted out Philip.

'You pity me,' she said, with rising colour.

'I can't help it—but I'll apologise if you like.'

Bryn turned away ; he thought she was offended ; it was a new sensation to her to be pitied ; perhaps there was a snaky fascination about it. At all events she recovered herself very quickly and said :

'Mr. Sandys, allow me to introduce you to Mr. Spong.'

Mr. Spong was a handsome middle-aged man with an iron-gray Vandyke beard. Though not tall he had a good figure and dressed rather well, while he affected the profoundest contempt for it. As he never made love to Bryn he was her most intimate friend ; for if there was one thing she respected, outside of religion, it was the lash of his tongue. She had modelled the style of conversation, which was to preserve her from stagnating, on his. He was an extraordinary man. He had been a Liberal member of Parliament when 'Liberal' still had some sort of meaning, and he once wrote a satire in the form of an allegory that went through a hundred editions, and was translated into Welsh. He said that he had come to Japan to get away from the Irish question, which led to the libellous assertion that Mr. Gladstone had, in some mysterious manner, made it worth his while to go ; though one would have thought it simpler to exile him to the House of Lords than to Japan. And it was more than intimated that the Home Rule question he sought to avoid was of a different kind. He was accused of exiling himself to get away from his wife ; but the better-informed people thought it was someone else's —or her husband. At any rate, he had never been openly convicted of marriage. As a man who has no ostensible profession is looked upon with suspicion in the East, unless he calls himself a globe-trotter, and globe-trotters don't generally spend five years in Japan, he got himself nominated Consul for Siam, it was currently reported, on the payment-by-results system. He chose Siam because Siam is the only Power which has consuls in places where its subjects never go. It gave him a terrible shock to see a coloured person land, for it might be a Siamese, and the Consul actually have something to do. He gave himself up for lost once ; but the supposed Siamese turned out to be a Cinghalese jeweller selling sapphires and cat's-eyes. An American female doctor with a touch of the tar-brush also gave him a severe shock.

The Consulate for Siam was over a *godown* on the *Bund*. There had never been anything in the *godown*—he said he rented it so as to be able to offer courtesies to Siamese traders when they came, though ill-natured people hinted that the Consul would have found it inconvenient living in a bungalow with only a ground-floor and French windows, at which friends familiarly disposed might pop in without notice. At any rate, it looked very imposing with the Siamese arms painted on a sort of hatchment suspended between his drawing-room windows ; and the Siamese flag, on a scale that would have suited the Eiffel Tower, hoisted from breakfast to dinner on the flagstaff in the front garden. The 8 A.M. to sunset period used for flying bunting on the men-of-war adopted at the other consulates seemed to him merely arbitrary, and he was a man who liked to be particular in trifles, so he hoisted the Siamese flag to inform his friends when he had done breakfast, and had it struck when he wished to go and dress for dinner. Dressing, if he was alone, meant undressing, more or less.

The only thing Siamese about the Consul, except the hatchment and the flag, were his servants. He had Siamese servants partly because he got them for nothing—they were supplied by Siam with a view to interpretation, if the Consul should ever have any duties — partly because, as they could not speak Japanese, they could not gossip much. Pigeon English was the medium of conversation in which the cook did his shopping.

Bryn meanwhile had resumed playing tennis, graciously inviting Lord Romney to be her partner; she felt it was necessary though she knew it was absurd—from a tennis point of view, their opponents being Mr. Mathdine and Mr. Dacres.

'These fellows tire me,' said Mr. Spong. 'This is their office; it wouldn't make the smallest difference to the head office in Japan of Sir Jocelyn Mathdine and Sons, or Dacres Brothers, if they burst with self-importance in this very game. Nobody'd miss 'em, not even Miss Bryn, except their creditors; and I suppose the firms would call in the chits. If they knew as much about 'em as I do, they would do it pretty readily. You can give chits for some very queer things in Japan. But they are the models of the community. What they do, all the young men, who have any pretence to style, pretend to do. Before they came out they left standing orders with their tailors, their hatters, and booters to send out every latest novelty that catches on, and the only reason they play tennis, which I must say they do d——d well, is to prevent their putting on flesh.'

'I don't think it seems a bad line with Miss Avon there.'

'No, d——n them. They are the type of the smart Englishman in the East, who races China ponies and drinks himself into a decline with whiskey and soda without ever getting what is called "the worse." If they were at home their *Malmaisons* would be the envy of the Row.'

'Their sashes are works of art, certainly.'

'I wouldn't trust a man who does his sash as well as that with my great-aunt.'

'You're rather down on them.'

'So would you be if you'd heard them for the last four years drawling out that Japan—from which their families draw revenues like princes—wouldn't be fit to live in if it wasn't for this house.'

'Miss Avon seems a very charming girl.'

'Do you mean what you say ?'

'Well, I suppose so.'

'Or do you mean Bryn ?'

'I meant Miss Bryn.'

'Oh, I thought you meant what you said.'

'Well, isn't Miss Bryn charming ?'

'Everyone in Japan thinks so.'

'Don't you ?'

'No ; I think she is irresistible.'

28

' I hardly understand you.'

' Well, it's like this. I don't think there is—beauty apart—much to draw between her and our friends, except that she doesn't drink and she does go to church.'

' I don't think she looks very churchy.'

' Oh, you don't know these girls. They are such good Low Church people. They have prayers morning and evening, and spend Sunday in going to church, and eating too much, and yawning. Mary goes to stay with the Bishop at short intervals. Bryn draws the line at that. She's as superstitious as the rest of them. I think old Avon regards it all as a sort of fire insurance against the wrath to come.'

' Well, but isn't Miss Bryn nice?'

' She's captivating; she can't help herself; but nobody ever did grow up such a spoiled child. I like it myself; it's so refreshing. It upsets all your ideas about women, and gives you a new start.'

' Mr. Spong,' said Bryn, coming up to him. She had just finished her set. ' I believe you are talking about me, my ears are burning so. I'm sure it isn't any good; but I'll forgive you because I want to make use of you. We are going to make a party to go to Tokyo to-morrow. We want to have a Japanese banquet at the Koyo Kwan, and the Club dancing-girls. We want you to manage it for us. Father says will you order the very best that can be got and let him know what it all costs? You know a member of the Club, don't you?'

' Oh yes; I'll send a boy over with the chit this evening. How many is the party going to consist of?'

'Yourself and us, Lord Romney, Mr. Mathdine and Mr. Dacres, and about six others, four ladies and two gentlemen. How many's that?'

'Thirteen.'

'Oh, father won't go thirteen; we must have fourteen. Won't you make one of the party, Mr. Sandys?'

'Certainly; I should be delighted.'

'Is that settled then, Mr. Spong?'

'Yes. You will have to leave Yokohama by the eleven o'clock train, to do the temples and get the banquet through in decent time. It will take about four hours with the dancing.'

She went back to her game.

'I thought you said they were so very religious,' said Philip. 'Isn't to-morrow Sunday?'

'Yes, but Sunday's the only day you can get the men to go anywhere till after four o'clock. They take such whacking long holidays in the summer, that they can only spare bank holidays for the rest of the year. Think of what might happen if I left Siam unrepresented.'

'What could happen?'

'Some God-damned Siamese would be sure to turn up just to spite me, and get led astray by a *riksha* boy; and the whole affair would come before King Chulalongkorn's Consular Court; and how the blazes should I hold a Court with nothing but these confounded Asiatics? I don't know what I should do unless I got Miss Bryn to come in and sit as my assessor. Except where religion is concerned, that girl has plenty of ruthless common sense at the back of her vagaries.'

'I can't reconcile the idea of religious prejudice and going to a banquet of dancing-girls on Sunday.'

'Don't you see, my dear fellow, these girls were born in Japan? They have grown up in a country of Continental Sundays.'

'H'm, very Continental.'

CHAPTER IV[1]

ON the next morning they rattled off to the station at Yokohama in *rikshas*, making, it must be confessed, a good deal of noise—for the Netheravon party was accustomed to behave like a Government House party in the colonies. Mr. Mathdine had been an A.D.C. in Australia, before he turned his attention to business. As *riksha* after *riksha* drew up, the party proved to consist of Mr. Avon and his two daughters, Lord Romney, Mr. Mathdine, Mr. Dacres, Mr. Spong and Mr, Sandys, with Mr. and Mrs. Sparling, Mrs. Phelps, Mrs. Prince and Mrs. Amory—thirteen. Mrs. Crosby had not turned up.

'She told me positively that she was coming,' said Charley Dacres ; 'but I don't think she often gets up quite so early.'

The train went at eleven.

'You see that fellow Sparling,' said Mr. Spong to Philip, whom he had taken under his protection for the day,. 'he's by way of being an artist. He tried

---

[1] The details of Japanese temples, dishes, dancing, and so on, are founded on the diary from which I wrote *The Japs at Home*. Such minutiœ must be taken from notes.

to be a journalist before he tried to be an artist, and
was such a failure in the latter capacity that he
accepted the Art professorship in a Tokyo university.
His duties are to show the Japanese how to forget
that wonderful touch with which they can make a
brushful of Indian ink indicate a whole landscape.
His own water colours look as if they had been
drawn in pen and ink and filled in with colour ; and
there's something quite Byzantine about his " oils."
The Japanese are delighted. The European style
of painting, as imparted by Professor Sparling, is so
easy to acquire. But he's a good-natured sort of
ass, though he has talked an unconscionable deal of
rot since he found that there was no one in the
settlement who knows enough to expose him. His
wife——'

'Is that his wife with him ? '

'Yes ; she is what is called a jolly little woman,
though I have been unable to find that her frankness
goes beyond her projecting teeth. She has steam
enough to run a Sunday School treat, and laughs
the whole time she is talking. But perhaps that is
to make the teeth look natural. They live in a
hotel at Yokohama, though his work is in Tokyo.
I think she must be afraid of the Japs running away
with her.'

'Who's the old lady ? '

'What, the old Mrs. Grundy with an 1860
face ? '

'I suppose so,' laughed Philip. 'I mean the one
with braids of black hair pulled down over each
temple in the old-fashioned way.'

'They're not black, only she thinks that we think

they are black. That's Mrs. Phelps, the wife of
one of the port officers, who can be useful to
Mr. Avon in business. Otherwise she wouldn't be
here, for she's the most awful old cat in the settlement.'

' And the others ? '

' Mrs. Prince and Mrs. Amory ; they're the wives
of American naval officers, whose ship is at present
in one of the other ports. Mrs. Amory is rather
pretty. Nice woman too, but a good deal of a fool.
I'd rather talk to Mrs. Prince. She looks sour, I
admit ; but those pale women with washed-out hair
and pinched faces sometimes make the truth sound
so sarcastic that it does more damage than a
lie.'

By this time the train was in, and the Japanese
were making their usual *hegira* for it—men, women,
and children, rich and poor, scuffing along as fast
as their clogs would let them run, and carrying
much of their worldly belongings in baskets tied up
in blue and green cloths, or stay-boxes done up in
oiled paper.

The Netheravon party got into a saloon, arranged
not like an American saloon carriage, but with a
seat running all round it. The train was so crowded
that several Japanese got in with them. The men,
as befitted the quality of Japanese rich enough to
travel first class, all in European clothes of a sort.
The women were in the exquisite dress of Japanese
ladies, *kimonos* of gray or dove-coloured silk made
with a graceful simplicity, open at the throat and
confined at the waist with handsome *obés*—broad
sashes of dark brocade folded double and tied in a

3

butterfly bow behind. Their hair was done to perfection, and they wore nothing on their heads.

The Japanese were shy in the presence of the foreigners. Their good taste would not have allowed them to enter the carriage with a party, if there had been room elsewhere. But as soon as the women had kicked their clogs off, and tucked their delicate feet in the snowy white *tabi* under them on the seat, Mary Avon, who happened to be sitting next to them, said something polite to them in Japanese. She and Bryn of course spoke it like natives, and could even read the letters in ordinary use.

The faces of the little women lighted up, and all the Japanese in the carriage bowed. Bryn did not seem to notice them ; she was trying to be interested in Lord Romney, Mr. Mathdine, and Mr. Dacres, whose conversation was at the ordinary level reached by competing lovers.

The gentleness which had prompted Mary was not lost upon Philip, who was growing more and more attracted to a woman who would have been charming if she had not been kept in the shade by her sister.

As they sped past the rice-fields beyond Kanagawa and the shrine of the holy man Nichiren at Ikegami, and the seaweed drying yards at Shinegawa, one of the Japanese gentlemen forgot his European dignity so far as to kick off his shoes and tuck his feet under him like the ladies. It did not take him much trouble. Most Japanese in Japan wear low shoes with elastic sides. To use their graphic expression, they do not make a street of their houses ;

and they pay the same respect to their gods when they go to a temple.

Arrived at Shimbashi, the terminus of Tokyo, Mr. Avon's Japanese house steward, whom he had brought to act as interpreter, and save the party from the trouble of having anything to do but eat, hired *jinrikshas*. The spectacle of fourteen *rikshas*, each with an extra coolie—the Avons did nothing by halves—created a great sensation in Tokyo, where one *riksha* generally does duty for two people (if Japs); the effect being heightened by their running, Japanese-fashion, in Indian file, especially when they turned out of the broad main road from Shinegawa into the narrow Shibaguchi, still further narrowed by the silks hanging outside the shops of the sellers of second-hand stuffs—the said silks having, not infrequently, once formed the garments of the priests of Shiba.

Shiba was a revelation to Philip, who had up to this not got beyond semi-European Yokohama. From the moment that they passed the big *torii*, and big scarlet gateway and Ama-inu and Koma-inu, the queer Japanese lion and unicorn, which guard the principal entrance, he was in fairyland. The fadedness of the temples mattered not to him. He had never seen them in their prime. He felt that he was in Asia at last.

Not that his party were very congenial to such thoughts, as the first exclamation proved.

'Where's that jolly little tea-house you took us to last time, Kano?' said Mr. Mathdine to the Avons' steward, quite with the air of one of the family.

A JAPANESE MARRIAGE

The steward explained in broken, but pretty fluent English, that it was by the Geographer's monument.

'Let's go there,' cried nearly all the party in a chorus.

It certainly was a very charming spot. On a little hill rose a tall obelisk with a bronze map let into its face, and a handsome bronze railing round it, recently erected to some Japanese *Mercator*, who had executed a map of the world known to the Japanese some hundreds of years before. But no one paid much heed to the monument; for right against it was a sweet little tea-house consisting only of a roof and a raised floor, covered with the delicate, primrose-coloured Japanese matting, and supported by a shaft at each corner. Along the eaves hung a row of brilliantly-coloured lanterns to allure patrons by night, and on its floor were some *fu-ton* —flat Japanese cushions for them to sit on, which the Japanese do, tailor-fashion, after kicking off their clogs, while the English sit on the edge with their feet dangling over.

The little *mousmees* came running round from the sort of kitchen attached, where they boiled the water for the tea, stooping and rubbing their knees together—the outdoor salute—while they sucked in their breath and called out *Ohayo*. They brought with them little trays of straw dyed brown, carrying tiny blue and white porcelain cups full of the local abomination, *sakurada*, tea flavoured with salted cherry-blossom, and the horrible Japanese confectionery, made for the most part of bean flour.

Mr. Spong waved them off majestically, and said in his vile Japanese:

A JAPANESE MARRIAGE

'*Irimasen—Yokohama Bieru-saké dozo.   Go!*'
and he held up five fingers.   The *mousmees* flew
back all smiles.   There was more profit to be made
on five bottles of *kirin* beer than on the tea-sales of
a whole day.   The ladies drank the tea (but minus
the cherry-blossom), a pale green decoction without
milk or sugar.   They were all long in the country
and accustomed to drink Japanese tea whenever
politeness demanded.   It is not easy to shop in
Japan without.

Philip meanwhile took stock of their exquisite
surroundings: the temples below peering out of the
dark cryptomerias and acres of pink cherry-blossom;
the tall scarlet pagoda on the hill-slope; the great
city stretching away to the left round the broad
river and the innumerable canals; the blue sea to
the right, with its row of geometrical islands in front
and blue hills on the horizon, dotted all over with
the white sails of junks, square at the top and gathered
almost into a point at the sheet.

Most of the others were too busy doing nothing to
attend to him, but Mr. Spong was always at everybody's disposal until he was bored—usually a matter
of seconds.

'Those islands!   Yes—the most entertaining
thing in Japan.   They're intended for forts.   In Sir
Harry Parkes's days the French had a Minister, who
was nothing more or less than a glorified commercial traveller.   He persuaded the Japanese to
give Frenchmen the orders for these forts.   The
French didn't know what it would cost them to carry
out the contract under such unfamiliar conditions,
and lost heavily by the job in which they hoped to

swindle the Japanese, and the Japanese have never been able to make any use of them since the day they were built. Why, the *Monocacy* could settle them.'

'The *Monocacy*,' said Philip; 'I don't understand.'

'Oh, she's been away at Kobe ever since you've been here. Well, the *Monocacy* is an ancient bone-shaker, a paddle-wheel sound boat, built somewhere about the time of the Civil War, which the Americans have had the temerity to send across the Pacific full of brave men. By some accident she didn't go down with all hands, and she's an admirable ship to give a dance in when she is behind a breakwater. But as a man-of-war you could sink her with a gatling.'

'Now, Punch,' said Bryn, touching Spong's arm with the tip of her parasol, 'you must get off the stump. We're going to be good little boys and girls, and do the pretty temples.'

With the exception of Philip, they trailed through the glorious mortuary shrines of the *Shoguns* in rather a perfunctory way. It was part of Mr. Spong's creed to scoff at all religions and their appurtenances; and the rest were dreadfully *blasés* in things Japanese. Mary, it is true, was quite interested when Philip appealed to her, but it was because she liked being appealed to, and not because the glorious gold lacquer, or riot of ancient carvings in red and green and gilt, or courts of lanterns in stone and bronze and brass, or tall tombs of princes in bronze that was half gold, touched her imagination.

Seeing that he was interested, Mr. Spong rejoined

him and called out, 'Here, Kano, come and tell Mr. Sandys all about these temples.'

'I was going to have asked, when Miss Bryn called you away,' said Philip.

Mr. Spong remembered the familiar 'Punch,' and made a grimace.

'I was going to have asked you,' said Philip, 'how that pagoda on the side of a hill managed to escape the earthquakes which we seem to get about once a week? And how all these temples have escaped?'

'Quite simple! Only a European is foolish enough to build his house on to a foundation in Japan. However big the building—whether it is a pagoda or a palace—the Japs stand it loose on the top of the foundation instead of building it into one structure. Then when the earthquake comes, your palace or pagoda may kick up its heels, but stands still again as soon as the earthquake is done.'

'I should like to go over that pagoda.'

'Dekimas! can do,' said Kano, 'if you stay here till July 16.'

'You had better come back,' said Mr. Spong; 'the others are in their *rikshas* waiting for us.'

'Mr. Sandys,' called out Bryn, 'I don't think I shall let you come again. You've corrupted even Mr. Spong. It must be very nice to be corrupted again, Punch.'

A short drive through a grove of needle-like cryptomerias brought them to the wooden portal of the Koyo-Kwan or Maple Club, so called from its fabric being entirely of maple wood, and its decorations inspired by that tree. Mr. Spong had brought

39

white linen bags to go over his feet, but the others
had to submit to the rather ridiculous operation of
having their boots taken off, an ordeal to which
dainty women like Bryn and her sister could submit
with a good deal more equanimity than some of the
party.

They were then conducted upstairs into the
banqueting chamber, a long low room divided into
two unequal parts by *shoji* (which were for the time
withdrawn), and flanked the whole length on one
side by a sun gallery decorated with a maple leaf
design. Everything was maple. The sunken
handles of the *shoji* were bronze maple leaves. The
white paper of the *shoji* themselves was flowered
with silver maple leaves, as were the silk cushions on
which fourteen unhappy Europeans were endeavour-
ing to do the Japanese squat, for Mrs. Crosby was at
the Koyo-Kwan awaiting them. She had gone
direct when she found herself too late to join them
in doing Shiba—a decidedly pretty woman with a
slim upright figure, auburn hair, and the brilliant
complexion that often goes with it, but rather a
weak mouth full of charming teeth. Mr. Dacres was
a good deal relieved by her arrival. He had come
off decidedly worst in the three-cornered competition
for Bryn's favours, and he fancied that Mr. Mathdine
was not meeting with marked success. The party
were arranged in a semicircle facing the *shoji* which
divided off the smaller room, Mr. Avon being in
the centre, supported by the Sparlings, for whom as
a merchant he felt a good-natured contempt ; but he
had Mrs. Phelps on his hands, and he knew that if
he cavaliered Mrs. Sparling she would tell her 'dear

A JAPANESE MARRIAGE

Coventry' to take charge of Mrs. Phelps. Bryn sat almost at one end, with Mr. Mathdine on the outside and Lord Romney between her and Mrs. Amory on the inside. Mrs. Prince, as the wife of a brother officer, and not likely to be in request, sat between Mrs. Amory and Mr. Avon's little *partie carrée*. At the other end of the crescent Philip sat between Mary on the outside and Mr. Spong on the inside, and Mrs. Crosby sat between Mr. Spong and Mr. Dacres, leaving the latter next to Mrs. Sparling. The banquet began of course with Japanese tea and *hiokwashi*(bean-flour cakes), tasting like the almonding on a wedding cake, flanked with sweets stamped into maple leaves of most poisonous reds and greens. These were brought in by fourteen exquisite little *mousmees* in soft gray *kimonos* with huge *obés*, and long hanging sleeves both lined with a marvellous scarlet. As pretty as peaches were these little *mousmees*, with their rosebud mouths, little white teeth, and damasked clear brown cheeks.

Lord Romney having made up his mind loyally to observe the promise he had given Bryn not to recur to the subject of matrimony, treated her so naturally and confidently that she attributed the opposite intention to him. She felt a morbid desire that he should propose to her again, and was not entirely confident of being able to refuse him, and yet so made up of contraries was the spoilt child that she kept him at arm's length lest he should do the very thing she desired him to do. The consequence was that she lent a particularly gracious ear to Mr. Mathdine, her neighbour on the other side. But by a strange irony Mr. Mathdine, who had

41

always been the slave of her beauty, had become so
alarmed about Lord Romney's intentions and so
doubtful of her strength to refuse so splendid a
match that he determined to try his own luck before
it was too late.   He had considerable tact in
humouring Bryn.   He had never said or done
anything which grated on her.   As the banquet
drew near its end he began to feel very satisfied.
He had ingratiated himself so successfully that
Lord Romney, in despair of getting in a word,
had turned his attentions to pretty Mrs. Amory on
his left hand, who dearly loved an Englishman, and
—being an American—a lord.   But Mr. Mathdine
did not get very far ; for when he bent towards Bryn
and whispered something to her, she turned very red
and then very white, as she made her reply with a
curtness, that would have been balm to Lord
Romney's heart, had he only noticed.

Meanwhile Philip was a good deal struck by
the interest Mary took in the little *mousmees* who
flitted round them like so many butterflies, and
by the intelligence with which she answered his
inquiries about the banquet.   She explained the
nature of the *suimono* which followed the *hiokwashi.*
The red and white fish served on the beautiful little
mats of fluted grass sewn together like the green
rush-mats used for cream cheeses in England were
the celebrated 'live fish' of Japanese epicures ; the
hors d'œuvres served with it were horse-radish
beaten into a paste with vinegar and green herbs ; a
slice of *daikon*, the gigantic Japanese radish which
grows a yard long and a foot round ; seaweed, raw
spinach and raw shrimps.   The soup in the lacquer

bowl, with the inverted bowl one size smaller on the top of it, was fish broth, and he was expected to swish the gobbets out with chopsticks, and dip them into a sauce concocted from the *hors d'œuvres*, before he ate the soup.

Philip had pictured himself holding up a kicking fish by the tail, and tearing hunks out of it with his teeth. He had not known that the Japanese are satisfied with a possible quiver, and the knowledge that the fish from which it was cut may still be alive, because the vital parts are avoided in the cutting.

Mary ate hers freely, and assured him that she enjoyed it, though he found a difficulty in keeping his down, after he had forced himself to swallow it.

Mr. Spong saw his struggles and said, 'Take some champagne.' Kano had just opened a case; for though Latimer Avon rather liked giving a Japanese banquet to a distinguished stranger like Lord Romney, he always took care to take a good supply of champagne and sandwiches to sustain life, and would have taken a whole picnic basket, but for the fact that Bryn, who had the digestion of an ostrich, rather enjoyed the strange delicacies of a Japanese banquet for a change, and said that a picnic basket spoiled the whole character of the thing.

Mr. Spong was munching sandwiches and drinking champagne.

'I call the whole thing disgusting,' he observed, 'except the dancing-girls; but there's no mistake about the dancing-girls here.'

'Are we going to have *guechas* then?'

'The finest in Japan. But you've got a lot to

get through before you will get to them. There's *sashimini* and *kuchi-tori*, prawns in butter, quails that look as if they had been put under a steam hammer; sugared-up oranges and walnuts; fish beaten up into paste till it's too immortally like pork fat; and potatoes—unfortunately sweet ones—worked up with bean flour and sugar till they would make a very fair substitute for *marrons-glacés*.'

'You must add to these *shiwoyaki*—fish baked with salt; *teriyaki*—plums preserved with salt; sweet potatoes syrupped, and *hachizakana*—fish in a bowl,' said Mary.

'*Hachizakana* wouldn't be bad,' said Mr. Spong; 'you can sometimes get a decently grilled piece of fish out of it—if you could rely on getting anything straightforward out of Japanese cooking; but when you do think you're on firm ground at last, you are sure to find that it is doctored up with syrup, or something else that utterly transforms its nature.'

'You're not drinking your *saké*, Mr. Sandys,' interrupted Mary, seeing the rueful face of the little *mousmee* who kept washing out his cup in the little tureen of hot water, and replacing it in its box-shaped tray of carved wood, full of freshly warmed *saké*.

'Don't you touch the beastly stuff,' retorted Mr. Spong. 'They may say it tastes like beer or un-fortified sherry, but it's much more like the cheap ammonia used for cleaning clothes.' .

Tinkle, tinkle, came the notes of a *samisen*, and the *shoji* were suddenly closed between the two rooms, only to be flung open the moment afterwards, and disclose little women playing on the *samisen* (guitar) and *koto*, which looked like a fender-stool about six feet long, fitted with fiddle-strings. A dancer had entered in a marvellous dress of scarlet brocade, made after the manner of Japanese costumes with long sleeves and two tunics, the under one very light, but covering white satin drawers which terminated in queer white linen *tabi*, shoes and stockings all in one with divided toes. The top tunic was loose, and fastened at the waist with a magnificent *obé* (sash) of green brocade. The colours were in admirable taste ; her hair was a work of art, pounded up with fat to the consistency of dough, and then moulded into a beautiful butterfly with large fat wings, profusely decorated with gemmed pins and flowers. And so, on a less elaborate scale, each of the pretty little girls who were waiting had hers done. The dancer gave a quantity of fan-play. She was an admirable actress ; good-looking too, not like the little waitresses, but an aristocratic beauty of the true type, with a long slender neck and a waxy oval face, thin eagle nose and bead-like eyes. It was some tragedy she was enacting, in which passion, represented by thunderous stamping and fierce rushings forward in a springing posture, was the prelude, followed by disdain, with pursed-up lips, thrown-up chin, and scornfully-averted eyes. Lastly, she swept from the room like a tragic queen.

'What do you think of it ?' asked Mary a little anxiously.

'Well, I don't call it exactly dancing in our sense of the word,' said Philip ; 'it's more posturing and dumb acting.'

'The Japanese dance with everything but their feet,' put in Mr. Spong. 'They can't do anything like other people; their screws turn the opposite way; and a woman puts on mourning when she is going to be married—though, perhaps, that isn't very surprising, when it's the woman who suffers at the hands of the mother-in-law, and not the man.'

Meanwhile Lord Romney had been partly consoled by pretty Mrs. Amory. She was so frank and gracious, though she never gave *Lootenant* Amory a moment's anxiety. And after Bryn she was very restful. She had her countrywomen's way of allowing themselves to enjoy the society of the man they are talking to, and allowing him to see how they enjoy it, just as if he was another woman instead of a man.

'Do you see the way that American minx is throwing herself at Lord Romney?' said Mrs. Phelps to Mr. Avon. 'The way these grass widows turn their opportunities to account is perfectly shocking. She isn't a fit associate for your Brynhild.' How far she might harm Mary did not seem a matter for consideration.

Mr. Avon, who was a kindly man, though not remarkable for moral courage, made a more outspoken reply than he generally ventured on.

'I should rather like to see the person who could move Bryn.' He spoke with a significance which Mrs. Phelps missed.

'Your sufferings are not over yet,' said Mr. Spong, as he poured himself out another glass of champagne. 'I can see *chawan* and *mizakaka* in

46

the offing, and you must go right through with them, my boy.'

'What are they?' asked Philip faintly.

'Don't be frightened, Mr. Sandys,' said Mary. '*Chawan* is a kind of white soup that even a European cook might make, as it only contains egg, chicken, mushrooms and watercress, and *mizakaka* simply means boiled with sauce.'

'Why, it's my old friend the *tai*-fish,' cried Mr. Spong, 'that has suffered *mizakaka*, and looks like a whiting gone out of curl. I wonder how they get its backbone out. By Jove, they must have got it out through this tiny hole in its belly, and I'm blessed if they haven't filled it with stuffing through the same keyhole. Really the ingenuity of these Japs! But I was going to tell you about the *tai*-fish. A party of us went out for the day from Tokyo to a lovely little place called—oh, I forget. We had the two most experienced fishermen of the neighbourhood with us, and all we caught was one wretched little *tai*-fish, small enough to be this one's grandchild, and that is why I am so affected.'

'Look, Mr. Sandys, there's a new dancer,' said Mary, who was far from sharing Bryn's enjoyment of Mr. Spong's flippant speeches.

She was dressed in rich white silk.

'I do believe they have forgotten the inevitable maple at last. No, d—— it, there it is on her fan,' said the irrepressible.

Hers was a softer tale, with death as a climax. She fell, like a shot bird, flat on her back; but she lost her head in the genuine burst of applause which

47

greeted her, and, with some inappropriateness, picking herself up, made a long salaam.

'That kind of thing sickens me,' cried Mr. Spong. 'Why couldn't they close the *shoji* while she was getting up?'

'Could you make anything out of the chanting of the musicians, Miss Avon?' asked Philip. 'It seemed to me a little monotonous, but I don't call it unmusical.'

'Oh yes, that was the story she was acting.'

'I hate their cracked voices,' growled Mr. Spong. 'Here, young man, you must go through *wan-mori* now; that will tax you.'

'What is *wan-mori*, Miss Avon?'

'Oh, a kind of custard soup with chicken, mushrooms, boiled fish and radishes mixed in.'

Before Philip had screwed up enough courage to tackle his *wan-mori* 'the maple dance' itself began, in which the maple leaf that gives the Club its name appears on the dancers' hair and fans, and every portion of their exquisite dress. The guests were enchanted, though all the idea of it they carried away with them was a swaying of graceful bodies in soft sensuous motions, a flutter of fans on the floor, and a gleam of dark heads bending over them.

The shades of night were now closing in, and the picturesqueness of the scene was heightened by the arrival of the tall black iron candlesticks, with straight slender stems and a spike to stick the candle on, so characteristic of Japan. The dancing was over; and as soon as the attendants had brought in the lights, they flew back for piles of little white wooden boxes, in which, with inconceivable rapidity, they packed away every remnant of the feast. Every dish had been left where it was brought in.

Mr. Avon grew a little pompous and impatient. 'Tell them we don't want it, Kano.'

'Custom of the house,' said Kano. 'You no take them, proprietor think you not satisfied.' Then he added in a lower voice, 'Can leave in *jinriksha.*'

'I simply won't take mine,' said Bryn.

'I won't, I won't,' said Mr. Mathdine and Mr. Dacres in chorus.

'I have a constitutional objection to making myself ridiculous,' said Mr. Spong.

'Please do take it,' said Mary, laying her hand impulsively on his arm. 'It hurts their feelings so if you don't.'

'Certainly, my dear young lady, if you wish it. I could not refuse anyone so charming.'

And she was looking very charming as she fled with heightened colour—it was an unusual display of spirit for her.

Bryn, when Philip rushed downstairs with his boxes and Mary's, was sitting on the doorstep scolding one of the *mousmees* in very voluble Japanese for having followed her with her boxes.

And Lord Romney, as he handed his to his *jinriksha* boy, looked at her in a pained way, which made her feel as she did not often feel.

CHAPTER V

PHILIP SANDYS had gone to the Club Hotel when he arrived, because it was homelier than the Grand Hotel, and he was not yet a member of the Club itself. And he had stayed there because it seemed to him the most homely place in Japan. In the Club itself he would have had to content himself with a bedroom for his Lares and Penates, and if he had lived in his *godown* he would have been isolated from Europeans. In the hotel he had a charming suite of rooms opening on the verandah, which was separated only by the roadway from the sea. His sitting-room had a beautiful bow window commanding a full view of all the shipping in the bay and the blue hills of Kanozan beyond ; and his dressing-room and bedroom led off it. He generally now breakfasted in the hotel and lunched and dined at the Club, which was next door. But he liked to get back from dinner in time to look at the harbour lights, when the approach of nine set the men-of-war a-bugling their crews to supper and bed. For there was no time when he seemed so near England. Japan was lost in the darkness—unless it was a twinkling *riksha* lantern ; every ray of light meant a ship that might be tripping her anchor, and hoisting the Blue Peter for England before another day was passed.

He never forgot the novelty of the first meal in the hotel, with its swarms of spindled-legged boys in dark blue doublets and hose, looking like so many pantomime imps as they ran about (Japanese waiters never walk), scuffing their straw sandals, which they dragged along with their big toes. It was unfamiliar too to order the dishes by numbers. Very few of the waiters understood any other English. 'Boy, you bring me number one—*ichi ban*—soup.' For as soon as their English got beyond this they were promoted to be bedroom boys, who were forced to know the difference between ordering a bath and ordering a whiskey and soda, though there were people who ordered them in about the same quantities.

It being April the hotel was brightened up with the uniforms of the English naval officers, whose wives were staying there. The husbands slept on board ship—seemingly the only duty they were called on to perform. The English naval officers' wives and American naval officers' wives always made a point of forgathering together. Most of the guests in the hotel hung about the front all day, though there was nothing to see but a few men-of-war and a few big merchant steamers lying at their moorings, and a dusty road bordered by a few starved fir trees, occupied by *jinriksha* men with big sun helmets and tiny brass pipes which they were eternally tapping against their wheels, until some one seemed about to leave the hotel, when they all made a rush for the gate. Both Mrs. Amory and Mrs. Prince lived in the Club Hotel. Philip had often noticed Mrs. Amory. She was such a wholesome-looking woman. She showed her white teeth so pleasantly; her auburnish hair was so glossy and well done, and she had such pretty little children. She would nod and give him a smile when they met in the hall, but he had never spoken to her before the banquet at the Maple Club.

On the next morning at breakfast her eyes said plainly, Join us at our table. Though they were so much with the American officers' wives during the day, the English officers' wives generally got their husbands to breakfast, and carried them off to corners to make their acquaintance.

'You are none the worse for your banquet?' said Mrs. Amory pleasantly, for something to say.

'I really took nothing but the sandwiches and a little champagne.'

'The Avons' champagne,' said Mrs. Prince, 'is about the only good thing in the country.'

'Come, Caroline,' said Daphne Amory. 'I hope Mr. Sandys will help me to stand up for Japan till the Sparlings come down ; you *are* so hard on it.'

'I can't think what the United States want to bother with Japan for. Our navy in these waters is kept up for the benefit of Frazar and Company and a few missionaries. And we wives have to stay away from our husbands till we are old women.'

'The Sparlings always take their meals with us,' said Mrs. Amory, changing the subject. 'They'll be down soon, for the boy took the bill of fare up to get their orders several minutes ago.'

'I don't see the use of ordering,' said Mrs. Prince. 'There are sixteen things on the bill, but they're none of them fit to eat.'

'But, Caroline, you never try anything but bacon and eggs.'

'I'm sure everything else is worse, Daff.'

'Good morning, dears,' said Mrs. Sparling, who had just made her appearance with the smile which Bryn compared to the key-board of a piano. She dressed the part of the jolly little woman by wearing a scarlet tie. Her shirt and skirt were dowdy enough for her children's German governess.

'Good morning, Mr. Sandys,' she said; 'so you've not been able to keep away from our fun. Charming people the Avons, aren't they?'

'I am more attracted to the girls than anyone I have met in Japan,' said Philip; 'present company of course excepted. I hardly know their father, though I am at the house fairly often.'

'Latimer Avon is a cypher in his own house,' said Mrs. Prince, 'and he always has been. A pretty dance they say Mrs. Avon led him while she was alive.'

'Has she been long dead?'

'Oh yes, she died at Bryn's birth. Bryn is just her double. If a child's too like its mother, it always kills her.'

'Did you know Mrs. Avon?'

'No, I didn't. But there are plenty of people left in Yokohama who did. She only lived here about two years. She came just before Mary was born and died with Bryn. There are two years between the girls, aren't there, Mrs. Sparling? I always look upon you as keeping the pedigrees of the settlement.'

'Well, I can't boast so much as that; but I know that there are two years between these girls. Coventry and I have always been such friends of the Avons.'

Mrs. Prince's face was a study.

'Mrs. Avon was a high-spirited creature,' flowed on Mrs. Sparling, 'the daughter of an Irish peer. She loathed Japan.'

'I'm high-spirited too,' said Mrs. Prince. 'I'd like to ring up Mrs. Avon's ghost, and *shake* on that. Dear me, what am I saying? I shall get into talking like Bryn Avon, if I don't take care.'

'You mustn't be too hard on dear Bryn,' said Mrs. Sparling. 'She's a good girl really. I'll take her in hand when I've got time.'

Mrs. Prince raised her eyebrows in holy astonishment. But she only said:

'You'll have your hands full.'

'I'm sure I shall make something of her. At present she may be a little selfish, shall we call it, to her sister, and a little wanting in consideration to her father, and a little assertive all round.'

'You're not over-stating it,' said Mrs. Prince. 'She's a regular cannibal to her sister, treats her father like a child who isn't quite all there, and treads on the whole white population, residents and visitors.'

'Bryn is certainly queen,' said Mrs. Amory with one of her charming smiles. 'But then she ought to be. The girl's a perfect goddess. Women fall in love with her beauty as well as men. I'm madly in love with her. And she never says anything but "How do you?" to me.'

'If their mother died when they were infants, who brought them up?' asked Philip. 'I don't think I could be surprised if you told me that Miss Bryn brought herself and her sister up from their cradles.'

'Not quite that,' said Mrs. Prince. 'Mr. Avon had one of the lady housekeepers of the pattern you English monopolise—a good fifty! with hair bandolined on the forehead! no indications of figure, a large bonnet, a black silk mantle, and a red stuff dress! She was as full of moral precepts as your Watts' hymns. She was in fact the pattern relations pick out for a widower, that there should be no possible chance of his wanting to marry her.'

'I should hardly have thought that Miss Bryn had been brought up by a guardian like that,' said Philip.

'She wasn't. At ten years old she stamped her foot till the old lady was turned out of the house, and her father did the only completely sensible thing he ever did in his life. He got a pretty young girl the children fell in love with. So did he. But he dared not face that awful child's "Papa!" There never was such an *enfante terrible* as Bryn. Her incorruptible candour almost plunged the settlement into battle and murder. If he and Miss Dasent were in any kind of proximity when Bryn came in, or if he said anything unnecessarily kind to her at meals, a childish voice trumpeted out " Papa " in the tones of a Junius. When Bryn was fourteen she married — I mean the governess-housekeeper did.'

'And since then?'

'Mary and she have brought themselves up. Bryn by and by sent herself to school at the Ladies' College from fourteen till she was sixteen and a half, when she grew tired of being top and knowing more than the governesses. She's got lots of brains, but

A JAPANESE MARRIAGE

I don't believe she has ever opened a book since she left school. She put her hair up and was quite a woman then. That's all the bringing-up Bryn Avon ever had. Their Japanese steward does the ordering, kept in order by the Chinese compradore in Mr. Avon's office.'

' Well, you must confess, Caroline,' put in Mrs. Amory, ' that she has brought herself up real well. Bryn may be a crocodile to her father and sister; she may be airsy and trample on the whole community; but no man ever could boast of a favour from Bryn Avon. She has been absolutely without a chaperone, and doesn't care what enemies she makes; but there never was a breath of scandal about her.'

' Well, I must say,' said Mrs. Prince, ' that of all the minxes I ever met Bryn Avon *takes the cake;* but she has spirit enough for the whole body that signed the Declaration of Independence.'

' I'll take her in hand,' said Mrs. Sparling again. ' Her father being the wealthiest man in the place, and the greatest entertainer, and the child having no mother, she wants some one to do this for her. I must do something to tone down that rebellious spirit.'

Mrs. Prince burst out laughing: harsh, disagreeable laughter which ended in a choke. When it was over she said that their waiter had such a comical face. But he had been waiting upon them for a month, and he could not have been winking at Mrs. Sparling's optimistic speeches, for he did not understand English.

' Was their mother really the daughter of an

Irish peer?' asked Philip, turning almost instinctively to Mrs. Amory.

'I believe so. She was a beautiful high-spirited creature, who loathed Japan so that she died of a broken heart when she had only been out here a year or two. They do say that the reason why Mr. Avon came to Japan was that his wife's relations thought her marriage such a *mésalliance*, that she had to leave England and go somewhere.'

'I think they must have been very poor,' put in Mrs. Prince. 'I can't picture an aristocratic beauty making a love match with Latimer Avon.'

'He's a good-looking man enough,' said Mrs. Sparling.

'Women don't care for good-looking men, unless they look bad as well. They do like a man to have a gentlemanly face and a gentlemanly figure. But the one thing they demand in a husband is power—the power of wealth above all, social power, political power, even brain power.'

'And you imply that Mr. Avon had the power of wealth?' asked Philip.

'Men have a motive for everything, and so do most women, except the good ones. I can't see what other motive she could have had. Out here she was the toast of all the army officers. They had an English regiment here in those days.'

'But they say she never would look at any of them, Caroline.'

'I know, Daff. Isn't her precious daughter just the same? I don't see any credit in her having no lovers, if she was as difficult to please as Bryn is.'

'How you do talk, Caroline; yet I daresay if

the girl was in trouble you'd be as good a friend to her as any one.'

'I might. She's as cussed as an Indian. People wouldn't have taken such a lot of interest in the Indians if they'd been as tame as niggers. Feni-more Cooper couldn't have lived in a Brooklyn boarding-house on what he could have made out of niggers. I like a bit of cussedness. Wives have it more than husbands in our country, or I might think diffcrent.'

CHAPTER VI

'DROP in whenever you like,' Bryn had said to Philip Sandys, as their party broke up at Yoko-hama station on their return from the banquet at the Maple Club. The Avons kept open house. Their friends were really at liberty to drop in at any hour or any meal, provided that Bryn tolerated them. If she did not, she had a very unmistakable way of showing it, so the practice never developed into a nuisance.

And it was such a privilege to be within the focus of her radiating beauty that Philip often did drop in for a couple of hours after business, which amounted to little more than sitting in the office, except on mail days, or when one of the Sandys ships had just come in, or was about to weigh for England. And yet he was by no means content to be a *fainéant* in the office.

Though he went for Bryn's sake, he was content

to remain at a very respectful distance, while the other men clustered round her, except when she made it plain that she did not want them. Thus insensibly he drifted into seeing a good deal of Mary, whose gentleness and habit of effacing herself appealed to him. He could not understand why this pale girl, who was so pretty and so dainty, could drop so completely out of notice.

The garden was so glorious in the April weather that he hardly ever set foot in the house, except when he was asked to a luncheon or dinner party. But one afternoon a heavy tropical shower drove them in, while Bryn and her court took refuge in the little tea ceremony chamber which acted as a summer-house and lent such a Japanese look to the landscape.

'What exquisite curios you have, Miss Avon. Some of these gold lacquer cabinets must be worth hundreds of pounds. I daresay a good many of these little ivories are worth a hundred.'

'Yes, I know they are. The only interest papa takes in them is their value—or in having the best that can be bought.' She felt that she had spoken too ungently of her father.

'They're all very beautiful.'

'Other people have said so. Bryn says it must be that the Japanese cannot make anything that isn't beautiful, when it's good. She's quite sure that it isn't papa's or the compradore's fault. The compradore buys most of our things, you know,' she explained, opening her eyes wider. 'We should be dreadfully cheated. But the Japanese cannot cheat a Chinaman.'

'I love those yellow silk *kakemonos* in the hall. They have faded to such a delicious tint.'

'Oh yes, they're very old. They were painted in fifteen hundred and something. That's the fifteenth century, isn't it? They came from one of the *daimios*' castles that was destroyed in the Revolution, I think.'

'You're too grand for me here. I'm so fond of the little domestic dodges of the Japs. We should call them curios in England.'

'Yes,' she said, as if she hardly understood.

'I mean such things as the little carved bamboo tobacco-boxes; the life-size bronze lotus leaves one just uses for trays; the bronze crabs and frogs and lizards; the old-fashioned satchels made of silk woven for the purpose, as one can see from the way the design fits in; little *netsukes* transformed from a root or a knot in the wood into a grotesque beast or reptile with a hot iron or a few strokes of a knife. I don't see any of them about.'

'We haven't got any.'

'Not even you and Miss Bryn, in your own rooms?'

She shook her head. 'I have seen things something like them in those little shops on the way up from the settlement. But they always seem to keep such rubbish there.'

'There is often a good deal of rubbish, but I hardly ever pass a curio shop that doesn't contain something quite beautiful. Personally, I find even those little shops on the way up far too high and mighty and civilised. I always mistrust a curio shop that hasn't got old boots mixed up with the curios. It shows that the natives don't deal there, for if there is one second-hand article which interests the humble Japanese more than anything else, it is a foreigner's worn-out boots.'

'I wish we had some of those things about—I don't mean the boots. I often feel that our house is not so homely as the Sparlings' suite in the Club Hotel; and yet Bryn says that Mrs. Sparling never spent a quarter all at once in her life.'

'A quarter!' he said tentatively.

'Twenty-five *sen*. Americans always call them "quarters."'

A day or two afterwards he brought her 'a *mousmee's* dressing-case,' which he had picked up, made of much-worn, but very curious leather, stamped with a Chinese scene, and lined with the same scene in rich brocade. It contained a metal mirror, a comb, and a little flat ivory box for the gold leaf *guechas* use for their extraordinary lips. The box was just the right length and breadth for ladies' visiting cards. It might have been deep enough to hold half a dozen. Cards, a comb, and a mirror and an empty pocket for dollar notes! What more could a lady want?

'What a delightful little thing.'

'It would do for Mrs. Sparling,' he said. 'It only cost a quarter.'

'Where do you get these bargains?'

'All sorts of places. In the cabinet-makers' street off the Theatre Street, for one. If you care to come I'll show you.'

'Oh yes, I'd love to come. When will you take me?'

He pulled out his watch. 'It's about five, and it's

done raining. Now, if you like. You don't dine till eight, do you?'

'No or yes. I mean that we do dine at eight.'

'Shall we start then?'

'Yes. You can use one of our *rikshas*. They'll be ready. The boys are always in except when they're doing messages.'

'I have my own *riksha* here, thanks.'

She rang the bell, and told a servant to send one of their *rikshas* to the door, and to call Mr. Sandys's boy.

She came home barely in time to dress for dinner, with an extra *riksha* to carry her purchases. The girls' purses were always bursting with pocket-money.

CHAPTER VII

'WELL, I call this too good,' said Mr. Spong, picking up an English newspaper which Bryn had just opened and thrown down contemptuously, when she saw that it did not contain any pictures. 'Here are the Conservatives thinking of taking up Woman's Suffrage.'

'But, Punch,' said Bryn, 'I thought you were in favour of introducing Woman's Suffrage yourself, when you were in Parliament.'

'My dear young lady, I was always in favour of introducing anything, to see the humours of a new situation.'

'I don't see what women want with rights,' said

A JAPANESE MARRIAGE

Bryn. 'If it is passed, I think they ought to call it *Men's* Sufferage.'

'Suffrage, not sufferage! I think you take about all the rights a woman could, except voting for the local member for the Japanese Diet.'

'The Japanese Diet!' said Bryn with concentrated scorn.

'I'm not talking about rice and seaweed.'

'Punch, you're talking to me as if I was a fool again ; this conversation's ended.'

'Well, seriously, Miss Bryn, what do you think about woman's rights ? '

'Well, I think the Japanese women seem as happy as most women ; and they haven't any rights to speak of.'

Bryn thought she detected an innuendo in his reply. She frowned and went on as if he hadn't said anything, addressing herself to Philip Sandys : 'In Japan, as in England, woman's rights largely depend on how badly she's dressed. If she has on the beautiful native dress, which very likely her grandmother or her husband's grandmother had before her, she has less rights than a dog. The dog is allowed to walk in front of its master, while she must always keep behind hers ; but if her poor little figure is disguised in a dress three sizes too big, of some heartrending colour, made in Germany, her lord and master would affect to treat her like a woman and a Christian.'

'I think,' said Mr. Spong, venturing once more to cut into the conversation, 'that they mightn't look so bad in their German finery if they put it on wrong side foremost, which would suit the Japanese ' . . . .

'Punch!' called out Bryn with a warning glance.

'I'm not going to particularise. I wasn't going to say anything very bad when you trod on me before. I was only going to say that in the *Onna Dai Gaku* it is expressly laid down that a woman should do all she can to please her husband's elder brother. As you swear you'll never marry, you'll have to be content with your elder sister's husband.'

· There was a general laugh at the idea of Mary being married first. Somehow or other no one ever contemplated Mary's being married.

'Husbands were made before brothers — for women!' said Bryn; 'but we are talking about woman's rights.'

'I always thought husbands were woman's rights,' said Punch.

Mr. Spong was called Punch at the Club, because his eyes had a leer curiously like that of the urbane old gentleman on the frontispiece of the world's most serious comic paper.

'The right kind of husband.'

'You don't seem to be able to make up your mind as to what is the right kind.'

'They're very rare.'

'Well, what do you think of me for a woman's right? I'm sure I'm rare enough.'

'I think you are more suitable for an illustration of a new woman's books.'

'What's the matter with me? I'm sure I looked very nice in " Our Legislators," No. 653 of Vanity Fair Item, a Spanish beard; the gray hairs don't signify; item, a face of a fine fresh colour : but they all have that—in Vanity Fair. The eyes had a kind of leer in them certainly, but I trust that was the ill-nature of the artist, and the clothes would have done credit to a book-maker.'

'You'll do.'

'You're very patronising—do for what?'

'What I said before.'

'I feel complimented.'

'But we are not talking about you, we are talking about woman's rights.'

'All right. To begin at the beginning, is a woman to have a vote for Parliament?'

'Oh, please no. A woman always insists on doing everything she has a right to do, and it would be such a bore to know whom to vote for. But after all it really wouldn't matter, because no woman ever does exactly as she's told, when there's no one looking on to see how she does it ; and as the ballot box is secret, three-quarters of the votes would be spoiled by filling them in in some idiotic way. Most women wouldn't vote for either of the regular candidates ; they would simply write the names of somebody else — their favourite curate or blackguard.'

'Seriously,' said Philip, striking into the conversation for the first time, 'I'm in favour of giving them a vote, though I'm a regular Tory. I'd much sooner consult Miss Bryn on a political subject than a stupid labourer who can't read about what he is voting for, or a man whose vote you can buy with a drink.'

'I object to the whole thing,' said Mr. Spong ; 'we can barely get women to pay enough attention to our dinners as it is ; and what should we do when they spent all day in getting over the tiresome secrecy of the ballot by going about telling every-body whom they had voted for?'

'Oh, I suppose you want us to go on with your "sufferage instead of suffrage" to the end of the chapter. You see I've laid your correction to heart, Punch.'

'Why not? It's the one ,thing the average woman is fit for.'

Bryn turned her back on him, and said to Philip, 'There's one weak point about woman's rights.'

'Oh, give it to us,' said Mr. Spong jubilantly, and quite unsnubbed.

'They want such a queer-looking crowd to take care of them. We've got a Woman's Rights Club even in Yokohama—the Minerva. They have a club-house of their own now, but they used to meet on the Bluff at the American Unitarian Missionary's. It's one of the best houses in the place—apart from its fittings. Everything, down to a Japanese lady's maid for his wife, is paid for by the faithful in Boston, whose hearts bleed for the way in which he has to rough it here in the savage East. It isn't half so savage as their own East, by all accounts. But the American's heart has to bleed for something — first his heart and then his pocket. It's the fashion. Their parsons have got them into the way of doing it, as a religious exercise.'

'The men call the Minerva the Spinsters' Club,' said Mr. Spong.

'They had much better call it the Skeletons'. A good many of the members are no longer spinsters in the eyes of the law. But there is hardly one of them who hasn't got a rattling skeleton in her cup-board.'

'I don't see why they shouldn't have a skeleton as the club badge. A death's head would be much more appropriate than Minerva for putting on the club envelopes.'

'They haven't got the sense of a squeezed orange, most of them. They are such a lot of misfits that if they had any sense of decency they'd insure themselves, and set the club on fire.'

'You don't seem to have much respect for woman's rights in the aggregate, Miss Bryn.'

'Aggregate! just think of the women that belong to it—Mrs. Prince for instance. The com-mander would never have married her if he hadn't remembered that he could not take her on board ship. She was cut out for a naval officer's wife—an American naval officer's. She's been left out in the cold all her life.'

'I think if she wore stays she might have had more chance of having a lover,' said Mr. Spong. 'She'd have something round her waist anyway.'

'She's a kind of a wind egg,' retorted Bryn.

He gave a ludicrous imitation of her warning glance.

'Don't you know what a wind egg is?' she said, with a faint increase of colour for once. 'It's an egg the hen's forgotten to put the shell on. There are such a lot of people,' she continued quite quickly, 'whose mothers have forgotten to finish them. The whole room is full of job lots at the Minerva.'

'But they are married, some of them.'

'That's nothing, if you can't keep your husband to yourself. I don't believe there's one of them can, except Mr. Measom's wife; and he had such a difficulty in getting a wife at all. He was seventy-five and had no money. The only way he could manage it was by becoming secretary or editor or something to a matrimonial bureau in a watering-place. He proposed to every woman that came in for a husband, and she had been on his books for five years. It was a toss-up between marrying him and becoming a life-member.'

'What do they belong to the Minerva for?' asked Philip.

'Because they've spoilt their homes. The men like it, because it's such a capital thing for keeping all the ugly women together. A sort of sink, you know. Mrs. Sparling is the only married woman in the club whose husband isn't glad that she belongs to it, and she generally takes him with her. I'm not sure that he isn't a member, but perhaps he'd have to wear petticoats.'

'What do they do there?'

'I don't suppose they take away characters,' said Mr. Spong. 'For one thing the club is such a glass house; and for another it would be a pretty tough job to damage the average exile's reputation. I should think they go in for trying to reform the Japs in some way or another: teach them how to kiss their husbands or something. Their rules were drawn up by the well-known platform speaker who is always expressing her doubts as to whether men are fit to marry at all, and sent out from England type-written, so as to go by book-post for a halfpenny.'

'Since the introspective lady novelists have become the fashion,' said Bryn, 'I should think they were mostly composing novels with themselves as the heroines.'

'Analysing your passions is the modern form of scandal, especially if you've had them all to yourself,' said Punch; 'and it's my belief that the time is fast coming when women will talk passions just as men talk sport. It suits all classes of intellect.'

'I should not like to see my wife going to this club,' said Philip seriously.

'Most men don't like to see them coming away. Their only objection to the club is that it shuts at ten,' said Bryn. 'Marriage is a good use for fools; but they never seem properly made for each other.'

'You seem to have very advanced ideas about marriage.'

'I know by observation, that though fools are made for each other they are usually badly matched.'

'Don't you think that there can be such a thing as a happy marriage?'

'If one's a big enough fool, and the other's a big enough knave.'

'Or when they've both learned by experience how little to expect,' put in Mr. Spong.

'Marriages are like cheap boots, they generally creak,' said Bryn.

'And they say they hurt,' said Punch; 'but, thank God, I never tried.'

'They say marriages are made in heaven,' observed Bryn. 'I think Japan must have a heaven all to itself. Though I really don't see how marriages can be made in heaven, when "they neither marry nor are given in marriage there." But perhaps it's only the match-making that's done up there. Anyhow there are an awful lot of misses. There's more risk about "taking the lady" at the altar than there is at loo.'

'By Jove, let's have a loo to-night,' said Mr. Spong.

'I think poker's more modern,' said Bryn languidly.

'That's what marriage is like,' said Punch. 'There's such a lot of bluffing about it—and the other fellow always goes one better. I shall "see you."'

'Well, upon my word,' said Mr. Mathdine—and this was his and Mr. Dacres's sole contribution to the afternoon's conversation.

'Tea,' called Mary, coming out of the summer-house. Philip hastened to her. His eyes had never before rested with so much satisfaction on her light figure, in reality almost as faultlessly dressed as Bryn's, though less markedly in the fashion. Mary had a good deal of grace, but she had not confidence. So she could not carry off a dress as Bryn could. Bryn would have made a cauliflower ornamental if she had worn it. The more bizarre the costume she would allow herself to wear (she had excellent taste), the more her beauty showed up.

As Mary met him with her face lit up by a smile of real pleasure, he felt that, superb as Bryn was, he would rather have Mary for a wife, even if he had contemplated the possibility of capturing the beauty, which his humility would never have permitted. Philip Sandys was a man of quiet tastes, rather plainly brought up. There was puritanical blood in the prosperous shipowner's family, and he was not yet accustomed to meet girls of twenty who could talk of marriage and sport in such a very *fin de siècle* way as Bryn had been doing. Positively there was hardly any difference between the views of life expressed by her and such an old *viveur* as Mr. Spong, except that she spoke with the stricter decorum natural to a well-bred woman. The others were some little time in joining them. Bryn and Mr. Spong were still waging their battle of wit, and Mr. Mathdine and Mr. Dacres were metaphorically wagging their tails beside their owner.

'Let's have our tea without waiting for the others, Miss Avon,' said Philip; 'and I'll take you to the curio-shops far along the creek. Or we might go out to the little village at the back of the 'Bluff, leave our *rikshas* and walk about looking at the Japanese farms. They'll be picking tea in that little garden.'

'Oh, it would be kind of you to take me out there,' said Mary; 'perhaps we should have time to go on to Negishi. Negishi has a tiny cemetery, with the funniest little Buddhas in rows.'

The Avon girls were accustomed to going out alone with gentlemen, like American girls, quite unquestioned, and they were just as worthy of the trust.

CHAPTER VIII

'LET'S get up a party for Kamakura on Sunday,' said Bryn.

Mary with some difficulty summoned up the courage to ask her to invite Philip Sandys. The Avons' parties were always Bryn's parties.

The idea struck Bryn as a good one. There were not many men who were in the habit of devoting themselves to Mary, and it was pleasanter to have Mary with her than to be alone with her father and a party of gentlemen. So she wrote a nice little note. And this is how Mr. Avon and Bryn and a bevy of her admirers and Mary and Philip found themselves at Kamakura that Sunday morning, just in time for an excellent lunch, ordered long enough in advance to enable the negro proprietor of the Kamakura hotel to lay in the delicacies which he knew would be paid for without a murmur. At a sufficient interval after lunch *rikshas* were ready to take them to the Kamakura Daibutsu, the great bronze Buddha fifty feet high, inferior to none of his known images in its beauty and its expression of the peace of God..

They went because they had been in the habit of going. To gaze at the huge idol, to find that it contains a temple, to learn that the counterfeits of the snails which crawl on the Buddha's head to protect him from sunstroke are silver, or that they could stand in the hollow of his hand, was no

72

novelty to them. Perhaps, as the day was hot, if they went a walk by the seashore or up to the temple of Hachiman Sama, they would get thirsty and buy the bottled beer, with the sale of which the priests eke out their scanty revenue in these days, when Buddhism is disestablished because it was the religion of the discrowned Shogun.

'Have you been to Enoshima, Mr. Sandys?' asked Mary, rather anxious to get away from hearing the beauty exchange the same old remarks with the same old set of men.

'No. Is that that wonderful island where they have the crabs fifteen feet long?'

'Yes.'

'And where they have that cavern temple to that important deity—the Japanese Venus?'

She nodded with a pretty little blush.

'Do let's go.'

They jumped into their *rikshas*, and were soon crossing the sandbank which links the island to the mainland.

Enoshima is very lovely. Nowhere in Japan is there such a quaint climbing street. It rivals Galata, and Amalfi, and Quebec, and totally eclipses Clovelly. Moreover, the island is one huge hill of camellia groves and bamboo brakes, interspersed with graceful temples, and ascended by picturesque stairways of mossy stone; and has beautiful paths round the edges of its woody precipices and delightful tea-houses.

Phil and Mary had examined the tunnelly cavern which constitutes the temple of Venus (Ben-ten). It reminded him of nothing so much as the grotto-bath at Banff in the Rocky Mountains (on a much inferior scale).

They were scrambling round the cliff path at the place where a wall of rock rose sheer above the narrow footway, and a wall of rock sheered down thirty or forty feet to a little recess of soft white sand, which shelved off so rapidly into deep water that egress from it, the walls being so precipitous, was impossible except by boats.

'That's a tight place,' said Philip, who was leading the way.

Just as he spoke the path gave way under him, and he was hurled down on the sand forty feet below.

For a little while he was stunned. When he was able to look about him, he saw a white scared face staring down at him from above. Mary was quite unable to get down to him.

'Are you injured badly?'

He picked himself up slowly. 'No, only a bit scratched, and beastly shaken.'

'What are we to do?'

'I don't know. I saw a house a little way ahead just before I got shot down here. But we haven't seen man or house for a mile or more behind, and you're the wrong side of the landslip, and the rocks are much too precipitous for you to climb up or down. I couldn't do it myself.'

'But the tide's coming in. If I go back all that long way it may be over your head before I get back.'

'I don't think that. I expect, as it is, a swim of a few yards round the corner would land me on dry land or in water shallow enough for wading. All the same, I would rather not look like a drowned dog all the time till I get to Yokohama,' he added, making light of any danger there might be, to cheer her. 'Besides, it wouldn't help you to get over the gap if I did.'

'I wonder if I couldn't scramble round. There is a tiny rim of the path left if it does not break away fresh.'

'For God's sake don't try. It's sure to give way again.' Then he added rather inconsequently, 'How wide is it?'

'About half a quarter of a yard, I think.

'It would be madness; there's a drop of forty feet.'

'There are some grasses growing in the cliff. I wonder if they would bear my weight to hold on by,' she said anxiously.

'You mustn't try.'

Mary was a delicate, and in most ways more than usually timid woman. But she was deeply in love with the man who had fallen below. He was the only real interest in life she had ever had —the one man who had ever treated her fairly when her beautiful sister was by. She pictured him drowned (not knowing how little danger he was in), if help did not come promptly. If he had to die, she did not, if fate were, mind dying with him. Life had been a barren affair for her in spite of her having more than her share of good looks, and more than her share of this world's goods. She took off her hat, a broad shady one which might have got in her way, and threw it with her parasol on the sand beside him.

'Stop, Mary,'—he had never called her by her Christian name before. It gave her fresh courage.

'No; I'm going to try it. If you see me not putting my foot in the right place, call out; and if I fall,' she added simply, 'try and keep me from striking anything with my head.'

For years after he could not get one picture out of his memory. The picture of a frail, pale girl creeping along a narrow slip of rock with a set, white, terrified face, and her hands stretched above her clinging to the grasses growing out of the crannies in the cliff. Once, with a sharp cry, followed by a low moan, she dislodged a mass of rock which almost struck him as he stood straining his eyes in case he might be able to give one saving warning. As the dislodged rock thundered down past his head, he expected in one second to have her flying through the air, and in a fragment of that second sent up a prayer that he might catch her in her fall, though the concussion might easily kill him. One second he saw the slight feet hanging limp in the air. Then he noticed the stump of a tree root broken off with the path. It projected out from the rock hardly more than a hand's thickness. 'Move your left foot back,' he cried. She felt the root. Providentially the grasses had held. From that poor foothold she was able to step upon a sound piece, and in a second more was on the full breadth of path again.

'Keep my hat and parasol till——'

He heard no more. When the tension was over he grew dizzy. He had not noticed that his head was bleeding.

He came to again quickly, as he heard the creaking of a *yulo*, and saw a *sampan*, propelled from the stern by a not by any means sufficiently clothed Japanese, shoot on to his little patch of sand, which was nearly all under water now, with Mary sitting in the stern bareheaded, and with a happy glow on her face which made her for the minute almost as beautiful as her sister.

The boatman landed them at the foot of the lovely winding stairway cut in the rock from which Mary had taken him. Speaking Japanese, she had had no difficulty in making him understand the importance of speed, and the pay Philip tossed him was as much as he could make out of Japanese in a week. He had been waiting for a party in the tea-house to which the stairway led, so he told Mary. Philip caught the word tea-house, and suggested that they should have tea to steady their nerves before they found their way back to their *rikshas*.

It was a lovely little tea-house, made of fragrant fir wood without a stain or scratch on it, and with the pale primrose matting inside as fresh as newly-fallen snow. The dainty little *mousmee* who came forward smiled gratefully when Mary, gathering at a glance that it was a house only frequented by Japanese, lifted her dress to have her boots unlaced, and asked Philip to take off his. The glimpses of her sumptuous white skirts, the idea of her being so helpless with her feet only stockinged (though his were no better off), added a touch of passion to Philip's admiration of the cool pluck shown by this dainty slip of a girl. It was not till she tried to take her gloves off to eat the bean-cake brought in with the tea that he saw what the girl had gone through in those awful seconds. The soft gray suede was sawn through, even forced into the gaping flesh by the knife-like blades of the tough, striped ribbon grass which had saved her, and she had never given her fingers — masses of bleeding pulp though they were — a thought till this second. When the *mousmee* who brought them their tea had disappeared with the sometimes rather embarrassing discreetness of Japanese hotel servants, his soul went out to Mary, and he and she found a great happiness.

There was a touch of humour almost at the birth of it. In Japanese rooms there is no furniture. It was so hard to be decorously affectionate on the floor, that they sneaked out and sat at the top of the ladder-like stair, listening guiltily for the step of the little *mousmee*.

CHAPTER IX

THIS was in May! As June grew insufferable in Yokohama under the heavy damp heat of the rainy season, the Avons made their summer flitting to Nikko, taking Mary's *fiancé* with them.

Although Nikko is far outside treaty limits, European residents in Japan are able to get special permission to have summer-houses there, the ports being so very oppressive in the height of summer. The Avons had owned an ideal place at Nikko, an ex-monastery no longer required for its original purpose owing to the disestablishment of Buddhism —a low one-story building of wood standing on the shores of an artificial lake surrounded by a Chinese garden, quaint and beautiful as only the loving patience of the Buddhist monks could make it.

But it had recently been burnt down, so this year they had to put up at the hotel.

It took them some time to get away from Utsonomiya, the railway station some thirty miles short of Nikko, where the train service terminated in those days. Not that they bothered about their luggage. The Japanese servants they brought with them were to take it up in one of the *stages*, which run between Utsonomiya and Nikko, and resemble nothing in the world but the vans in which half and quarter carcase; are conveyed from the shambles to butchers' shops in England. They crawl along, or rather hobble at the rate of about three miles an hour, and a European would die of asphyxia in them before he had gone a mile.

Kano the inevitable, whose English was fluent though mangled, and Bryn's maid were to accompany the family in *jinrikshas*. Now it might have been supposed that jumping into *rikshas*, when there were other people to look after the luggage, could have been done in no time. But nothing is done in no time in Japan. Nothing would satisfy Kano. He wished to put on airs; to show the good people of Utsonomiya what poor trash they were compared to a Japanese who was a European's steward. One *riksha* was old; another was dirty; the *kurumayas* (*riksha*-men) were not good runners; and so on.

Finally they started ; Phil and Mary in front, followed by Bryn and her father, with Kano and Otori-san bringing up the rear, each drawn by two strong runners, bowling out of the town at their best pace.

The journey was quite a new experience for Bryn. They generally went up to Nikko in a large party, but as they were not going to their own house, only Phil, who, as Mary's *fiancé*, was in a way one of the family, was with them, and he was quite absorbed in Mary ; so Bryn had to ride beside her father, who bored her, and whom she rather pitied. She soon got rid of him, however, for two *riksha*-men will never run side by side for two minutes, unless their occupants keep them up to it. There is possibly a police regulation on the subject.

Before this afternoon Bryn had no idea that her sister was so pretty and attractive. But as Mary rode in the *riksha* in front of her, sitting upright and with her head inclined towards Phil, with whom she was keeping up an animated conversation, Bryn noticed that her little well-bred head was uncommonly well set on her neck, and that when the excitement of being thoroughly appreciated and happy brought colour into her cheeks and a sparkle into her eyes, her delicate features made her almost a lovely girl.

Mary was of a chameleon nature. When the people round her thought her 'poor Mary,' she felt and looked 'poor Mary.' When the man she was with thought her as capable as himself of appreciating the humours and picturesquities of the Pilgrims' Road, she rose to the occasion and thoroughly enjoyed them.

Mr. Avon smoked.

And Bryn did something very like sulking while Phil and Mary were calling out to each other to look at the queer Japanese pilgrims with their enormous umbrella hats and all their worldly belongings in stay-boxes tied up in oiled paper ; or the crawling stages which they overtook full of every variety of poor Jap stolidly enduring ; or a *jinriksha* with two big Japs inside and one little one drawing it ; or a troupe of acrobats and jugglers who generally were performing something or other as they went along : at all events when there were *jinrikshas* in sight.

The whole thirty miles lay through an avenue of tall cryptomerias, planted the day that the ashes of Iyeyasu, the founder of the mighty dynasty of the Tokugawas, were carried to rest in the plain bronze urn on the hillside, which is the end of all human greatness. And they were hardly ever out of sight of a wayside tea-house, with its cluster of *riksha*-boys squatting on the edge of the raised floor shovelling down bowlfuls of smoking rice, and its gay little *mousmees* rushing out to call ‘ *Ohayo*,’ and proffer the inevitable tea ; or the shops where they sell the straw-rope sandals worn by *jinriksha*-men, which cost about a penny a pair.

Now and then their boys would halt for a few minutes, pull out their *kiseru*—tiny brass pipes— smoke a few whiffs, tap the ashes, and then on again ; and about half-way they made a longer halt for a meal. *Riksha*-boys must have digestions like locomotives, for they are very fond of eating in the middle of a long run. The boys would have liked to stop much oftener than they did, but they had

Kano to deal with, and he had told them that they would be well paid if they tried no nonsense. It is purgatory for an unprotected European to go a long journey with lazy *riksha*-boys.

At the principal halt the travellers themselves had tea in a pretty little tea-room with glass *shoji*.

They had started fairly late from home, so it was dark as they entered the mile-long street which constitutes the dwelling-town of Nikko. By night it did not seem a very imposing place, with its low houses, and dim lights glimmering through paper *shoji*. The hotel in which they were going to stay was across the river, close by the temples. Mary was quite disappointed that the darkness prevented Phil beginning his impressions of the approach to the Golden Shrines with the view of Mihashi, that exquisite arc of red lacquer which spans the foaming sky-blue Kamman-gawa, and is never used but for a burial or procession of the house of Tokugawa, or a glimpse of the little red shrine at the entrance to the dark wood which shrouds the road to the shrines.

At the door of the hotel they were met by Mr. Mathdine and Mr. Dacres. Mr. Spong always went to Miyanoshita, where he found the baths and other arrangements to his liking. Mr. Mathdine had volunteered to come up the day before to see that the rooms and preparations were to the Avons' liking. One of their servants could have done it equally well; only this was a way in which he could show anxiety for Bryn's pleasure.

Bryn showed rather more appreciation than he had ventured to expect.

Dinner was ready almost before she and Mary had slipped into cool silk *kimonos* from the dress-box which Otori-san had been hugging all the way up from Utsonomiya.

CHAPTER X

THE next day Mr. Avon and Bryn and her cavaliers went to inspect the damage done by the fire. The monastery which had formed their pleasant summer home, being all wood and paper, had been burned to the ground. But the tennis lawn and the old monastery garden, with its lake and wistaria arbour overhanging the water, were undamaged.

'What a bore that there's no fourth,' said Bryn; 'we might have had a knock up.'

'Let's go fishing instead,' suggested Mr. Mathdine. 'There was a Jap fishing in that little stream at Taki-no-jinja yesterday who caught four or five dozen —little ones, of course.'

'Yes; let's go fishing,' said Bryn. 'Kano, go and find that Japanese who caught those fish yesterday, and bring him and his tackle and bait.'

Kano always carried out orders somehow, and soon after lunch they were industriously fishing the clear little runnel that sped along a leet with a crumbling, picturesque wooden paling on one side and a thicket of hydrangea on the other. The stones were slippery with moss, and Mr. Mathdine was for helping Bryn. Every time he touched her fingers he would have a thrill of secret and passionate pleasure. Bryn was either suspicious or wayward. She refused his aid. 'I'm going to walk in the water.'

'But you'll spoil your things.'

'I don't care.'

She was less afraid of that than of losing a friend, and when their fingers had met, as he helped her over a gate coming down from the temples, his hand was tingling in a way which put her on her guard.

They did not catch any fish, and eventually handed the tackle over to its owner, who caught a few. They did not wish to return empty-handed.

Then they wandered along the ancient causeway of footworn stones towards the shrines of the three Gon-gen, the original patron-saints of the holy mountains of Nikko-San—Bryn and Mr. Mathdine. Mr. Dacres had torn his clothes in crossing the fence, and hastened home to repair the damage in a costume that it was his business in life to keep immaculate.

The other two wandered on till they came to the waterfall, which the Japanese love to compare to a bowl of macaroni for its filaments of white foam. They climbed the crumbling stairway past the *hon-den* and the *hai-den;* loitered awhile on the little hunchbacked bridge of mossy stone, which leads to the Gon-gen's fallen trees behind the exquisite balustrade, to hear the pooh-pooh belling its strange note in the depths of the forest; and passed on to the magic stone, where barren women lay their offerings and pray to be blest with children. Here they sat down by the banks of the clear fern-arched stream.

Robert Mathdine forbore to seize an advantage. He played Bryn as he would play a big fish. He loved her passionately. She could make of him any kind of man, good or frivolous. But the time had not come to strike. He thought it best to quietly ingratiate himself.

And Bryn was in the mood to be gracious, so long as he refrained from heroïcs ; but somehow she could not help wishing that he saw more difference between Yokohama and Takinojinga woods. New arrivers thought so much of Nikko.

In the evening, when they were all sitting in the broad verandah, outside the big bedroom which had been turned into a drawing-room for them, Phil kept by the window, through which the light was streaming, to read up Murray's pages and pages about Nikko. Bryn came across to him more than usually lovely, as the rays fell on her ruddy fairness and tawny golden hair, toned down by the pale apple green (flowered with bunches of daisies) of the soft silk crepe *kimono*, opened at the throat, which the heavy moist heat had driven her to wear in place of an evening dress.

Though he had first frequented Netheravon for the love of her, and though he still thought her the finest and loveliest woman in the world, he hardly ever addressed her. It was sufficient for him to be one of the family, to have the right of always being near her. .

He was a good talker ; and had the talk at

dinner not been so much of the Mathdine and Dacres order, he and Bryn would doubtless have been drawn into many a keen conversational skirmish. As it was, he generally sat quietly talking to his *fiancée*. For one thing, it gave her so much pleasure. She had generally been the negligible quantity at her father's table.

Why Bryn crossed over from Mr. Mathdine to Phil did not appear. To leave anyone who was talking to her with scant warning was one of the prerogatives assumed by the queen of the Settlement.

'What have you two being doing this afternoon, Phil?' she asked, drawing a folding chair up beside him.

'Well, first we did the Murderer's Temple!'

'What's that?'

'Don't you know that tiny temple across the river, high up in that big patch of azaleas half-way up the hillside?'

'I love those wild azaleas. We've got a thicket of them at the back of our garden. Is it really a murderer's temple?'

'Well, there are two or three rusty swords there with dark stains on them.'

'That's quite exciting. What did you do then?'

'Walked along the river bank, down the Avenue of the Hundred Buddhas.'

'Oh, what's all that? those mouldy images?'

'Oh, Bryn, haven't you ever noticed any beauty in them—the repose, the infinite compassion, in the faces?'

'I've never looked at them. I've tried to count them often, and got a different number every time.'

'Well, I think that little glacier river, blue as the sky, goodness knows how deep, foaming away between banks of stone, that look as if they had been cut with a knife, past those solemn Buddhas, and the rock on which Kobo Daishi carved his message, and the acres of scarlet azaleas, and the sacred groves, is about as beautiful a thing as anything in the world.'

'I hadn't thought of it,' said Bryn simply.

CHAPTER XI

BRYN had 'developed' a Hungarian count, who played tennis quite decently, so that they could get up a four. This made the days pass easily, and in the evening he taught her the *tsardas* and other picturesque Hungarian dances, whistling the tunes.

Phil and Mary had done the sights of Nikko as exhaustively as if they had to pass an examination in them. The priests were getting quite accustomed to them, and would let them linger on long after the temples were closed to the public to see the sun set over the dark wood where Iyeyasu sleeps his long sleep; or watch the water swimming over the four sides of the cistern, which the Prince of Bizen set up under that indescribable canopy in memory of Iyemitsu. The water flows so evenly that the cistern looks like a block of ice.

One day they all arranged to walk over the mountains, past the Seven Waterfalls, to the lake of

Chiusenji. Bryn and Mary were to go shares in a
pony whenever they were tired, as they insisted on
walking like the gentlemen.

The walk was lovely. Now they were crossing
a thicket afire with azalea blossom, now passing
between a lofty waterfall and the rock over which
it leapt. Now they were scrambling along on a
ledge above a mountain torrent, or threading a dark
wood, starred with red and white camellia trees
thirty feet high. Once they halted among the charred
ruins of a temple. It was strewn with broken gods.
The Count was very funny. Calling his guide, a
weak, broken-kneed wretch, he handed him the
head of a good-sized Buddha, weighing somewhere
between ten and twenty pounds.

'You verstehe—understand, Shundo, that I vish to
take god back mit me to Hungary. In Hungary
I have kein Gott——' (He twisted his fingers in
his anxiety to explain)—'Ah, I have it! In
Hungary I have no god—I am a Christian.'

There were another dozen or two of idols' heads
lying about, and the guide, wishing to be obliging,
for the Count was generous and most autocratic,
asked if he should take all.

'Man on Eart,' said the Count, 'is not vun god
enough?'

Chiusenji they duly reached, with its huge *torii*
reflected in the mirror-like waters of the lake; and
the great mountain Nantaizan towering above it;
and the huge old tea-houses, built on piles driven
into its bosom.

They went into the first, and found it very clean
and highly picturesque; but they would have had

to put up with Japanese fare if the Count's guide had not laid in for him enough lunch for six. The Count had a great objection to Japanese food. The guide at first produced hardly enough for one person ; but the Count, whose inclination for strong measures had betrayed him into nine duels, took hold of him by the nape of the neck and shook him till he confessed about the rest. He knew his little weakness for ordering six times too much of everything. It was astonishing how such a puny little man could have managed to carry such a quantity besides the head of the Buddha.

But though the hotel-keeper was unable to supply European food, he offered the services of a couple of *guechas* (singing-women) to enliven the feast, which gave it an Oriental tone to the globe-trotting Count and the newly-arrived Philip, though the singers were not of a class to impress the old stagers.

. . . . . .

The two girls had not got far on the way back before they began to regret that they had not brought two ponies instead of one.

'Oh, Bryn,' said Mary, when they were about a mile and a half from home, 'I do wish you'd let me get on now. I feel dead beat.'

'I can't walk any more,' answered Bryn pettishly. 'You've had all your time (which was hardly the case), and if I walk any more my feet will be sore, and I shan't be able to take my lesson in the *tsardas* from the Count.'

'N'importe,' said the Count, shrugging his shoulders. 'Your sister is more white than my teet'.'

'Oh, nonsense, Mary, you're all right.'

'Bryn,' quietly interposed Philip, who had only just gathered the drift of what was going on, 'you must give up the pony to Mary. I'm not going to tell you that she's your elder, but at any rate she is positively ill with tiredness. Now that I have a right to interfere, I'm not going to stand by and see you trade on her gentleness, as you used to.'

It was about the first time that the beauty had ever been told a home truth since she was a child. At first she looked as if some one had struck her a heavy blow, then she flushed scarlet, then she turned white with passion ; then she said to Mr. Mathdine in icy tones, 'Will you help me to get down ? I'll stay in that little tea-house by the bridge, and you can send the pony back for me.'

'I'll stay with you,' cried all the gentlemen but Philip.

'No. No one shall stay with me,' said Bryn passionately ; but as she sat waiting in the tea-house she saw her future brother-in-law pacing up and down about fifty yards off, to guard her from any possible unpleasantness. When the pony came back he struck into the wood, and reappeared about fifty yards behind. She thought he might be loitering to make his peace with her ; but he never came near her either on the journey or during the evening.

Bryn danced the *tsardas* with the Count, and behaved generally as if nothing had happened, with the exception of not addressing Philip. And it was not his custom to take the initiative in addressing her.

CHAPTER XII

'LET'S do the big temple, Iyeyasu's, again to-day, Mary,' said Philip next morning at breakfast.

'Oh, Phil, I'm so sorry ; but I've got a splitting nervous headache. I'm afraid I rather overdid myself yesterday. I mean I ought not to have gone.' She suddenly reflected that it looked like raking up old sores.

'You're as white as a sheet, little woman. You'd better rest in the verandah. But I think I'll go up alone—unless you want me particularly. I can't take a thing like the shrine of Iyeyasu in, until I've been to it over and over again.'

'Don't stay at home for me. It will rest me more to be quite alone, I can close my eyes. Otori-san is sure to be within call. She sits and watches like a dog, without making a sound, when there is anything the matter with either of us.'

'I'll go with you, Phil,' said Bryn rather shyly. 'I'm not a fool, really.'

'And so will I,' said Mr. Mathdine and Mr. Dacres and the Count.

'No,' said Bryn firmly. 'I won't have any of you. I'm going to "do" the temples—not to make a background of them. Will you take me, Phil ?'

'Of course I will, Bryn.'

'Off we go then. Imagine that I'm an American willing to be personally conducted over any mortal thing, from the working of a phonograph to the interior of a pyramid.'

'Well then, we'll just walk down to the sacred bridge and begin at the beginning.'

When they reached the sacred red lacquer bridge known as Mihashi, a beautiful shallow single arch resting on two vast stone *torii*, Bryn, laughingly saying that she was going to do everything in style, tripped round by the ordinary bridge, and, climbing the barriers, crossed Mihashi.

'The police will be after you,' said Philip.

'Not they. They'd hardly raise a finger to save the temples being burnt. I don't read much, but I was born in Japan, and have never been out of it, and Japanese has been my native language as much as English, and I know by popular acceptation what an eyesore in one way these shrines of the Shoguns here and at Shiba and Ueno are to the present Government. They represent loyalty to the Tokugawas.'

'The who?'

'The family of the Shogun who was deposed in 1868.'

They entered the sacred grove by the little red shrine of Jinja Daio, wandered slowly up the broad Naga-saka, with a clear brook running down a stone channel in its midst, and stately cryptomerias towering on each side ; skirted the south wall of the great monastery of Mangwanji ; then ascending some broad steps shaded by a double line of cryptomerias planted in stone-faced banks, and passing through the great *torii* of the Prince of Chikuzen, made of beams of stone four feet thick, stood on the piazza outside the temple, which soared in front of them. On their left stood a tall scarlet pagoda ; on their right, at the top of some crumbling, mossy steps, a beautiful little temple with some fine decorations and a large Buddhist bell.

'This,' said Philip, halting at the foot of the steps to turn it up in the guide-book, 'is only used when the large temple is undergoing repairs, isn't it ? '

'I don't know,' said Bryn, running up the steps, and standing knee-deep in the flower-spangled hay-grass which had grown up round the disused shrine. 'But come and look at the view.' She led the way to the brow overlooking the woods of Taki-no-jinga. 'It's almost the only spot in all Nikko where you can see a vista and a slice of sky between the mountains,' she said, pointing to the blue distance stretching away in the fork between the tall pine-clad hills. 'It's like my life,' she added. 'There never was a break in the mountains which ring it in, till yesterday. I like your pluck, Phil,' she continued, laying her hand on his arm just below the elbow. 'I was mad with you at first, but while I was in the tea-house, and saw you on guard lest anything should befall a lonely woman, though you would not move an inch to make friends, my heart went out to you, and I said to myself, "Thank God, a man has come along at last, a real man, to tell me when I am a fool." '

He began to stammer out something about being sorry that he had had to speak.

'Phil,' said the girl, taking his arm lightly with the hand she had laid on it, and walking him back towards the entrance of the main temple, 'I want to make you my friend. All the rest are lovers, more or less declared, whom I have to keep at arm's length.'

She showed no suspicion of the feelings he had once entertained for her. Now he was candidly prepared to be her friend, and to love her, if he could, no more than a brother-in-law should.

'All right, Bryn,' he said, withdrawing her arm and taking her hand into his for a second or two, as an earnest. 'I'll be your friend. You can come to me, and if I think it necessary, I won't wait for you to come. Let's go into the temple now, because I'd like to be back with Mary by the time she feels rested.'

Handing their queer little silky paper tickets, which looked like Buddhist prayers, to the priest who sat outside at the seat of change, to be sealed, they trailed lazily through the outer gateway, the Niomon, containing no more the grotesque images of the two kings who gave it its name, but only Ama-Inu and Koma-Inu, very highly gilt.

'Do you recognise our old friends, Bryn?'

'No, what?'

'The lion and the unicorn. Don't you see the little horn on Koma-Inu's forehead?'

'I'm afraid they look more like poodles to me. They have them everywhere in Japan; we always used to call them Corean lions when we were children. I haven't seen very much of the lion and the unicorn, you must remember,' she added, with one of her frank smiles, which went straight to every man's heart. 'I've never been out of Japan except for the Hong-Kong races.'

'It seems hard to realise. You've got our Tudor rose, as well as our lion and unicorn—only you call it a peony. The guide-book says there's a very fine one round the back of this gate.'

'How do you account for it all? I never talk sense, you must understand, so I know nothing.'

'I hardly know either. Some story as old as the world, I suppose, connecting these animals and flowers with kingship.'

'I wish you had your camera here. There's an awfully rare beast carved upon this gate. An old priest used to tell us about it when we were children —the Taku-jin. It can talk like a man, but it has not been seen within living memory, because it only appears when a virtuous sovereign occupies the throne. Perhaps it is in England now. We do have your Queen's virtues rather rammed down our throats.'

'*Our Queen's*, you should say : you're an English-woman.'

'I suppose I am.'

They passed into a courtyard with a timber wall painted bright red.

There were three handsome buildings inside with heavy gables, arranged in a zigzag, ornamented with magnificent gilt brasses and painted carvings.

'What curious carvings,' said Philip. 'Do you see the elephant on the near gable? His legs bend the wrong way.'

'Do they?' said Bryn. 'I'm not up in elephants ; but you mustn't let the Japs hear you. The carvings are by their great left-handed sculptor, Hidaro-Jingoro.'

'Well, the carvings are very curious, correct or not.'

'Those aren't the ones to look at. The show carvings are on the other side on the sacred stables. The monkeys that everyone takes away photographs of.'

'Oh, the san goku no saru,' he cried, pulling the guide-book out of his pocket wildly.

'That only means the monkeys of three countries. The old Japs only recognised India, China, and Japan.'

'What's all this Kika Zaru, Iwa Zaru, and Mi Zaru?'

'Oh, that's just the not-hearing, not-speaking, and not-seeing monkeys.'

'What's the stable for?'

'Oh, it has one of the small white ponies they generally keep in a Japanese temple when it's dedicated to a deified hero, so that he may not have to walk if he should take it into his head to come back to earth. This one has such fierce blue eyes. They blaze up if you offer him beans.'

He smiled. She smiled too.

'Real beans. Selling *sen*'s worth of beans is one of the principal sources of income in the temple. And I don't think the god-like hero would be altogether satisfied with the pony, because I grieve to say that it's piebald. We who have been brought up here as children can't help seeing the funny side. That tree outside always tickled us enormously, that huge koya-maki,' she said, pointing with her left hand. Iyeyasu used to carry it about in his palanquin in a little blue flower-pot.

'I expect koya-makis grow very fast. But, to be serious, could anything be more lovely than that fountain with that exquisite canopy on those twelve light shafts? There's nothing to beat that in Constantinople. Why, it's got another of those cisterns like the one in the temple of Iyemitsu, with the water running over all its sides exactly level. It was built by the same man, the ancestor of that dear old Marquis Nabeshima you've met at our house so often—almost the only Jap who can meet you like a European. He is one of the new marquises, but his ancestors were princes of Bizen. The water comes from that Somendaki fall we were at yesterday, through goodness knows how many miles of bamboo pipes.'

'And what lovely carvings there are on that red building next to the fountain.'

'Oh, that's the library. Would you like an instalment of salvation on the cheap?'

'What do you mean?'

'Come inside and I'll show you,' she said.

Inside there was an enormous circular cupboard made of lacquer, fixed into a sort of capstan with a pole sticking out of it.

'Stand in front of that pole,' she said. He did. 'Now push it as hard as you can.'

The cupboard swung slowly round one, two, three times.

'You're safe,' cried Bryn.

'What's it all about?' he asked.

'Well, you see a man would never have time to read all the Buddhist scriptures if he lived to be a hundred and did nothing else. There are about

7000 volumes of them, 6771 or something of that sort, so they put them all into this spinning-wheel affair, and adopted the useful fiction, that if you can make it go round three times without stopping, it does your soul as much good as if you had read them all.'

'Really, Bryn, you mustn't tell me any more of your nursery tales, or I shall have no reverence left for the temple of Iyeyasu, and it's said to be the most beautiful thing in the whole Buddhist world.'

'Well, I'll be serious.'

They passed under a magnificent bronze *torii* and up a flight of stately steps to a terrace with a picturesque balustrade of lichened stone, with two stone lions in the act of leaping down, given by the great Shogun Iyemitsu, who is buried in the other principal shrine of Nikko. On this terrace stood the funny bell tower and drum tower of Buddhist temples, looking for all the world like a couple of huge scarlet windmills without their sails. Crowded round these under the sky were some of the finest bronzes the world possesses; the candelabrum given as tribute by the king of Loochoo, and the candelabrum given as a kind of tribute by the Dutch of the old factory at Nagasaki. They must have been great novelties 250 years ago, because they had sockets for the candles, a thing unheard of in the far East, where candles are hollow and go on their sticks instead of into them.

Bryn took no notice of them or the noble Corean lantern; they did not belong to her childhood. She took him straight to a great bronze bell, and made him stand underneath it. There was a little tiny hole in the top close to the ring.

'We call that the moth-eaten bell. In Japanese it has some legend. I can't remember what.'

'The guide-book has something to say about that bell.'

'Come on,' said Bryn, 'there's a lot more to see yet. You can't look at all those *daimio* lanterns, there are a hundred and eighteen of them.' He was lost in admiration of the great bronze votive lanterns cunningly wrought and chased, which the chief feudatories of the house of Tokugawa had erected in pairs when the body of Iyeyasu was brought here. Then he climbed the lofty flight of steps, at the top of which he stood before one of the crowning glories of Nikko, the great white gate Yomeimon, a riot of fantastic Eastern carving.

As usual, Bryn had her child's curiosity to show him. She made him examine the delicate carvings of the pillars. 'Do you see anything?' she said. He shook his head.

'Well, look at this one.'

He looked closely and found that the pattern was upside down, though it was so cunningly managed that it did not in the least interfere with the general effect.

'We call that Mayoke-No-Hashira—the evil-averting pillar.' From Yomeimon they walked across the outer courtyard to its rival, the Karamon, the tiny little white gate with miniature carvings of Chinese sages and scenes, as delicate as ivories. This Karamon was in the centre of the front of a stockade. They hardly noticed the carvings, for they passed under a plain white wooden shed into the temple itself, leaving their shoes outside. Neither of them could repress a cry of admiration, often as they had been in it before. The famous lacquer of the Golden Shrine, the most costly effort of the lacquerer's art, was so exquisitely soft and unobtrusive. The great *hai-den*, or hall of the temple, was so majestic in its costly simplicity. The exquisite doors of the *hon-den*, the Holy of Holies, the holiest Buddhistic spot in Japan, had such an air of splendour and mystery.

Philip was not prepared for Bryn's being so impressed with the quiet, rich taste of old Japan. She appeared to genuinely enjoy it. It was he who suggested that they must be moving on.

As they left the temple she drew his attention to a building on the right, adjoining the scarlet cloister. 'That's where they keep the *mikoshi*, the three sacred cars, looking like huge sarcophaguses of scarlet and gold, which the images of Iyeyasu, Yoritomo, and Hideyoshi ride in at the To-sho-gu festival, carried on the shoulders of about a hundred coolies.'

'What is the To-sho-gu festival?'

'Unfortunately it's just over. It's the festival of the deified Iyeyasu; but really it's a sort of demonstration of discontented Buddhists, and adherents of the Shogun. Do you remember the San-gin-ko, the three treasuries where they had that carving of an elephant? They're full of the dresses worn at this ceremony, and of various relics of Iyeyasu, which are carried in state. If we'd only thought of it we'd have brought you up here in time for the To-sho-gu. It's great fun. You sit up above and throw "cash," twisted up in tissue paper, for the crowd to scramble

for. You never saw such a crowd in your life;
Nikko goes wild with excitement. It's a sort of
carnival with all the coolies in the place dressed up
in feudal array.'

Philip turned round to go to the tomb. 'Those
two buildings in front,' he said, consulting his guide-
book, 'are the Goma-Do, and the Kagura-Do. . I
suppose they dance in the Kagura-Do. What do
they do in the Goma-Do, Bryn?'

'Burn cedar, and make a nice smell. I don't
know what else they do. They have very nice
screens, and the priests always look awfully clean in
their white robes.'

'Shall we go in and have a look?'

'Oh yes.'

The priests received them most graciously, and
said something in Japanese. They did not know
Bryn by sight, and were quite surprised at the young
English beauty's answering them back fluently and
idiomatically in their own language.

'What did they say, Bryn?'

'They asked if we wanted to buy any prayers;
they have them specially printed for people who are
not educated enough to formulate a prayer for themselves. They cost the poor Japs a *rin* each, but we
must pay 10 *rin*—1 *sen*, what you call a halfpenny
—for the good of the house, as gentlemen say.
You just throw them into the grating in front of the
god, and the prayer is answered if it goes right in,
especially if you weight it with a few *rin*.'

The prayers were very pretty little things, printed
in dainty characters on silky white paper, and
stamped with the priest's little red seal, that the deity

might know they were authentic. Philip bought a whole handful to use as Christmas cards. Thus encouraged, the priest volunteered something else in Japanese.

'What does he say?' said Philip.

'He says "Will you buy the *Good Counsel of Iyeyasu?*"' answered Bryn, pulling a broad sheet of tissue paper with large black characters on it, which made it look like a police notice, out of a pretty blue and white wrapper, such as they put round head towels for New Year's gifts to coolies.

'Read it.'

'Oh, I can't. It's in the classical character; and I only know the newspaper alphabet, and that's more than most white people do,' said Bryn, tossing her chin.

'Does the priest know what it means?'

'Oh yes, I suppose so.'

She plunged into a long conversation in Japanese. At the end, 'It's the usual thing,' she said. 'Iyeyasu, having reached the very height of human wealth and power, says it's all vanity, and that it's better to be a virtuous peasant or something of the kind. Have you seen the Kagura dance?'

'No.'

'Well, it isn't worth much, but it doesn't cost much; she'll go through a performance for 10 *sen*. She's the mother of a family, and has black teeth. The only picturesque thing about her is the scarlet and white dress; but she does the fan-play rather well; that's all the dancing amounts to. I think we had better go straight to the "sleeping cat."'

'What is the "sleeping cat"?'

'Oh, a very wooden-looking pussy by our friend Hidaro-Jingoro, who carved the elephant wrong. It's over the little archway through which we have to go to the tomb.'

'Oh, let's get on to the tomb.'

'By all means; the way up to it is about the prettiest thing in Nikko.'

Bryn had not exaggerated. To people sauntering along as they did, chatting all the while, in the way that two friends will who have known each other long in a perfunctory way, but have only just discovered something in common, nothing could be more charming than the ascent to the tomb, now sunk between high ramparts full of ferns, now climbing up winding, moss-grown stairways of hoary masonry, now carried along the side of a brow with a picturesque balustrade of carved stone. All gradual.

At the top they passed through another *torii*, and, walking round a beautiful little temple, intended for use in case anything happened to the great temple in this land of fires, they came to the hero's tomb, a plain bronze urn of the pattern used for princes in Japan, with a stork, a censer, and a vase of the same metal in front of it. It stood on a stone platform surrounded by a simple stone balustrade, entered by a flight of steps, and was guarded by a massive bronze door, simple and beautiful, the largest bronze ever made in a single casting, with Ama-Inu and Koma-Inu on each side of it.

The great stork standing on a tortoise, the emblem of immortality, held on his back a brass candlestick. The great vase, made like the censer, of inch-thick bronze, had a spray of brazen lotus flowers. There was nothing to distinguish the tomb of the most powerful of all Japanese except that the bronze was of the strange light colour which shows the plentiful admixture of gold. Up to the very edge of the little court in which the platform stood came the dark and solemn grove.

Bryn sat down on the steps to the tomb quite unimpressed. It did not appeal to her; it did not touch her sense of beauty as the interior of the *hai-den* had done. 'Our old Japanese *amah*,' she said, 'that is, our nurse, used to say that Iyeyasu had himself buried in this very plain style after piling up the agony in the magnificence of the temples down below, to show that, no matter how great a man may be in his lifetime, he can only end one way. She was a funny old Judy, but she really was very interesting if we had been more appreciative.' They sat in silence for a minute or two; then Bryn said, 'I am afraid you have found me rather a fool, Phil. Mary seems so much better at these things than I am, though I was always above her at school.'

'On the contrary, I think you're awfully appreciative. I had no idea you cared about these things.'

'No more had I; though I find they interest me immensely. I came because I thought talking to you would be such a nice change. I had a hope that you might not talk to me about myself quite all the time as the others do—when they are not talking about themselves.'

CHAPTER XIII

IT was not such a blow to the Avons, as it well might have been, to have lost the pleasant habitation that was their summer home at Nikko. They did not feel the overpowering regret some people—Philip for instance—would have felt at the destruction of the ancient *shoji* painted by master hands in the seventeenth century, which had been the glory of the house in the days when it was a monastery; or the exquisite woodwork of fir that had never known paint or varnish, but mellowed almost to a gray by the gentle influence of a couple of centuries. The Avon girls felt that they had their garden still for entertainments; and, apart from that, it was almost more fun living in the hotel. There is much to divert one in a hotel kept by Japanese on the foreign plan. Except wars and such, the Japanese have little idea of running a thing on a large scale. Their genius is particular and not general. In this hotel there were never enough servants, never really enough food, and the very agreeable young manager never thought of fulfilling a promise, until a guest took the law into his own hands—except when there was a thoroughly competent Japanese intermediary like Kano to be reckoned with. But he and all his employés had such pleasant manners that people just laughed and forgave them.

Bryn knew the Japanese too well ever to be much surprised at anything they did; but she did give a little start when she awoke the first morning and found a Japanese man standing by her bed in the act of touching her shoulder again. However he smiled benignantly, and said, ' Bath riddy—please examine. Gentleman want soon.' The morning after she had done the temples he was particularly importunate, so Bryn packed him out of her road, hurriedly slipped on a *kimono*, and flew barefoot after him, only to find the bath so far from being ' riddy' that the man who ought to have brought up the hot water could not be found.

He turned out to have taken the water into the bathroom down the passage for Philip, who had bribed him to try for once to be quick. To crown all, Philip made his appearance *en route*, and was almost passing Bryn before he noticed her. He pretended not to see, and muttering ' Hullo, I've only got one towel,' turned and fled. But Bryn, reflecting that he was just about to become her brother-in-law ; . . . to do her justice she did not give a thought to the fact that her *kimono* was so chic, and her slim white feet as unspoiled as a well-bred Japanese's, and her hair a flood of sunshine when it was let down,—called out with a fine disregard of grammar, ' It's only me, Phil. I didn't expect to meet like this quite so soon ; but I suppose it won't be the last time.' Whereupon he gallantly insisted upon her taking his bath, and kicked up his heels until his hired villain brought up a fresh relay of hot water for the bath which was to have been hers. After this Bryn always sent Otori-san to make sure before she proceeded to her bath.

Another time they came in late for lunch.

'Toku,' roared Mr. Mathdine to the head waiter, 'bring some lunch.'

There was no reply. 'Tora.' Still no reply. 'Here Toku, Tora, Cauliflower, one of you, confound you, bring lunch.'

Still no reply, though there was rustling and smothered laughter behind a big screen at the end of the room. The local head of that eminent shipping firm strode up to the screen, boiling with indignation, and pulled it down, and discovered the comical little waiter, known as 'Cauliflower' from the shape of his curly hair, struggling to get back into his European trousers. But though it looked for the moment shocking, it was really perfectly decent, because he always wore his European clothes over his Japanese. The waiters at this hotel were so impressed with their importance that they would almost as soon have died as waited at table in native dress. But they were so supremely uncomfortable in their suits of dark blue serge (made like officers' in the merchant service without their brass buttons) that they always kicked off their trousers and relapsed into *kimonos* the very moment that the last guest was served. Cauliflower had evidently unshelled before their arrival, and the rustling and laughing denoted his frantic struggle to readorn before he came out, and yet to come out before their patience was exhausted.

The food, too, was food for laughter. For dinner there was an ambitious programme of sixteen items. 'Forgotten soup' was the variety which oftenest filled the tureen—a name invented by Bryn, because they had forgotten to put any meat in the pot, and sliced pea-pods were the most usual vegetable, mixed occasionally with carrots and turnips stamped into little stars of the vermicelli pattern. The hotel had an alarming habit too of running out of bread, and was always short of butter and potatoes. These were only issued in famine rations. The dearth of the former was almost condoned for by Cauliflower's brief and witty explanation, ' Cow at Kobe.'

Philip discovered to his cost that Japanese houses can be extended or even moved from their sites without their inmates paying the slightest heed. Imagine his state of mind when on going to bed one night he found one side of his bedroom gone. He slept on the first floor, and if he had gone into his bedroom without a light, would very likely have ' walked the plank.' But with the thermometer at 80 there was no fear of draughts, and, the hotel being of wood, he found himself in possession of a whole room again on the following night, and of largely increased proportions, including a bow window.

He very soon had an object lesson in the way Japanese servants will feign stupidity to get out of doing anything which they dislike.

A rich Australian came to the hotel, doing everything in a very swaggering, damn-the-expense way. Now, there is nothing the Japanese dislike more than the swagger of the rough rich, with which their proximity to San Francisco has made them familiar. So when, a night or two afterwards, he drank a little too much, all the servants began to mimic him and make fun of him behind his back. Turning round suddenly, he caught them, and kicked a couple of them out of the room pretty roughly. After this not a thing would any of them do for him. He complained to the manager, who asserted that they were terrified to come near him, except when he was sitting down at table—which may have been partly true, though it was none the less annoying to the victim.

On another night, when he had been in the bar 'shouting' and 'being shouted' in colonial fashion, he went out for a long walk to work it off. He was by no means a drunkard, though he would go on drinking with boon companions till he had taken too much. It was a beautiful moonlight night, and he walked on and on, so that it was long past midnight before he got back. The watchman took care not to hear him, though he thundered and thundered with his stick and cursed till he was hoarse and like a wild beast with rage. At last Bryn, whose room was almost over the door, heard him, and hastily flinging something on, went down in search of the night watchman. She found him seemingly fast asleep. When she succeeded in making him confess himself awake, he swore that he was afraid of his life to open the door, for Mr. Murphy would certainly kill him.

'You coward,' hissed out Bryn, and told him in Japanese that if he undid all the bolts she would give him time to get away and turn the key herself. He obeyed trembling, and then she began to parley.

'Is that you, Mr. Murphy?'

'Yes. Who are you? Why the devil don't you open this d——d door?'

'I'm Miss Avon; nobody else seems to have heard you.'

'I'm sure I beg your pardon, Miss Avon,' said Mr. Murphy, who was quite himself again as far as drink was concerned, though he had been going on like a maniac when he found himself locked out.

'Mr. Murphy!'

'Yes, Miss Avon.'

'If I unlock the door will you count a hundred before you open it, so that I may get back to my room?'

'I promise you I will, thanks.'

The key turned. Mr. Murphy counted two hundred out aloud in a deliberate voice, and then walked in, and found that Bryn had lit a candle before she went upstairs.

With it he searched the best part of an hour for the night porter, who had gone into the manager's room and taken refuge under his bed, never to re-appear until Mr. Murphy left the hotel for the more congenial atmosphere of Yokohama.

The hotel door was not locked again that night.

CHAPTER XIV

'Do you really like poking about old temples and going those long walks with Sandys, Miss Bryn?'

'Honestly, Mr. Mathdine, did you ever know me do anything I didn't like twice?'

'Oh, well, I don't know. I don't think anybody would ever want you to.'

'Not unless they were in love with me. Lovers have absolutely no conscience as a rule.'

'You're hard on us, Miss Bryn.'

She gave him a swift glance.

'Most men are in love with some woman, I mean. And what a life they'd lead her, if they had their own way. A pretty woman ought to be a mighty good listener, and have a very poor memory.'

'I'd like to have a walk with you, Miss Bryn ; but I don't think we'd better do any temples.'

'No, I don't think we had.'

'Will you go for a walk ? '

'I suppose so. You heard me telling Mary I wanted to.'

'That's why I asked you. Where shall we go ? '

'Oh, a good brisk walk,' said Bryn warily. 'Men say such silly things when they're "loafing."'

'Where shall it be, then ? '

'The top of Toyama.' Bryn was a healthy creature and hardly knew what fatigue meant, and she had an idea that Mr. Mathdine was only moderately enthusiastic about walking.

'All right,' he said, and off they started at a good brisk pace.

Bryn was in a mischievous mood, so when they came to the red pagoda of the three Gon-gen, she suggested, ' Let's strike a bee-line across the river.' The river being a broad sheet of dry stones of all sizes, from a pebble to a precipice, with a tiny rill losing itself about the middle in this dry weather, though it ought to be a foaming torrent a couple of hundred yards broad, as it was now the rainy season. 'And the wistaria is so lovely.'

Now the wild wistaria is not a very showy flower, as Japanese flowers go. Its pale lilac racemes are only about a foot long, instead of three or four feet as it grows on arbours, and are rather raggedy. But what it lacks in flower it makes up in wood, as they soon found out, for there was a thicket of it to cross before they could get to 'the river.'

The vines were simply appalling to get through. Now they caught her under the chin and nearly strangled her, now they tripped her, now one would take her round the waist, and bring her to a dead stop.

'Let me take your hat,' said Mr. Mathdine: it was being dragged off her head every other minute. The quick eye which made him so brilliant at tennis kept him out of difficulties except where the vines were absolutely so interlaced that he had to take out his knife.

After a moment's hesitation Bryn gave it to him. It was a confession of weakness, and she had intended the weakness to be on his side. But it was making him useful to her too, and Bryn was accustomed to humble service.

Presently he said, 'I think you'd better let me go in front.' She demurred at this second confession of weakness.

'It's getting thicker,' he said chivalrously, 'and I shall break a way through.'

It was not, as a matter of fact, but he wanted to let her down easily.

She allowed him to pass then, but she was rather angry with herself.

At last they emerged and, stumbling across the stony bed, commenced the ascent.

Toyama was not high, nor particularly steep, till
the last hundred feet or so, and its lower slopes
were carpeted with the gorgeous wild scarlet azalea
growing on shrubs three or four feet high. Bryn
picked a spray of the almost oppressively aromatic
blossom, and pinned it at her throat. She must have
been very anxious to have scarlet round her face.
A month ago she could not have blushed. She
walked on briskly, paying no heed to the beautiful
pine-clad mountains opposite, which held the famous
shrines in their solemn groves. As the path rose, it
wound through rustling bamboo brakes, with an
occasional trail of wistaria. Here and there the
pale blossoms hung across the path.

Still that healthy, slender figure with its pride of
youth and conquests sped on, Mr. Mathdine purposely
hanging a little behind to feast his eyes on its poetry
of motion.

The top of Toyama was decidedly steep. It was
something after the manner of the Great Pyramid.
It was pure climbing—now scrambling up a rock a
yard or more high, now swinging yourself up by the
bough of a tree, for it was quite thickly wooded.

The girl clambered up with surprising activity,
disdaining his offers of assistance.

Up above this steep, wooded belt there was a
grassy knoll bare but for a tiny shrine, and a row of
little images of Buddha, such as one sees in graveyards.

Bryn threw herself down, panting with exertion,
against the little gray gods, and Mr. Mathdine seated
himself with some degree of ceremony beside her.
She was afraid that he meant business. And, indeed,

before she knew where she was, he had asked her, in rather a manly and taking way, to marry him.

'Don't be absurd, Bob,' said Bryn. He was always called Bob Mathdine, but she had never addressed him by his Christian name before. 'Mayn't I have *any* friends? I suppose you thought you had to.'

'Miss Bryn—Bryn, don't be offended. You've been so awfully nice to Sandys, who's going to marry your sister, that——'

'How blind men are! Don't you see that the reason I am so "nice," as you call it, to Philip Sandys, is that I don't have to keep him at arm's length, as I have to keep you? He's going to marry my sister for one thing, and for another thing I can depend upon him to treat me like an ordinary being. He's the first man who ever did, except old Spong: and he's old.'

'I suppose you'll never want to see me again,' he said bitterly.

'If only you'll be content to be the oldest friend I've got. I don't want to marry you, Bob Mathdine. I should get sick of honouring and obeying you in a week, because—because I want a lot of things which wouldn't interest you, and wouldn't have interested me last year. I'm not the old Bryn, but I wish you would continue the old Bob.'

'All right, Bryn,' he said frankly. 'I'll just be your friend. I shall love you all the same. And sometimes perhaps you'll let me tell you that I love you. But I shan't want any answer; and when you are bored beyond endurance you can just shut me up.'

'Oh, if you won't bother me to marry you, you
can tell me you love me ; and very likely I love you
a little.   Only it would never do for us to marry.'
Then suddenly looking more feminine than he had
ever seen her before, she added quite shyly, 'You
won't grow familiar, Bob, will you ? '

'Before God, I won't, Bryn.'   And she knew he
meant it, for he was what he looked, a well-bred
Scottish gentleman.

'And I won't forget the Miss, if I may call you
Bryn in private.'

'I wish you hadn't said that, though I know
how you mean it.   I'd rather you called me Bryn
always, if you do it at all.   I don't know that there
is any particular reason why you shouldn't.   You're
my oldest man friend.   Only I'm afraid——'

She smiled.

'Afraid of what ? '

'That people will put it down to its true reason.'

'But I'm not ashamed of having asked you.'

'Well, be guided by circumstances.   I'm not
going to call you "Bob."'

CHAPTER XV

GOOD-BYE to beautiful Nikko, and good-bye to
beautiful Japan in its glory of autumn maple and
autumn weather.

It was with great pleasure that Philip's father
heard of his wish to marry Mary Avon.   For there

could be no such earnest of his intention to settle down in Japan seriously as his marrying the daughter of one of the principal residents.

For two reasons old Mr. Sandys thought it advisable that Philip should come to England for a visit immediately after his marriage in the autumn, —that Mary might see something of England and her new relations before Philip started a five years' sojourn in Japan ; and that Philip, whose six months in the East would have taught him what he was likely to want, might make arrangements with tailors and the like and take out whatever he required for setting up house.

And Philip had a third reason. It was not Bryn's nature to do things by halves, and when once she had chosen to make a chum of him, she did it with all the frankness of her strong nature. She was irresistible when she chose to be engaging ; and he had always thought her the most beautiful thing he had ever seen. He doubted himself if he remained within reach of her fascinations, and he felt that it would be cruelly unjust to Mary to be near Bryn in the first flush of their wedded life. Not that Mary had ever felt any disquietude or suspicion. It was merely his own conscience which told him that it would be unjust to her.

The wedding had gone off with special *éclat ;* it was the finest ever given in Japan. And now the great Canadian Pacific liner which was to carry them from Yokohama to Vancouver had given her first snort of departure, and Bryn had come down into their cabin to say good-bye to Mary.

Bryn was hardly herself, certainly not the old

Bryn who had so lightly given Lord Romney and a dozen other doughty suitors their *congé*. Mary was of course sobbing.

'You oughtn't to mind leaving me, Mary. You haven't much to thank me for. I'm afraid that I never really considered you. And it isn't as if I was going to run any risks. I shall just potter on here till you come back. But for me it's different. You're going a great many thousand miles and anything might happen to you, though of course nothing will.' (This was partly from her old common-sensible optimism, partly to avoid frightening Mary by saying anything ill-omened.) 'I know—now that you are going for so long—how good you have been to me, the thousand and ten thousand sacrifices you have made to me. Good-bye, dear, dear Mary. Come back to me safe and sound,' she said, for the first time since childhood folding her sister to her and taking long kisses.

The sisters talked on in their too-late-awakened confidences until a second snort from the steamer warned Bryn that she must go up on deck and step on to the tender. All Yokohama seemed to be on the deck of the steamer to say good-bye to the bride and bridegroom. There was quite a flotilla of launches among the *sampans* still packed round the great ship by the score, in spite of the ominous green water seething round her screw. Then came the third snort.

Mary sobbed, while Philip shook a perfect wind-mill of hands. 'Good-bye sir' (to Mr. Avon), 'Good-bye Spong, Good-bye Mathdine, Good-bye Dacres, Good-bye Bryn.' He had kept her till the last to linger over the handshake. His only real good-bye was not to Japan, not to his hearty men friends, who grudged letting one of the little outpost of Englishmen go away for but a few months, but to Bryn, whom he was really going away to avoid.

'Good-bye, old Bryn,' he said, holding out his hand. She did not shake it, but taking it in hers, there on the steamer's deck, in front of all Yoko-hama, Bryn, with something very like tears in her rebellious blue eyes, kissed his mouth as she kissed Mary's, simply, spontaneously. Bryn Avon !

CHAPTER XVI

THAT journey to England was the happiest period of Mary's life. After his parting with Bryn, Philip felt his heart burning within him to show his pretty gentle wife his desire for her. And she for her part, never dreaming that he felt there was anything to make amends for, received his advances as gratuitous, and thanked God for a good husband.

They did not loiter on their way to England, but flew through the majestic 'Rockies,' with their first autumn caps of snow, across the great plains, and past the picturesque old towns of New France, till at Quebec they joined the last steamer of the year. At Liverpool they were met by the family, and carried off first for a month in London—the sight of the world to one born in an out-of-the-way spot like Japan—and afterwards to spend Christmas at the old home, bought by the rich shipowner from an impoverished squire, where Philip had been brought up.

Mary wrote much in her letters to Bryn about the noble old mansion, and the position taken by Philip's sisters in the county, though the hospitalities at Latchford Towers seemed rather constrained after the 'open house' at Netheravon. For the rest they were chiefly about the dresses she was ordering, and the furniture they were buying for the house they had chosen in Yokohama just before they left.

Mary's nature was too refined to allow her to mention that Philip's people were solidly wealthy, and Philip the only son—facts which Philip had mentioned to her father but not to either of the girls.

Then came letters that they were starting for New York; letters that they had arrived in New York, with the usual exclamations about American prices; and a letter announcing that they were just off to Montreal for the Carnival.

CHAPTER XVII

THE Carnival week at Montreal breathed almost of enchantment. From the warm sensuous air of the softly-carpeted colonnade of the delightful Windsor Hotel, wrapped in such a wealth of furs as to defy the cold, Mary had only to step into a sleigh with a pair of fine horses and a pile of the now costly buffalo robes to be whirled along the hard-trodden snow high above the level of the pavement—now up Mount Royal in the wake of the four-in-hand club for its far-stretching views over the frozen land ; now out to Lachine to see the ancient store-house and mill, which formed part of the great La Salle's outpost against the Iroquois two centuries ago. There were Carnival processions and living arches to watch in the streets, masked balls and hockey matches on the ice of the Victoria rink (there is little skating outside in that land of deep snows), in which women and men displayed the marvellous Canadian grace on skates. There was a Carnival ball in the hotel itself.

Mary was gratified to find, though the thermometer stood at five-and-twenty below zero, that, wrapped as Canadians wrap themselves whenever they go outside, she could stand about by the hour watching the sights of the Carnival, even at night, so dry was the clear sparkling air. By day, when the sun was shining, she saw to her surprise little children in their warm blanket suits sitting or rolling about in the snow, on which they had been turned out to play, generally in the middle of the road, till the jingle of sleigh bells drove them to the high piles of snow on each side, down which they ran their 'coasters.' And when the crowning event came, the storming of the ice-palace with every description of explosive firework, though it was right opposite their windows, she found herself standing out on the balcony, so as to catch the inspiration of sharing a sight with a great crowd of white people. It was so exciting when the hum of the vast assemblage greeted the appearance of the torch-bearing snow-shoers gliding down the mountain like a fiery serpent. On they came swiftly gliding, till the head of the column reached the stately palace of ice with its tall keep and flanking turrets reared between the hotel and the St. Peter's of the New World. Then the fusillade of rockets, bombs, shells, Roman candles and every explosive firework under heaven poured into the defenderless fort.

And so the week sped,—inside a luxurious hotel, with soft sensuous air, bands of music, and elegant women at every turn; outside—the exhilarating Canadian winter with its brilliant display of unfamiliar sports.

The Carnival proper was over, but they determined to have one more night with the torches at the Tuque Bleue slides before they left for a home where ice and snow are rarer than earthquakes, and laid on with a cat's paw.

Mary was all excitement, looking her very prettiest. They had already been experiencing for half-an-hour the truth of the Chinaman's summary of tobogganing, 'Swish! swish! walkee back-a-mile,' when two well-known tobogganers came up to practise for a toboggan race.

The light, fine racing toboggans made of special woods were as different from the ordinary as an Oxford and Cambridge racing boat is from the 'Eights' let out for hire at Richmond. And there are sundry methods known to the initiated for working up their racing pace.

Mary's eyes sparkled. She had finished for the day; but she would probably never go on a toboggan again. She asked the gentleman who had brought her out for the evening if he thought she might try one of the racing toboggans.

'I know both men. But those toboggans are hardly made for two, and you couldn't go alone. Can you hold on tight? They're pretty dangerous things if you're not accustomed to them.'

'May I, Phil?' asked his wife, her pretty pleading face flushed to actual beauty with exercise and excitement.

'Oh yes. If it's perfectly safe.'

'Well, you can hardly use the words "perfectly safe" of tobogganing,' said their Canadian friend, who was not particularly anxious for Mary to try, though he would have tobogganed down anything short of an elevator-shoot himself. Canadians rival the most exacting fox-hunter in their appreciation of the Gordonian saw :—

> ' No game was ever yet worth a rap
> For a rational man to play,
> Into which no accident, no mishap,
> Can possibly find its way.'

So he added, to save his character, 'Millions toboggan every year, yet you hardly ever see an accident.'

It was a pretty sight—the light of the torches thrown on the slip of a girl in her elegant furs, with little more than two sparkling blue eyes exposed, perched in front of a slip of a toboggan, with the brawny Montrealler in his blanket coat and bright blue *tuque* behind her. For a minute they were balanced on the hill-top, with the steep slide of glittering ice in front looking black against the snow on either side under the dark blue starlit night.

There were little groups of men and girls standing round, nearly all of them in blanket suits—some on snow shoes, some with the toboggans which they had just wearily dragged up the hill after the few seconds' rapture of the shoot. The air was full of merry shouts and the jingling of sleigh bells as parties flew along the road for this or the other junketing.

'Are you ready?' asked the gentleman who was going to start them.

'Rather,' cried out Mary, full of happiness and excitement.

'Off you go then!'

Suddenly that indescribable noise which is neither groan nor moan nor cry swelled out. Everyone was watching to see how the young English girl (they just knew that she was not a Canadian) would get through the ordeal. Suddenly she lost her hold and her balance, and was hurled many feet. The man too was upset by the sudden withdrawal of her weight, but he held on to the toboggan and merely rolled over and over in the deep snow.

There was a rush for where the girl lay stunned, probably dead. She had struck a sunken paling. Strong arms bore her swiftly and gently on a toboggan used stretcher-wise, with her head resting on a cushion thrown over the curled end, to her sleigh.

Few weirder sights could be imagined than the inanimate bundle of seal and sable, which a minute before had been a pretty young bride, in the zenith of her happiness, borne on the shoulders of the snow-shoers in their pantomime-like uniforms amid the glare of torches, over a world of snow.

Arrived at the sleigh, they held a council of war, which resulted in their deciding that it would jolt her less if they carried her on their shoulders right into the hotel. For in the interval the whiskey poured down her throat had brought her back to consciousness, and she was suffering agonies. 'Phil, darling,' she said, 'I think my back's broken.'

The sorrowful *cortége*—for most of the people who had been tobogganing sent their sleighs home, and walked behind to show their sympathy—wound slowly into Montreal. Outside the quaint, steepled, round towers which De Maisonneuve reared for the earliest defence of the infant 'Ville Marie' against the implacable Iroquois, a sleigh which had flown from the slide the moment after the accident dashed up with a doctor.

BOOK II

CHAPTER I

THE telegram of his daughter's accident had an effect on Latimer Avon which no one could have predicted. He was found in his sanctum at the office dead of heart disease. Possibly Philip guessed why, when on his return he found that the large portion which Mary was to have inherited was dust. Latimer Avon died just solvent, as it proved when his accounts were squared up. From his books it appeared that he had sometimes been in possession of a large fortune, at other times many thousand pounds in debt. Probably if he had not lived so extravagantly he might have amassed a good deal of money. But his ambition had been to live ambitiously until Bryn had made a brilliant (and if possible a titled) marriage, and then, seizing a favourable moment, to retire, and live quietly with Mary, with whom he felt more comfortable than with the beautiful younger daughter, of whom he was so inordinately proud that he had surrendered his whole life to her.

When his elder daughter had been married off

so suddenly his plans were modified a little ; it seemed as if the crash he had always dreaded—the fear of which prevented him taking his daughters to see England when they grew up—might be indefinitely averted. He had a high opinion of his son-in-law's business capacity, and he thought that if he chose an opportunity when things were going well he might be able to transfer the business to him in return for ·an annuity.

Mr. Avon had stated the position in which he expected to be at such a date frankly and truthfully, if things turned out as he expected. Philip was willing to accept his terms, one half of the annuity reverting to Mary on her father's death. If affairs had turned out as Mr. Avon had almost a right to anticipate, Philip would have had a large accession of income by the bargain. But they were not turning out at all right, and he dreaded meeting Philip. Consequently, when he heard both of Mary's accident and their immediate return, the shock affected his heart.

Philip and his head clerk were his executors. The head clerk, knowing how affairs stood, thought it best to spare Bryn by refusing to do anything till Philip's return. He knew Philip's sound business position and his generous disposition, and felt sure that he would smooth matters over somehow.

The loneliness of that month, living in the great house by herself, was the most awful thing Bryn had ever experienced. Of her financial position fortunately no one knew anything. The firm was able to meet its liabilities, so the faithful head clerk was able to keep the shortness of the surplus a secret.

Everybody was of course willing to be kindness itself
to the beautiful young heiress. But only certain
men—an old *viveur* like Mr. Spong, or a young
blood like Mr. Mathdine—knew her intimately. And
it was obviously impossible for her to see much of
them, when she was living alone and just orphaned.

How she longed for Philip's return. She hardly
told herself how terrible it would be to meet Mary in
her shattered state. She just felt that Philip was
the one person in the world against whom she could
lean in her trouble.

Mr. Mathdine took her out in his firm's launch to
meet the ship, and there at the companion-head stood
Philip, strong, brown, and modest. Mary was of
course in her present condition below, and as Philip
had not been near a port since Mr. Avon died, his
feelings were quite cheerful, for he anticipated much
towards Mary's recovery in her return to Japan.

The moment the great Pacific liner had dropped
her anchor the launch puffed alongside, and Bryn
flew up the companion to Philip.

'Oh, Phil dear, I am glad you have come.'

'But, Bryn, why this mourning? Mary isn't
dead. She's quite better, I hope,' he said, with a
little quiver of his lip.

'It's father—didn't you hear?'

'Dead?'

'Yes, and I'm living up at Netheravon all alone.
You and Mary must come there to-night.'

Philip was too shocked—too sorry to speak at
first. When he mastered himself all he could say
was, 'Come down to Mary. I know you'll break it
gently to her, Bryn.'

CHAPTER II

THE double blow had a terrible effect on Mary. The inherent weakness, which in the old days before Philip's love and interest in her had inspired her, more than returned. She was often querulous, and from time to time the injury to her spine affected her brain. Some such affection mercifully set in with the shock of the news about her father, so she did not feel as poignantly as she might have, its happening during her first absence from him. For her father and she had been much nearer than either Bryn and she, or Bryn and her father, had ever been to each other.

Philip behaved more than handsomely in business matters. Though the house of Avon Brothers (Pierce Avon had been lost at sea with all his family many a year ago) was so barely solvent, he at once declared his readiness to take the business over, as bequeathed to him in his father-in-law's will, rather than throw so many employés out of work and allow the slur on his wife's family. He even declared his readiness to pay Bryn half of the annuity which he was to have paid her father if he had taken the business over during Mr. Avon's lifetime, though this would have involved a heavy pecuniary sacrifice from his own pocket. He gave the head clerk strict injunctions that she was to know nothing of the real state of affairs. But his generous precautions were in vain. For on Philip's arrival, Mr. Avon's lawyer

produced a codicil, which associated Bryn with Philip
Sandys and the chief clerk as executors, so that she
had to know everything. It was not easy to see
why this codicil should have been added, except as
an act of justice to Philip. Mr. Avon, though so
weak in character, had plenty of shrewdness in
reading the character of others, and he may have
done this to let Bryn's pride checkmate Philip's
quixotic generosity.

Bryn flatly refused to receive a penny from Philip
that the property did not fairly yield, which at present, after all debts were paid, would be practically
nothing. 'You can offer me a home,' she said; 'in
fact, while Mary is in her present state, it is my plain
duty to be with her. But anyhow, I should throw
myself upon you for a home, Philip, because I know
the spirit in which you'd give it. And you're the
only relative I have, except a cousin in England I
have never seen.'

Nor were her affairs hopeless. Philip had no
doubts of the ultimate value of the business—and
over and above the business property, there still
remained Netheravon with its wealth of curios.

'Bryn,' said Philip, 'I want you to do me a
favour. I want your consent as co-executor not to
sell the curios, when we sell Netheravon. This you
will probably agree to as an executor, because to
throw all these curios on the market together might
result in a total sacrifice; but you are also a legatee,
looking to the sale of these curios for the bulk of
your income. So I want you to do me the further
favour of letting me pay you your half of the
interest on the sum at which they may be valued

by a professional valuator, until such time as they
have been sold, when we can adjust accounts.'

'Of course you can put off the sales, Philip. I
can only rely on your judgment in that ; but how
can I take money from you before it has been
made ? '

'But, Bryn, it will be made for one thing ; and,
for another, can't you see that you are doing me an
equal favour in return ? For half the money which
the curios fetch goes to Mary and myself, and if they
are sold now we shall hardly get anything. And
you won't be receiving money that has not been
made either. For putting down the income you
would receive from this source at two thousand
dollars a year, which is my lowest estimate, or five
thousand, which is quite possible, I am certain to
have sold pieces to that amount as the money
becomes due.'

'You're saying all this to persuade me over,
Philip. But I won't let you cheat yourself like
this. You shall sell the curios as you like, but I'm
not going to take the income till they're all sold, and
the money is re-invested in something which will
really yield an income. I suppose the sale of Netheravon will bring me in just something, Philip, won't
it ? ' she asked rather anxiously. 'It won't be
swamped in the business, will it ? '

'No. You will get that income clear.'

'Honestly ? '

'Yes, honestly.'

'That is half of the income from the sale. You
and Mary will get the other half, won't you ? '

'Yes,' he said, and this relieved her a good deal.

'How much shall I get?' she asked with some embarrassment.

'From five hundred to a thousand dollars a year.'

'That will give me plenty to dress on really, though I used to have two or three thousand, I suppose; but then I shall be living on you.'

'No, you won't; you will be keeping house for me, without taking anything for it.'

'Well, Phil, don't let's put any gloss on it. I'm the daughter of a bankrupt, and I'm just going to live on you till the better times, which you tell me truly are coming. It is true, isn't it, Phil? If I thought it wasn't, I'd go out at once and earn my living as a companion or stewardess or anything.'

'It is absolutely true, Bryn.'

'Well, I'm going to live on you till better times, because you're my nearest relation—no, not really for that — partly because I'm coward enough to care that the world can't sneer at me for eating my brother-in-law's bread and butter, and partly because you're the only person in the world I like well enough to ask a favour from.'

There were tears in Philip's eyes.

'Tell me your plan about the curios, Phil,' said Bryn, to relieve their emotion.

'Well, instead of sacrificing them, I hope to make a big profit out of them. In taking over the business of Avon Brothers, I don't see why I should not deal in curios as well as in other kinds of merchandise. You know what an interest I take in curios, and I hope gradually to buy some of my favourite pieces myself. If I sell the curios only in the ordinary course of business, I shall only sell them when I can do so at a sufficient profit; and if I do not pay any money out for them, but merely sell them on behalf of the estate, it won't cripple the business in any way. I should like to have bought them right out for myself, with the idea of reselling the pieces I did not want, but I shall be investing all my capital in the business of Avon Brothers. My father fortunately provided for this before I left home. It suited him so well as a ship-owner in the Japan trade to have a son possessed of a large merchant's business in Japan, that he at once fell in with your father's suggestion that I should take over the business and pay your father an annuity, half of which was to go to you, and half to Mary and myself at his decease. To speak quite frankly, he had no idea, of course, that affairs would have gone so unluckily. But as a set-off against this, half the annuity is payable to Mary and myself, and of the other half you have generously refused to accept more than your actual share of the earnings.'

'But won't your father be wild at your taking over such a—such a—shaky concern?'

'No. As a man of business he knew that, being so far away from Japan himself, he must rely upon my judgment in this affair, so he gave me *carte blanche*. Besides, I don't consider the firm of Avon Brothers shaky.'

'Phil, you're saying this to please me. You're too generous to fight against. Do as you will. All I can do is rigorously to spend as little as possible; and to insist that if I have any money over, it shall be at your disposal.'

CHAPTER III

PHILIP'S forethought in making the sale of the curios a branch of his business was justified by the fact that Netheravon, the carriages, horses, and such furniture as they did not keep, sold only very moderately well. There was a house on the Kanagawa Bluff—the quarter of the wealthier Japanese—which would have suited him admirably, for, while not too large or too expensive, it had a very charming 'Chinese garden,' with all kinds of Japanese fancy gardening in it and some very fine palmettos. But Mary, in her present nervous and crippled condition, was thrown almost into hysterics at the idea of having to go anywhere except 'the Bluff.' This was the one thing which seemed to bring her father's death and the blow to his fortune home to her. So to the Bluff they went, to the house they had chosen before they went to England—a very nice house with a fair garden, but nothing to be compared to the garden at Netheravon, nor above the ordinary. They had chosen it principally for its being vacant at the time and its proximity to her father's.

By this time it was clear that Mary Sandys would never be on her feet again, though there was apparently no limit to the number of years she might live, unless her symptoms took an unexpectedly unfavourable turn.

She was, of course, dreadfully altered in face—a little haggard, and aged a good deal. But except in her bad moments, which sometimes lasted a few hours, sometimes it might be for days, when she was querulous almost beyond endurance and practically insane, she was the old gentle Mary, profoundly happy in Bryn's unwearying care of her; for she had never known the magic of sisterhood in the old days.

In due time, while they were up in the country for the summer, she became a mother, and aunthood developed an unexpected tenderness in Bryn, though she was not allowed to exercise the function much, for the baby proved a godsend towards saving Mary's threatened reason. The doctor pronounced the girl strong in every particular, and Mary perfectly healthy and capable as far as the rearing of children was concerned. Motherhood proved to be her *métier*. She was both an excellent mother, and also far less subject to her attacks while nursing.

And what of the outside world in the interval?

Some rumours of the financial crisis, of course, got about, but Philip's business position was known to be excellent; and no sane son-in-law could be expected to keep up the insane expenditure of Netheravon, nor did it seem remarkable that Bryn should not care to live there by herself.

Again, Bryn's admirers could not expect open house from Philip as they had received it from his late father-in-law.

Netheravon had been a kind of tennis club for the smart set. There was only the most ordinary court at Philip's new house. So there was no excuse for men like Bob Mathdine and Charley Dacres to drop in upon Bryn nearly every afternoon. But their manner to her was absolutely unchanged, though she was no longer the heiress as well as the beauty.

And globe-trotting lords were, of course, a thing of the past as far as she was concerned—or as far as Yokohama society generally was concerned. For there was no house to take the place of Netheravon socially. Among smart globe-trotters, not to have been at Netheravon was not to have been at Yokohama. Its hospitalities were in its day world-famous—as far as the travelling-world was concerned.

Of course, there was never a function to which Bryn was not asked. She was still the most beautiful and best-dressed woman in Japan. And to do a community, which may have a good many shortcomings, justice, turning its back upon those who are in financial troubles is so far from being one of its failings, that rather more attention than usual is shown to the victims. And after her mourning was over Bryn went about a good deal. She saw no reason why she should not.

Offers of marriage were certainly less frequent. She no longer had the opportunity of having many globe-trotters for suitors; and her old lovers in the settlement, though the first thought which occurred to one and all, was that she perhaps would consent now, somehow felt that Bryn was not an easy girl to patronise. In fact, the queenliness of the girl had never been so conspicuously shown.

Not an iota lower did she hold her chin. She wished it to be abundantly clear to people that it was no favour their continuing to ask her to everything. She intended to be exactly the haughty, wayward Bryn she had been when her father's house was a palace of delight and hospitality. In fact, she hugged her *hauteur* for two reasons—one that she was hypersensitive about being suspected of coming down a peg for her altered circumstances, the other that she laid her armour off nowadays when she was alone with Mary and Phil. For she was happier now than she ever had been in her life. It was such an infinite rest to her to be an ordinary woman in her own home; expected to have the ordinary interests, eager to do the ordinary little but constantly-recurring things which a woman does for the happiness of a household. In the old days life had been one perpetual party—all champagne and trifle—no bread and butter, or if there was, only the shavings of the loaf used for afternoon teas. Now she was gradually achieving woman's heritage.

For the baby when it came she had all the exaggerated affection which spoilt beauties, whose sway has been absolute, because there has been no traitor within the keep in the shape of the instinct of sex, so often display for other people's children.

But this baby received also the deeper love born of pathos. For with the baby at her breast Mary's face grew young and happy and almost healthy, though every one knew she could never bear children again; and when the lusty little thing was away from her side she relapsed into the incurable.

CHAPTER IV

THE Japanese are said to be fickle, treacherous, ungrateful, but they do not waver in their attachment to a chief, or their love of beauty.

When the Avon establishment was broken up, first Kano refused to go. Philip had called him in (with Bryn present to act as interpreter in case there was anything to explain beyond Kano's comprehension in English) to give him his *congé*, and find out if a few of the inferior servants would like to follow Bryn to her new home. It was in vain that he explained that his steward would have to be satisfied with lower wages, and that there would be no perquisites such as there had been in the wasteful Avon *ménage*. Kano bowed with grave Japanese politeness and said, 'Bryn San, go with you?' Philip nodded. 'Then you say how much wages I take,' and added something in Japanese to Bryn.

'He says that it is all right about the perquisites, that he has made a good deal of money out of us.'

The last remark was characteristic of the *naïveté*, so curiously mixed up with the cunning of Orientals.

Philip asked Kano if he thought any others of the servants would go with them, mentioning that they would want a few, not nearly so many as Mr. Avon had. There was no question of reduced wages with them. They had, of course, been paid at the (liberal) current rate.

' *Yoroshi*, I ask. I think all—as many as you take.'

He came back in the evening to say that there were none of them who were not willing to go. They were all homesick for Bryn's fair beauty. That was intelligible enough. Blue eyes and golden hair have always had an irresistible attraction for Orientals since the days of Solomon. But that, it appeared, was not the only or even the main reason. Deep-engrained in the Japanese is their respect for aristocracy, and the imperious, imperial Bryn had been the delight of the household. 'Any of them,' said Kano with Oriental hyperbole, ' would follow Bryn San, even if they received no wages at all.'

Then the question arose which should be engaged. There were two or three like Otori-san, Bryn's maid, who must, of course, be included, and Kano was allowed to choose the rest, as he would have to find a substitute if any of them had to be sent away for anything.

Philip had never kept a private *riksha* before, and the girls had hitherto had horses and carriages as well, so they were able to find employment for all the Avon *riksha*-boys.

They were not long to wait in idleness.

' Phil,' said Bryn, ' that's a jolly little sitting-room you have made for me out of the dressing-room off my bedroom. I want to make it homely with didgy little curios like you did in your old rooms at the Club Hotel. Take me to the dear, dirty little curio-shops you used to take Mary to, where you got all your treasures.'

' All right ; wait a day or two, and Mary can go

with us. I think that's a thing which would give her
a great deal of amusement, and that she very well
could do, as soon as " the chair," which I wired for
to Hong-Kong, comes. There is one of our ships
on her way up now. W—— said that with a few
adaptations a Hong-Kong chair ought to do very
well ; and he advised me to tell our agent at Hong-
Kong to send two strong Chinese bearers up with
it, for he thought they would be steadier than the
Japs.'

' And did you ? '

' No. I thought Mary would feel more comfortable with Japs. They know her and she knows
them, and she can talk the language.'

' You might have got the chair from Miyanoshita,
I should think.'

' By George, I didn't think of that ; but I tell you
what, it would be a jolly good place to get the
bearers from. I'll go and ask M—— to write for
them. He invented the place, so he's sure to know
of some.'

In a few days Mary's chair arrived. It was
rather heavy for Japanese bearers, but fortunately
she was very light — since her accident a mere
shadow. The skilful Japanese cabinet-makers soon
made the requisite alterations. She had to lie at a
slope instead of sitting.

' A chair ' is not a usual sight in Yokohama.
People stared a little the first time it was carried out
of Philip's compound, with him on one side and Bryn
on the other in *jinrikshas*. This was three or four
months before the baby was born.

' Where shall we go, Mary ? '

'I'd love to go down the cabinet-makers' street again. It was the first place you ever took me to alone.'

The chair was a success. It swung with delightfully easy motion down the Bluff; along the Hon-Mura-Cho, with its rubbishy little toyshops and the like, across and beside creek and canal—Yokohama has its network of water like Tokyo and Ozaka, on a smaller scale, and banished from genteel quarters —till they came to one of the big red police stations, with which the Japanese love to bestrew their cities, marked by a huge gilt conventionalised chrysanthemum, just under the roof.

Here they turned down the broad Theatre Street, with its great native theatres adorned with twenty-foot-long panels, sloping outwards at an absurd angle, of blood-curdling scenes from their plays; and its public baths; and its bazaars for Japanese holiday-makers, full of cheap soap, and combs, and hairpins, and pipe-cases, and every variety of lacquer and leather rubbish.

'Bazaar very good,' said Philip's *riksha*-boy, who had not been out shopping with him before. 'More good than cabinet-makers' street.'

'*Hayaku, hayaku.* Get on! Quick!' said Philip.

'*Yoroshi.* All-er-right.'

The cabinet-makers' street was a little bye-street, so little used that they could not go up it in *rikshas*, for it had never been levelled. There were hillocks of hard yellow loam like ant-heaps in the middle of the street.

They stopped at the first shop, which seemed the best in the street. A boy of about the usual age to be left in charge of a big Japanese shop came running out, scuffing with his hastily-donned sandals, rubbing his knees together, and drawing in his breath as he bowed.

When he recognised Mary his face fell. She had often been to his shop, and was the only English lady he knew who could talk to him in his own tongue.

'Is the Honourable little Missis badly hurt?' he asked sympathetically in Japanese.

'No, not badly,' she said, with a sad conviction of the untruth. 'I shall get well soon, I hope.'

'Ah! I hope so,' he said cheerfully, taking her at her word. Then addressing himself to Philip in broken English, he added, 'Very good curio have got—temple banner, temple burnt not so long ago. You come see. *Yasui!* very cheap!'

'I'll go in with you,' said Bryn, and, bending over her sister, who was almost sitting up bright and smiling with the excitement of being carried back to old times, she whispered, 'Don't let on that I understand Japanese.'

'*Ikura*, how much?' asked Philip, after they had duly inspected the banners and found them to be in first-rate condition.

'Ten dollar. Very fine. *Daimio* temple. No can get more.'

'Ten dollars,' repeated Philip, turning away loftily. 'I'll give you two—*Ni yen*,' and he held up two fingers.

The Japanese laughed—a courteous little laugh that was merely to show the absurdity of Philip's proposition. He waited for a new one; but Philip was an old hand. After all, the first price named always partook of the nature of skirmishing. Neither side ever considered it as serious.

Presently, seeing that Philip had laid the banners down, as if he was thinking no more of them, and was looking at some little brass knife-handles, worth from five to ten *sen* apiece, according as he wanted them or not, the boy said, '*Shti yen, go ji*—seven dollars fifty.'

Philip shook his head. '*Irimasen.* I do not want them.'

'*Shti.*'

'No.' He picked up a cracked china bowl which had been beautifully cemented together out of a score of pieces. It was a bluish white in colour, and for a pattern had grass growing all round it in blue. It must have been exquisite when whole, for the shape was lovely. 'How much this?'

'*Go-sen*—five cents,' said the boy dubiously.

'*Yoroshi*, I'll have it,' said Philip, preparing to leave the shop.

The boy was frightened. He had been fully prepared to be beaten down, and take three cents or even two. He feared that Philip's agreeing to the price at once meant that he was just buying a trifle, so as not to have given him trouble for nothing. Philip had so often done this, when he could not find anything he really wanted.

The boy said, '*Mati, mati*—wait, wait'—pushed back the *shoji* of an inner room and consulted his father, who took up the *soroba*, the abacus of British village schools, on which all Japanese do their reckoning.

Mary, of course, could see the whole proceedings, for the purely native shops have no fronts when the *ama-do*, or outside wooden shutters, are taken down for the day.

But she was out of earshot, and the Japanese never give Europeans credit for understanding the *soroba*, as Mary and Bryn did, having been brought up to it from their childhood.

In a few seconds the boy came out and said, ' *Go yen*, five dollar, sair.'

Bryn said quickly, 'Don't give it. They only cost him 1.75. I thought I heard him saying so, and I saw him figuring it out directly afterwards.'

'Come on, Bryn,' said Phil, leaving the shop. The boy was rather disconcerted, and followed them to the door. 'Tell him that he makes me tired, Mary,' said her husband, 'that I will give him two dollars and fifty cents, and not one *sen* more.' He did not ask Bryn, because he did not wish to divulge that she spoke Japanese.

Mary laughed, and did as she was asked ; and then her chair was carried a few doors up the street to a shop where they sold hardly anything but woodwork. Here there were cabinets three feet high, with a sliding cupboard and two or three drawers, to be bought for eighteenpence ; queer clog cupboards, perhaps four feet long by about a foot high, having sliding doors, with the bark still left on them like the Italian rustic work—fetching as high as two-and-threepence or half-a-crown second-hand ; and still queerer old-fashioned Japanese desks, about two feet long by a foot high and broad. They were made of some heavy, hard wood like teak, and had a large sort of well at the top, surrounded by various smaller hollows, perhaps for rolls of paper, envelopes, and so on ; and underneath these the usual nest of drawers. While Philip was buying one of these the boy came running along from the first shop with the banners, which he laid in Philip's *riksha*-boy's arms.

'*Dekimas! Dekimas!* All-er-right. Master say can take two dollars fifty. He want money to-day.'

Philip gravely handed him two of the bright blue and white dollar notes with one of the gods of wealth squatting on them, and a fifty-*sen* piece, about seven-and-sixpence in all, as exchange was going then.

'You open,' he said to the *riksha*-boys, beginning to unroll them. The quick-witted Japanese caught his meaning, and his and Bryn's boys stretched them out to their full length to show Mary. They were twenty feet long and perhaps a couple of feet wide, made of a coarse sort of sail-cloth, painted one side with two cross stripes and the crest of the *daimio* who had presented them, in black, and on the other side with historico-mythological subjects in all the colours of the rainbow. One represented the great Japanese warrior Toyotomo Hideyoshi accepting an offering of fire from a Korean. There was a very conventional and blue sea in front to typify the geographical difficulties in the way of conquering Korea. The other was a picture of the famous fight on the bridge of Uji between the boy Yoshitsune and the veteran Ben-Kei, in which the former won by his extraordinary activity, typified in the picture by representing him in high wooden clogs, balanced on the rounded top of one of the bridge rail-posts.

In both banners the drawing and colour were very spirited.

'How lovely,' said Mary. 'I'm so glad that I was able to help you buy them, and that you actually bought them out here beside me.'

'You'll soon be able to come in with me, little woman,' he replied. But he had misgivings.

'Oh, let's go to that shop across the way,' said Bryn. 'That's a regular curio-shop—a second-hand shop, where they sell anything that's not in first-rate order.'

They certainly had a pretty wide selection. Cheap but rather curious old *kakemonos*, curious old screens mellowed with age and lovely and rich in colouring, rejected from some good house for a burst made by a jagged corner of a box after two hundred years of careful custody; sweet little scarlet lacquer tables standing on tall spindle-legs, discarded because the old world lacquer lamps they were made to support had given way to paraffin; little black lacquer shrines (with fine brass fittings and the image of Amida or Kwannon Sama inside), fallen from higher estate by reason of their chippings; magic mirrors which reflected the Chinese characters on their backs; finely embossed hand-gongs, once carried in processions by priestly hands; sweet little *inros* of chased silver or brass, now sorely dinted, and of sealing-wax lacquer or *nashiji*, battered beyond all value, which once were the liliput medicine-chests of fine ladies; swords, and copper lamp-ends; china of all sorts and conditions; and what not.

'There's a fascinating nest of trays here, Mary,' said her husband; 'they fit into each other one above the other, so that they can be slung at one end of a shoulder bamboo; and they're full of all sorts of delightful odds and ends, like we used to buy before we went " home." '

He said " home." She called it home too, like a Colonial.

'Take that to the lady outside,' said Philip, pointing to the tray and then to his wife. The little Jap understood either the words or the gesture, and carried out to Mary tray after tray full of seals and *netsukes* and *inros* and queer little silver spoons shaped like lotus-leaves; not to mention charms, compasses, fantastic silver beads, forgeries of rare coins, quaint old-fashioned *tsubas* and *menuki* (swords, guards, and hilt ornaments), some of them good; little bronze Buddhas, damaged ivory pipe-cases, and a most fascinating set of tea-cups with pentagonal saucers, apparently carved out of cocoa-nut, but really fine bronze. These at twenty-five cents (about 9d.) for five of them were Mary's great prize of the afternoon. Bryn's cost five cents less, a tall antique iron candlestick, like the iron beak of a gondola at Venice, which slid up its stem till it stood nearly three feet high.

And as they were going home they bought for a good deal less than a dollar an old image, made in plaster, of Binzuru, the faithful servant of Buddha, curiously coloured, and standing two or three feet high, in the attitude of saluting.

This they bought to keep the drawing-room door open.

As Mary swung home, happy and excited, on the backs of her sturdy carriers, after a long afternoon's shopping, it seemed as if her era of youth and health had come back.

But, crossing the hogs-backed bridge by the big police station, a thing of ill-omen met them, which sent a cold chill through Philip.

CHAPTER V

IT was a young girl's funeral.

In front, with a peculiar dancing stride, pranced two coolies, carrying tall staves with huge white lanterns at the top, under queer little white wood roofs. They wore two enormous flat limpet-shaped hats. One was bare-legged except his sandals, the other wore the blue wrappings of the coolie class. They were followed by *jinrikshas* containing young girls with very carefully-dressed hair, carrying large bunches of real flowers on their laps, followed in turn by two more coolies carrying square white wooden jars, containing huge silver tinsel flowers. Then came priests in white robes with wide bell sleeves, and curious mitres on their heads—half-way between a bishop's mitre and a cap of liberty; then, borne on the shoulders of four sturdy coolies, wearing the same limpet hats, came the corpse, sitting up in a little wooden shell, which measured about a couple of feet each way, and had a beautiful white wood cover, made (especially the graceful roof) in almost exact imitation of a temple.

This palanquin hearse was decorated with more

tinsel flowers, like those carried before it by the bearers, but not so large. And the whole *cortége* wound up with two more coolies carrying the tall staves with the white lanterns and the little white wood roofs.

There was not much in it—the poor little funeral of a girl, who was not rich—though the whole was carried out with a grace which Philip had never seen equalled in the mournful procession of a human body to its long home.

At any other time he would have been delighted with its beauty, feeling just the least chastening touch in its message of mortality.

But at this moment it seemed to him to have a further message—this funeral meeting his girl wife on her return—the very first time that she had ventured out for a long ride since she had come back so mutilated to her native shores.

He could only hope that Mary had not read any omen in this inauspicious encounter.

Bryn had merely been struck by the picturesqueness of the funeral. She did not know when she had enjoyed an afternoon so much. It opened a new world of amusement to her. Owing to the ambitiousness of Latimer Avon's *ménage*, such a thing as curio-hunting in the little jack-of-all-trades shops, or among the stalls which congregate in the evening in the Basha Michi, had never been suffered to enter the children's heads.

'Here, Bryn,' Phil had said in the shop where they bought the bronze saucers and the ancient forged iron candlestick, 'have you noticed this old wooden *hibachi* (charcoal brazier) with the charred rim?'

'Yes, what a splendid fox there is on the back of it—in the middle of what is it?—oh, wheat sheaves. Why, it's that old fable you were telling me about; but where's the man?'

Phil turned the *hibachi* upside down, and there was the man, lying in wait underneath, carved with the same spirit and finish as the figures round the sides.

'What a pity putting such a good thing where it would never be seen,' said Bryn.

'That's the whole spirit of Japanese art,' he replied. '*Ikura*, how much?' he asked the boy.

'*Ju-ni sen*—twelve cents.'

'About fourpence, by Jove! Well, I'll have it.'

'What are you going to do with it?'

'Have it worked up into a footstool for you. I don't know what this light wood is, but it will go very well with the oak of your room.'

'How perfectly lovely to pick things up like this, and have them dodged. Just think what a lovely lot of things I might have collected in my twenty years in Japan.'

'Are you only twenty, Bryn?'

'Twenty-one next month,' she said, with a gentle toss of that chin, and one of her incomparable smiles. 'Don't you like my age?'

'There's nothing I don't like about you, little sister.'

'Not so very little,' she objected, drawing herself up to the full of her five feet six inches; 'but not too big to look up to you, Philip.'

CHAPTER VI

WHAT a change it was from that delightful afternoon to the next morning!

Mary had overdone herself, and was in a frenzy
of nervous irritation and exhaustion.

The blinds were down and the curtains drawn in
her room. Up to this it had not been too hot, and
she liked them so in order that she might have the
long sleeps which she seemed to need so much in
her present condition.

'Philip,' she called crossly; 'Philip,' she repeated,
raising her voice, though he flew to her side at the
first call, from the dressing-room leading off her room,
in which he slept.

'I wish to goodness you'd let some light in.
I'm sick of lying here in the dark. I wonder what
those lazy servants are doing. Why haven't I had
my breakfast brought to me?'

'But, my dear, it's only about seven, and you
never will have your breakfast till nine,' he said to
soothe her, as he groped to the windows and, drawing
back the curtains, pulled up the venetians.

'Do you want to blind me with that blaze of
light? How inconsiderate you are, Philip.'

'I'm so sorry, dear. I thought you were pining
for light because you couldn't sleep.'

'I never said so. I don't see why you should
take it for granted. When are you going to give me
my breakfast?'

He rang the bell, and a servant came to the door.
'Come in,' said Mary, and, addressing him in the
most good-natured way, ordered breakfast, telling
him not to hurry if it was inconvenient.

The moment the servant was out of the room, she
turned upon her husband to know if he was going to
let her lie there and starve.

Bryn had heard Mary's voice, and, fearing that
she was ill, tore down in a dressing-gown. When
she came in to know how Mary was, 'You and
Philip think of nothing but yourselves,' was the
gracious reply.

Then the servant brought breakfast and she told
him that he needn't have hurried about it, and that
she hoped she had not given them too much trouble.
Yet no sooner was he gone than she cried out—

'I wonder who it is that wants to poison me.
Some one has been putting something into this tea.
Bryn, if you cared for me in the least, instead of
standing star-gazing there, you'd go off to the kitchen
and insist on having some fresh tea made.'

Bryn flew to the kitchen.

'Why, this egg's hard,' Mary almost yelled. 'If
there's one thing in the world that kills me with
indigestion it's a hard-boiled egg.'

'But, Mary, you told Taki to boil it for ten
minutes,' said Philip, gently remonstrating.

'What if I did? I didn't tell them to boil it
hard. You're all in conspiracy against me,' she said,
as Bryn, in her dressing-gown and with bare feet,
hurried in with a fresh pot of tea and a fresh cup and
saucer on a tray.

'I washed the teapot out myself,' said Bryn, 'and

tied the tea up in a muslin bag, so that you might be sure of a nice cup this time.'

'I hate those horrid bags. They make the tea taste, and you didn't use boiling water to make it.'

'I did really, Mary. I was so particular.'

'I tell you you didn't. You treat me as if I was a dog.'

Bryn received her sister's ill-temper with a tact and gentleness which went straight to Philip's heart. She had always been a queen to him : her humanity made her more than human.

As he stood invincible in his strength of patience by her temporarily distraught sister's bedside, she asked herself, Why had not God let her win this man also, as she had won every other man from her sister and all around her ? She did not know that the one armour which had been proof against the shafts of her beauty was the lowliness that dared not aspire to thinking of her.

That was a terrible April day. From sunrise to sunset Mary tossed as far as her wounded spine would let her, cursing the heat and glare, but refusing to have the room darkened.

'Why don't you do something to amuse me, Philip ?' she cried.

He was so anxious about her that he had not gone to his business. He told her all the gossip of the settlement.

'Why do you take up my time with talking about those stupid people ? I have something better to do.'

Philip thought that she might feel irritated, because she wanted to rest, having woke so early, so sat in silence. It was torture to him to be doing nothing, but he did not move lest he should disturb her.

'Are you going to sit there like a stone all day? Why don't you tell me something?'

He began to tell her how he was doing with her father's business, which he had just taken over.

'Don't bother me with your old business,' she said curtly and ungraciously. 'I've enough things of my own to think of.'

Once more he was silent.

'Oh, do say something. Aren't you going to try and do anything to amuse me?'

'Is there anything you would like to look at?' he asked kindly.

'I can't be bothered looking at things.'

'Would you like Bryn to play to you? the drawing-room is underneath, so you can hear quite well.'

'What's she want to bang at the piano for, when I am ill?'

'But she doesn't *want* to, Mary. I only asked if I should get her to play to amuse you.'

'Oh, you two will drive me wild.'

Philip went up and kissed her; and took her hand in his.

At last she seemed pleased. 'Stay like that,' she said, ignoring the fact that he was stooping over her in a most uncomfortable position, and able to do nothing.

'I'll get a chair and a book,' he said kindly, 'and then I can sit and hold your hand as long as ever it soothes you.'

'That's always you,' she said. 'One for me and two for yourself.'

He kept hold of her hand, and simply knelt, when it was impossible for human nature to stand any longer in that stooping position.

She appeared to forgive the kneeling in consideration of its ridiculousness and discomfort.

Not a word or a gesture was lost upon Bryn, as she stood by the window gazing out on the perfect Japanese spring day with its sunshine and blue sky, and the merry sparkle on the sea, mournfully contrasting the scene without and within the house. Why had not she instead of Mary married such a man? She longed to have had the opportunity of showing him what a wife she would have made him.

Towards sunset the fever, or whatever it was, seemed to leave Mary; for, suddenly drawing her husband to the head of her bed, she threw her arms round his neck and kissed him passionately. 'Dear old Phil; it is nice to have you and Bryn with me,' she said. 'We must have another of those jolly expeditions like we had yesterday, soon. I'm so happy.'

CHAPTER VII

'PHIL,' said Mary, on the next day, 'I've got a queer fancy. I expect it is that I am so weak after yesterday; but I can't help feeling that I should be much better if I had that big crystal ball that we saw at Arthur and Bond's. It wasn't theirs. They were trying to sell it for some hard-up *daimio*. My countrymen, you know '—it was always her habit to talk of the Japanese as her countrymen, because she was born in the country—' attach all kinds of magical properties to these crystal balls, when they are flawless and of great size ; and that particular ball is historical for its virtues. I read the long roll of Japanese writing which was in the box—a sort of pedigree of the ball. They are awfully lucky.'

' I'll see if we can afford it, dear. A talisman will often restore health, because it restores nerve, which is the key of health.'

Philip opened negotiations through the Chinese compradore who had bought all Latimer Avon's curios for him. The price demanded was very large, for the ball was nearly three inches in diameter, and the crystal peculiarly pure, apart from its historic and magic value ; and the sum which eventually secured it, after three or four journeys on the part of the compradore, ran into hundreds of dollars.

At first Philip demurred at the price. He simply felt that he could not afford it, but the compradore said, ' You no want, I take any time myself, ten per cent off.'

Seeing then that if ever he was in absolute need of the money, he could be sure of realising almost the price he gave, Philip no longer felt justified in not purchasing a thing for which his wife in her present condition felt such a craving.

' Tell Mr. Sandys,' said the vendor, ' to lock it up very carefully in his *godown*. There are a good many Japanese know of its existence, and might be tempted to try and steal it for its value ; and fanatical Japanese have the greatest objection to famous crystals passing into the possession of foreigners, which might be an even stronger motive for the robbery.'

Philip, however, like most able-bodied English-men, had a supreme contempt for danger at the hands of the Japanese, so he paid no heed.

If Philip had doubted for a minute whether he ought to incur the expense, all his doubts vanished when he saw the effect that its possession had on Mary. She picked up wonderfully both in health and spirits, and was handling the beautiful crystal all day in her bedroom or the adjoining sitting-room, into which she was carried on a sloping invalid chair.

Not many days afterwards she happened to look up while she was playing with it, and was astonished to see the face of a Japanese she did not know watching her intently from the window, which was perhaps fifteen feet from the ground. She could not get up, of course, and by the time that Otori-san had answered the electric bell lying on her mistress's lap (connected by a flexible wire as long as the room, so that she could use it in whatever part she might happen to be sitting) the face had disappeared ; but Kano, who was summoned, detected the scratches of a bamboo ladder on the wall just below the win-dow. He thought that the man who was mending the waste-water pipe, a few feet away, had heard of the crystal and wished to catch a peep of it. The Japanese are very fond of seeing treasures, and the servants, who were in a great state of excitement over the presence of such a treasure in the house,

might easily have told him something about it—one
of them. If his mistress liked he would bring the
man who was mending the water-pipe to her room
that she might identify him.

Mary said no ; that it was all right.

Of course the man protested that he had never
been near the room, when Kano questioned him.
Japanese duplicity is not easy to fathom, so Kano
gave up in despair.

When Philip heard of it, he merely told Kano
not to allow any ladders near the house again unless
he himself was by to see that Mrs. Sandys was not
subjected to this kind of annoyance. In her weak
state it might have disastrous effects.

That night Philip, who slept in the little dressing-
room adjoining Mary's bedroom, heard footsteps.
Mary's illness had made him a very light sleeper ;
she so often wanted something in the night. Leaping from his bed in his *pyjamas*, he did not wait to
slip on the *kimono* he had caught up, but, switching
on the electric light, rushed to the head of the stairs.
With an Englishman's contempt for Eastern races,
he kept no arms in the house, in spite of the fre-
quency of burglaries in Yokohama ; but, seeing two
Japanese advancing towards him with drawn swords,
he twisted the *kimono* round his arm as a sort of
shield, and advanced towards them.

' The crystal,' they cried. ' Give us the crystal,
and we will not harm you.'

He knew enough Japanese by this time to understand the drift of what they were saying, but in
answer he flung himself at them to hurl them downstairs,

Both cut at him, but fortunately they had brought their long fighting swords, and the ceiling was so low that they had to shorten their sweep a little, and Philip managed to receive their blades on his shielded arm with very slight wounds, and at the same time closed with them, judging that his only chance of life was to crash them through the flimsy banisters on to the stone flags of the hall below.

Prevented as they were from stabbing or swinging their swords, they yet managed to deal him some terrible cuts on the head with the razor-like blades. The blood pouring over his face began to blind him. He felt that he must risk everything upon disposing of one of his assailants. The banisters were apparently too strong for him to fling his assailants through them, and if he went on engaging both he would be tired out or blinded and fall an easy victim. So, suddenly ignoring one, he seized the other round the waist with both his strong arms and swung him on to the rail of the banisters. The man gave a wild yell, and his comrade, detecting Philip's change of tactics, in an instant slipped behind, and dropping on one knee, so as to get the full sweep of the sword, slashed down at the most fatal place between the neck and the left shoulder. Philip, in an Englishman's supreme effort for his life, tossed the man he was tackling like a great log into the air, and like a log the assassin landed, breaking his neck against the hall table as he fell.

He had noted the other slipping behind him even in his terrible struggle, and now he hardly knew if he had received his stroke. For the peculiarity of the razor-edged Japanese sword is that if the cut be

heavy enough you hardly feel it. Every instant he
expected to die. All he knew was that for the
moment he felt life enough in him to tackle the
other miscreant, and he turned on him.

There he saw a sight which gave him the strength
of fury. Bryn, her delicate nightdress soaked with
blood, clutching the assassin's sword with streaming
hands.

Phil was on him before he could wrench it free,
and in an instant he had the man on the ground,
with an iron finger-grasp round his throat. And
then a fierce joy took him, for he felt that he was
tearing the man's throat out. And then he gave up
all hope, for he knew that he was fainting.

CHAPTER VIII

WHEN he recovered he was lying on his bed.
For a while he was in a state of half-consciousness,
and kept murmuring, ' It's nothing, Mary, darling.
I'll be all right in a minute. It's just the shock.'

He dreamed that he was once more lying sense-
less at the foot of that cliff at Enoshima, and that
his wife, restored to health and strength as he knew
her then, was kneeling beside him bathing his head.
He could have sworn that he felt her lips.

When he did come to, it was not Mary kneeling
beside him, but Bryn, still in her nightdress, with
both hands pitifully bandaged. Just as consciousness returned, he heard her say, ' Oh, Philip, come

back to me.' Her arms were round him, her cheek against his, and she was sobbing her heart out.

'Oh, Philip, I thought you were dead.'

'Is the doctor coming?' he asked faintly.

'Taro has gone for one. He'll be here in a minute.'

.   .   .   .   .   .

Mary, waking suddenly, had heard ghastly sounds on the landing outside her door. With her injured spine she could not move a foot to her husband's aid, or she would have flown to it as Bryn flew, for the graceful, timid little creature in supreme moments knew no fear. But action has no terrors like suspense. And as Mary lay there listening to the short grim snorts of men fighting for their lives, to the rubbing of struggling bodies against each other and the banisters, the swish of the sword-cuts, and then to Bryn's agonised shriek as Philip fainted, it was like dying half a dozen times over.

But she did the one thing helpful. The electric bell lay on her bed, and she rang it for dear life straight on. Kano heard it even before Otori-san, and came bounding along the back upstairs passage, expecting to find Mary at death's door, instead of which he found Philip desperately wounded and fainting away with a throttled Japanese in his grasp, from whom Bryn, with mangled hands, was trying to tear the sword-hilt. Kano realised the situation at a glance, and seizing the sword from the relaxing fingers of his countryman, stabbed it through his eyes into the brain, for he was ignorant of the use of the sword, not being of *Samurai* birth.

Bryn was spared the sight, for she had flown

to her room for sponge and jug to try and revive
Philip before life had fled. Wounded as she was,
every movement gave her exquisite pain ; but Kano,
with Japanese tact, left her to do it for a minute or
two while he glided in to assure his mistress that
Philip was not dead (though he felt sure that he was
dead) but only badly hurt, and flew back along the
passage to rouse the household, and send for a
doctor. He was back in an instant with all the
other servants at his heels, and laid the dying Philip
out on his bed, while Otori-san bound up Bryn's
poor hands with strips of soft white calico torn
from some Japanese garment.

Then Bryn let Otori-san bathe the four gaping
wounds in Philip's head while she clung to him, and
the servants saw with wonder and ready Japanese
sympathy, how their haughty Bryn San, whom they
had worshipped as beyond the scope of lovers, loved
that plain man, her sister's husband, like a wife and
a mother. They listened with awe as she poured
out her heart to the body, utterly unmindful of their,
presence ; and they thanked whatever gods they had
when his eyes opened, and Bryn's sad beauty was
illuminated with hope.

Bryn had heard the sounds even before Mary,
and, seeing the struggle when she put her head out,
flown barefoot to the rescue, though she did not see
what she could do except die with Philip. But she
was a stranger to fear, and knew that Heaven helps
those who help themselves, and came up just in the
nick of time to save Philip's life by clutching the
sword of the assassin behind him as he knelt to get
his sweep. A struggle ensued, in which her hands

got horribly gashed, but her antagonist being on his knee, and an Asiatic, while she was a tall healthy Englishwoman, she engaged him just long enough to enable Philip to despatch the other assassin. Then followed the second combat, in which Philip had throttled his adversary at the very moment that he fainted.

When the doctor came he stumbled over the dead body at the foot of the stairs, with its hands still grasping a long sword with a broken blade.

'Foul work,' he exclaimed. Kano had packed Taro off without telling him more than that the doctor was wanted for sword wounds.

At the head of the stairs the other body was lying, a revolting sight, with face blackened by suffocation and jabbed out of recognition with the sword. The doctor did not stay to examine it, or to ask questions, but passed straight on to Philip.

'Take your mistress to her room,' he bade Otori-san. 'Even on a summer night she may catch cold in her night-dress.'

Which was true, though he said it more as the likeliest excuse for getting her to leave him with Philip, who opened his eyes faintly as he felt the withdrawal of Bryn's arms.

'This is a bad business, Sandys. Do you feel much hurt?' asked the doctor as cheerily as possible.

'The cuts don't hurt, doctor, but I feel very weak.'

'Of course.'

After a few minutes' anxious examination the doctor said with a great sigh of relief, 'There is nothing mortal. A healthy liver like you, Sandys,

will pull through all right.   Tell Mrs. Sandys, Kano,
Mr. Sandys no danger,' and then he proceeded to
bandage up the wounds.   In a minute or two he
noticed Otori-san waiting to catch his eye in the
patient Japanese fashion.

'Bryn San, can come?' she asked.   'Riddy now.'
'Yes.   She can come now.'

Bryn came in, partly dressed, in a warm *kimono*.
It would not have been easy for her to get into a
dressing-gown with her lacerated and thickly-ban-
daged hands.

The doctor, strong man as he was, and accustomed
to wounds and death, when he gently stripped off
the bandages to replace them more scientifically, felt
a big lump in his throat as he saw her fingers, and
thought of the courage of this lovely girl in seizing
the razor blade in her bare hands to give Philip that
precious half-minute on which everything hung.

Bandaging those slight fingers, and laying the
sliced-off pieces exactly on their places, so as to
leave as faint a scar as possible, took three or four
times as long as the great gashes on Philip's head
had done.   It was a labour of chivalry.   Then the
doctor passed in to Mary to briefly reassure her—no
easy task, till his heart told him that the right thing
to do was to lay Philip on the marriage bed he
had never occupied in his own home, and let the
paralysed woman think she was nursing him.

As Philip sank into an uneasy sleep he edged
nearer to the loving little wife, and his dream of the
Enoshima accident returning, he kept murmuring, ' It's
all right, Mary.   I'm not hurt '—the sweetest music
she could have heard.

The doctor went out and, aided by the servants, began to examine the bodies of the assassins.

'Send for the police, Kano, and carry the other body into the hall.'

When the police arrived, Kano explained to them as far as he knew what had happened.

'Who did this?' they asked, pointing to the sword-jabs in the smaller assassin's face.

'I,' said Kano.

They said something more in Japanese.

'Policeman ask which kill first, this one or this,' said Kano to the doctor, first pointing to his eyes and then his throat.

The doctor examined the body carefully. Life had evidently not been extinct when Kano did his work, but the assassin could not have survived the throttling, because the muscles of the throat were so torn, though he might have recovered consciousness sufficiently to have despatched Philip.

So that paralysed Mary had saved her husband's life. The other man had been killed outright by his fall. He was still holding the stump of his sword, as he gripped it in the fight.

'*Samurai*,' pronounced one of the police curtly. Then they examined the dead men's clothes, and found a lozenge containing a sort of Tudor rose

'*Chosen-no-Daimio*,' he exclaimed. 'Daimio of Chosen,' said Kano to the doctor.

'Poor fellows,' mused the doctor; 'starving *Samurai* driven to burglary and murder by the loss of their ancient honourable occupation of cutting throats for the Daimio of Chosen.'

And then, having given Bryn a sleeping draught,

he went home. Philip had lost so much blood that he might be trusted to sleep.

When the inquest was held in the presence of the British Consul it was proved beyond doubt that this was no ordinary burglary. The men were two *Samurai* formerly in the retinue of the Daimio of Chosen. Now the Daimio of Chosen was the ruined noble who had sold the crystal ball through Arthur and Bond to Philip, and it was, no doubt, to recover this sacred and historical crystal from the sacrilegious clutch of the foreigner that the raid had been made. It is credible that its money value had not been considered by the men, poor as they were, and that they wished to recover the crystal merely for the honour of their clan. The Japanese *Samurai* is capable of any sacrifice to feudal fidelity.

It was possible that the *daimio* himself might have experienced so much resistance from his own household to the sale of this crystal that he personally had originated the warning which had reached Philip through the compradore.

Of course, the settlement was convulsed by the news, and would have been still more convulsed if the servants had divulged what Bryn said and did when she thought Philip was dead. As it was, Yokohama rang with her heroism, as well it might, for it had her bandaged hands to keep it in mind for a month and more. She had saved Philip's life, without any doubt, by her courage. What the poor little wife did would have been forgotten but for Philip, who trumpeted it forth.

Phil lay for a long time between life and death, but his simplicity and wholesomeness of living turned the balance, and he slowly mended. It was a source of impatience to Bryn that she could not wait upon him, but the state of her hands precluded it. Until he was out of danger he lay on a bed put up beside his wife's, and Bryn sat by him from the very beginning, with Otori-san to do the fetching and carrying.

It showed great tact and sagacity on the doctor's part to have laid Philip by his wife's side, for, instead of her health being irretrievably damaged by the shock, the creation of a new interest—watching by her husband—rather improved it than otherwise.

She was almost sorry when he was sufficiently recovered to get up.

CHAPTER IX

THOUGH she had not the regular use of her hands for weeks, a superbly healthy creature like Bryn was naturally not long in recovering her general health.

Her newly-formed passion for Philip—if one may use the word where the question of sexual feeling did not enter—would have carried her through a much more severe trial.

She thought the grandest sight she had ever seen in her life was Philip, unarmed, and in his night-clothes, first hurling one sworded assailant over the banisters to break his neck on the flags below, and then tearing the life out of the other's throat. She did not think that she would ever see the ridiculous side of *pyjamas* again. Philip, though strongly built, and wearing habitually an air of quiet resolution, had been her ideal of gentleness. She was not prepared for the change in him as he stood at bay. Though Bryn was quite shrewd enough a reader of character to know that deadly snakes seldom bite unless they are taken at a disadvantage—that the ugliest man to corner will often give danger a wide berth. Her own share in the victory she promptly forgot. Even while the second assassin's sword blade was sawing through her hands she had noted how magnificent Philip looked as he swung the other into the air to toss him to his death.

And Philip always made so light of his wounds. 'They're nothing,' he would say in answer to her anxious inquiries of a morning. 'It's just that feeding up and blood-making is such a long business.'

As the doctor would not let him transact any business, he was able to spend much more of the day with the little wife, whose back kept her so confined. Her accident, and the quiet, gentle, uncomplaining fortitude with which she endured her pain, had made him feel tenderer and tenderer to her—the first object he had had to love in the new home, which was so far from the old home and all home ties—to her, whose whole being had been wrapped up in him, since he had first wooed her.

So that his period of convalescence was perfectly delightful to him.

Bryn would watch them through the half-opened door. There was no more taint of jealousy than there was of sexualism in her passion for Philip. She did not desire his caresses, though they gave her a dog's pleasure. The strongest characteristic about her new feeling for Philip was an intense satisfaction in being in his presence, and finding evidences of the eternal fitness in everything that he did—an ordinary enough feeling in a man towards a beautiful woman, but rare in a woman, not weak, towards a man.

'Oh, Bryn, how can I thank you for saving me my Philip!' said Mary one day. 'My heart bleeds every time I see the bandages on your hands.'

'It was you who saved him, Mary, by ringing till Kano came,' Bryn replied quite sincerely, not knowing the deep sense of compensation for the shattered spine which her words gave the invalid.

Mary blushed with pleasure. 'And they were such pretty hands too, Bryn.'

'Never mind,' said Bryn, 'the doctor says I shan't be minus any digits; and sword-cuts are honourable things when they are not received behind the back. I suppose it doesn't matter so long as it's somebody else's back.'

CHAPTER X

THE crystal ball was locked up in the *godown* while the household was in this battered condition. 'It will be mine all the same, won't it, Phil?' said his wife, 'and perhaps it's the possession that brings the luck. One can't for ever be handling it.'

But whether it was that she pined for it, though she did not like to have it in the house while Philip's feebleness made it so tempting to burglars, or whether the reaction after the splendid way in which she had risen to the crisis was now setting in, she began to get very much worse.

Morning after morning, when they had perhaps been up half the night with her, she would wake up complaining that nobody ever paid her the slightest attention. The malady took the old form of an incapacity to distinguish degree. She would protest that the room was boiling when the temperature was below 50°; she would swear that it was freezing when it was nearer 80° than 70°. She would shriek with anger at the venetians being closed, and ask if Philip wished to blind her with the glare when he gave them a quarter turn. If he stood there patiently turning them by fractions of an inch and asking her to say when it was just right, she would snarl out to him not to bother her. Once more it was impossible to get her the right temperature. She did not want the right temperature. She wanted to complain.

She always did complain of being tired to death, and the worst of it was that nothing ever did tire her. She would talk, complain, scold, yell, for days together almost without intermission, while Phil and Bryn, robust in health as they were, were utterly exhausted.

Fortunately, the Japanese servants are very affectionate in their service, and as they regard all English people as mad, are never surprised at anything any one English can do. Again, they did not understand half she said, and what they did understand seemed only to amuse them, though, of course, they were far too decorous to let her see their amusement.

With English servants Philip would have been compelled to call in a nurse. And he had wished to do so all along, but Mary went into paroxysms of fury at the idea of a nurse. In her wildest moments she was quite shrewd enough to know that a nurse simply would not put up with the vagaries that her patient, loving husband and sister tried to parry with such affectionate care. In fact, she dreaded having to behave herself, and though the doctor begged Philip to have a nurse in spite of her objections, assuring him that she probably would accept the inevitable inside of a day, when Philip found out that it could not be certain of improving her condition, he thought any suffering on his part was better than overriding her wishes, until the time came when she would require a nurse of a different kind. In the near future she would be a mother.

And then the doctor, seeing that it was already April, and that the season promised to be a hot one, said that he thought the only thing for them to do was to go up to some place in the mountains like Miyanoshita at once. Miyanoshita for a choice, because it was nearest Yokohama, and because Yamaguchi of the Fujiya hotel was the only Japanese country innkeeper who thoroughly understood European requirements.

CHAPTER XI

THEY went up to Miyanoshita as soon as Mary could be moved after the baby was born. It suited Philip better than Nikko, because he could get down to Yokohama and back in the day when need was, and he was leaving town before the summer holidays had really begun. He had noticed the advantages of Miyanoshita when he went up there to get fresh bearers for Mary's chair. The first had been unsuitable, the Japanese to whom Mr. M—— had written having been faithful to their tradition of thinking that any trash would do for an order.

Mary's acquiescence he had secured by suggesting Nikko. With the perversity which had become almost characteristic of her since the injury to her spine, she at once said, 'Oh, why can't we go to Miyanoshita?' (the other summering place of Europeans), and Philip gave in.

They ventured to take her by train from Yokohama to Odawara, the curious old castle-town which is the railway terminus for Miyanoshita. It was the first railway journey she had ventured on since her accident, but it did not seem to affect her unfavourably. For the remaining seven or eight miles she was carried at a very gentle pace in her modified Hong-Kong chair, which was really very little more than a litter. Bryn and Philip, and Kano and Otori-san, who were taken up to see that the hotel servants attended properly to Mary, went in *jinrik-*

shas as far as Yumoto, and walked the other three miles, the mountain climb being almost too steep for *rikshas*, though the sturdy little Japanese porters carried huge trunks on their backs, fastened to a sort of frame, like those used for large sheets of glass by glaziers in England.

Mary said she did not want to talk, she was a little tired, so Phil and Bryn strode on. Both were in raptures over that glorious glen—one of Fuji-yama's vistas to the sea, with its sides now walls of black rock, now thickets of flowering trees, and its breast a clear brown river charging over and between great mossy boulders.

At every vantage point of view—bold gorge or sylvan softness—there was the inevitable tea-house with its gay little *mousmees*, who barred their way, holding out a tray with little cups of pale green tea, and, generally, a group or two of quite poor Japs, who had often walked from great distances, carrying their flimsy luggage, to see some famous bit of scenery or some well-known patch of flowering trees in bloom. These pilgrims stood gazing at the 'lions' in a way that was childlike and bland—the gaze being transferred in a respectful manner to the Euro-peans as they passed. The *mousmees* were quite willing to let one go without drinking the tea if one threw them three *sen* (halfpence) on the tray.

When they reached the hotel, which looked all windows as it stretched across the head of the valley, Mary was soon in the sleep of exhaustion, but Bryn spent the hour before dinner in taking Phil down to Dogashima, the quaint little Japanese village with its beehive roofs of mellow thatch almost lost in the

woods which hide the waterfall—the very antipodes
of the fashionable semi-European watering-place
above.

. . . . . .

Days passed quickly at Miyanoshita. It gave
Mary positive pleasure for the others to go away
and leave her with the baby. She seemed to have
a sort of presentiment that the baby would some day
be theirs and not hers, and she was nursing it herself. She had a healthy and plentiful supply of
milk.

So Philip and Bryn were thrown upon their own
resources, and for a young man and young woman
in full vigour and fond of each other's society few
places have more attractions than Miyanoshita with
its mountain walks and woodland nooks.

The baths, too, large sunken wooden boxes filled
with highly sulphuretted, almost boiling water, carried
down from the bosom of Ojigoku—the Mountain of
Hell—in a mile or two of jointed bamboo piping,
were the most delightful Phil had ever known, though
it took him some time to get accustomed to being
taken to them by girls who were not at all particular whether he was in his bath or not if they had
any question to ask him.

A *posse* of careful Japanese easily bore Mary in a
kimono to the edge, where Otori-san and the women
were able to help her strip and slip in.

CHAPTER XII

NURSING the baby and a month or more of Miyanoshita did wonders for Mary. She was still, and
always would be, on her back, but she was so much
better in general health, and so much more her old
gentle self. Bryn's baby-idolatry, moreover, brought
the sisters almost closer together than they had
ever been.

Mary had had a good many short rides in her
chair along the brow of that exquisite gorge, in air
which had the invigorativeness of mountains and the
softness of summer.

One day she said, 'Phil dear, I should dearly
love to go a picnic I went in my childhood, which I
think was the most beautiful day I ever had in my
life till I knew you. I can't help feeling that I may
never come to Miyanoshita again, so I should love
better than anything in the world to do this picnic
once more.'

' What is it, dear?' he asked.

' To be carried in my chair over Ojigoku—we
went in chairs when we did it before, I remember—
to the Hakone lake, to go down the lake in a *sampan*, with my chair and bearers in another *sampan*,
and then to be carried back from Hakone past
Ashinoyu.'

' But, Mary dear, it is far too far; it would kill
you.'

' Dr. Williams is here, our doctor; he came up

here last night. May I ask him? If he gives his permission, it will be all right, I suppose.'

'I suppose so,' said Philip, anxious to humour her, and not dreaming that the doctor would extend his sanction to such a mad-sounding project.

But the doctor said that in her highly nervous condition it might do her more harm to be refused and brood over it, as she had the presentiment that she would never come to Miyanoshita again.

And so they made the preparations to go.

Philip and Bryn walked. Bryn, who had hardly ever walked a yard in the old days, was so naturally hardy and active that she took the keenest zest in long walks now.

As soon as they were away from the village their path lay mostly through parched woodlands, where women-woodcutters, with their heads tied up in bright blue kerchiefs, were chopping faggots or carrying them on the same glaziers' frames. The path all the time wound along the mountain side with sharp turns.

First went Mary's chair, swinging along, followed by Bryn and Philip, generally in single file—the path was narrow for two Europeans. Then came Kano, and a coolie carrying a heavy luncheon basket, and then Otori-san in a *kago*, in case Mary might want her. It was long before Philip got that picture out of his mind—the tall chair with his ill wife looking so marvellously better, and the supple figure speeding up the mountain path before him, in its fresh white blouse and well-hung skirt, caught up with the left hand in the soft clinging gray glove, which matched the skirt so well, high enough to clear the sharp bamboo stumps at the edge of the path.

It was hot work toiling up Ojigoku, which being interpreted, literally means " big hell "—fortunately, not for Mary on her chair, well shaded with a preposterous Japanese umbrella. But Bryn, however much she felt it, managed not to turn too painfully red.

' Kano,' said Mary in Japanese, ' tell them to stop when we get to the place where we can hear the lava boiling and bubbling under us. You've not been up here before, Phil, so you must be careful to follow the luncheon coolie, or a heavy man like you might sink through and get fearfully burned, the crust is so thin. There have been several accidents like that up here. Oh, this is the place, is it? I thought so. See the steam rolling up through the cracks ! '

' Oh, I must go on,' cried Bryn ; ' it's scorching the soles of my feet.'

But the coolies, with worn-out straw rope sandals, did not seem to mind it.

On they climbed, the walking growing very rough and the mountain very bare and wild.

Suddenly it became much easier again—with little clumps of bamboo here and there. Not far above them on the right were a small and apparently unused hut and a little row of stone Buddhas, and just above those a smooth bank.

' That top,' said Kano, with a fine disregard of grammar.

Bryn rushed up and stood with her beautiful figure and fluttering skirt outlined against the sky as she shaded her eyes with her hand.

'Phil, Phil,' she cried—'Fuji!'

But Philip, excited as he was, waited a few seconds to let his wife get up at the same time with him.

There, right in front of their eyes, rose from base to summit the most beautiful mountain in the world, like the inverted head of a palm-tree in the exquisite curves of its truncated cone, the muzzle of which was hoary with thousands of feet of snow.

'Give me your hand, Phil,' asked Mary, and then she cried, 'O Fuji, I feel that I don't mind dying now, when I have seen you again in all your beauty rising from your blue lake with my husband by me. I was afraid, Phil, that this was never going to be. I believe I should have died of grief and anger at my helplessness if you had not let me come.'

'Don't talk of dying, Mary,' begged Philip with tears in his eyes. 'You're not going to die yet for many a year, and it is so ill-omened to talk of it.'

'Very well, Phil, though I do feel that just now is the moment that I would choose. When you are like I am, dear,' she said quite simply, ignorant of the pathos, 'you will be able to think of it quite calmly—to think about choosing your time.'

'No see lake well here,' said the practical Kano, probably without any idea of stemming the mournfulness of the conversation. 'By and by good place; lying tree sit on; have tiffin.'

'Go on,' said Mary, laughing.

She spoke a few words to Kano in Japanese.

'I thought so,' she said. 'It is a fallen tree which you are to sit on while you have lunch.'

'It's almost lunch enough for me to see the

dainty way in which it is packed,' said Bryn, in high spirits. She had not heard the conversation on the top of ' Big Hell.'

First from a spotless napkin came cold fried fish, and from another equally immaculate, bread. Butter, mustard, pepper and salt were in little blue and white earthenware crocks, with cunningly-fitted lids that fastened in some mysterious way.

More napkins were forthcoming for personal use, and from yet others two daintily-roasted chickens and a tiny loin made their appearance as the fish disappeared. The knives and forks fitted into each other, and were all one long handle when out of use. Highly-ambitious tartlets came out of a partitioned box ; a cake from the tin it was baked in (as the smallest receptacle which would hold it), vigorously sand-papered outside ; mandarin oranges without any pips from a sweet little basket—all of which, with a good many other kickshaws, and half a dozen pints of champagne and glasses, had been packed into a folding basket of the most modest dimensions, but no trifling weight carried mountain-fashion like faggots or portmanteaus.

It was Mary's picnic, and yearningly they drank her speedy return to full health and activity.

When lunch was over Kano said, ' You no want pack up. Coolie go more fast than you. At lake same time.'

Going down the sharp slope it was natural for Bryn and Phil to get a good deal ahead of the chair, which had to be carried down with great gentleness to prevent Mary being shaken.

Presently, in the midst of a charming grove, a

little off the path, they saw a beautiful little building of fresh white wood.

'Do let's go in, Bryn,' cried Phil. 'Hurry up so as to get back to the path by the time that Mary is there.' They tore in and came out like a flash of lightning. It was a bath, and in the steaming sulphur-pool men and women stark naked were observing the Government regulation against promiscuous bathing by letting a bamboo float on the top of the water between them.

Bryn showed no *mauvaise honte*, though she flew out so quickly. 'I thought it was rash,' she said, 'plunging in in that unguarded way; but don't expect me to be too shocked; remember that I'm a Jap by birth.'

After passing through lovely feathery, wavy brakes of bamboo, and groves of dark camellia trees, with their beautiful single scarlet blossoms, they found themselves by the dark blue waters of the lake of Hakone. There, sure enough, was the coolie who had carried the lunch sitting in the bows of the more unseaworthy-looking of the two *sampans* which were to carry them across the lake. Into this *sampan* went the bearers of the chair, and, a good deal to their disappointment, Kano and Otori-san. They went instead of the chair, from which Philip would not hear of Mary's stirring. Each of these long heavy *sampans* had several rowers. Philip judged that the swaying motions of the *yulos* or gondoliers' oars, with which they were paddled, would be quite as much as Mary could bear, even if she were lying back in her chair. The boats had masts, but the wind was not right for hoisting the picturesque, banner-like sails with their black stripes, which would have given a great deal easier motion.

Down the few miles of this exquisite icy sapphire lake, literally under the shadow of the immortal grace of Fujiyama, past the summer palace of the Mikado, moved the quaint Oriental boats, till they grated against the steps of a tea-house overlooking the lake in the little village of Hakone—famous for its high-pitched roofs of matchless thatch. Here they had tea—Chinese tea—Nankin tea, the little *mousmée* called it. To the uneducated Jap everything Chinese comes from Nankin. At Hakone Europeans are by no means *rarae aves*, so provisions are made for their comfort.

After tea they marched along the broad, paved roadway of the Tokaido, close to one of its most historical and picturesque portions, though none of them remembered the fact. They were more taken up with the beautiful temple and stately cryptomeria avenue by the lake-side.

It was an infinitely restful scene. On the left the blue lake with the majestic mountain brooding over it; behind, the ancient avenue of tall trees; round hills of tangled green ahead; and, immediately in front, the tall stone votive lanterns and the elegant *torii* of a temple.

Here, too, the flags of the road were smoother and better cared for, and the chair swung along with an easy swimming motion on the bearers' shoulders, while Phil and Bryn strode along with the sense of ease natural when one comes to a level after a sharp incline.

But from this point on the walk was one long climb.

A JAPANESE MARRIAGE

This often seemed typical to Philip afterwards. The climb rose sharply behind the temple, mainly through grass as high as a man, and bamboo brakes, already yellow with summer. Though, as it were, only a bridle-path through scrub, it must have been a track trodden for centuries, for at every *cho* was a tiny Buddha of gray stone mellowed by the weather of ages, and just off the road, in a thicket into which Kano led Phil and Bryn, were three ancient tombs of the peculiar cushion-topped shape which symbolises the five elements.

'Those tombs,' said Kano enigmatically, 'Japanese kill dragon men. One time big dragon live in Ojigoku. Kill every man, woman in Miyanoshita, Hakone, Yumoto. Three brothers no can kill.'

He was very much insulted because Bryn asked him about it in Japanese. He considered this a reflection on his English. As they had gathered, there was a big dragon in Ojigoku once upon a time. After the manner of dragons, east and west, he had insisted upon a maiden-tribute from Hakone, Miyanoshita, and Yumoto, until he fell a victim to the wiles of the three brothers, who were honoured with the style of tomb generally reserved for princes and prelates. After all it was not much for a dragon to have lived in a mountain that was always struggling to be a volcano.

Half-way to Ashinoyu they halted in front of the vast and beautiful image of Jizo-Sama, carved out of the living rock, about thirty feet high.

Mary was in pain for the moment. Perhaps the journey was a little long.

'Do you know, Phil dear, that since my accident

181

I have sometimes felt inclined to pray to the gods of my country. They seem so much nearer to me than the imported Christ. He has only a church here and there, opened only once a week by a man who seems just one of us till he puts on a white surplice and goes up to the reading-desk or pulpit. But the gods of my country are everywhere.'

As she spoke, Philip saw the gods of her country everywhere outside the foreign settlements. No matter where she stood, she could hardly sweep the horizon without her eye falling on a *torii*, that mystical double-cruciform Japanese arch, of which no one knows the origin or the significance. Not a day could pass without her hearing the tinkle of the bells pulled by poor worshippers to call heaven to listen to a prayer, or the boom of mellow gongs. And the priests ever wore white raiment.

' It does me good to look at Jizo-Sama to-day,' said Mary, in a low voice. ' His face seems full of that peace of God which passeth all understanding spoken of in our prayer-book. And Jizo sounds quite like our Jesus, doesn't it ? There is so much about Jizo like Him.'

' Cheer up, little woman. It's your picnic,' said her husband, rather inconsequently it might have seemed, except that most people only think about religion when they feel frightened.

' Did you think I felt bad, Phil ? I'm only a little tired, I think.'

' We can rest here as long as ever you like. I love this great merciful-looking god.'

Mary closed her eyes, and Phil and Bryn sat musing.

Presently Mary looked up and said, ' I feel better now. Let's go on.'

When they were upon the tableland overlooking the reedy pool of clear warm water which gives Ashinoyu its name, and the far silvery sea beyond the gorge of Miyanoshita, their spirits rose, and they were able to laugh over the humours of the humble tea-houses dotted along this rough walk, often mere. cupboards in the wilderness.

And they lingered happily by the little waterfall above the town, till Bryn said, laughingly, ' It is getting dusk ; we must be quick home, or we shall see all the *riksha*-boys having their baths in the open. There's a leak in the pipe which carries the hot water from Ojigoku down to the hotel.'

CHAPTER XIII

THAT night Mary was in a high fever and ex- cruciating agony, with Dr. Williams constantly in attendance. The journey had been far too much for her.

And in less than a month, in which there were many days like that first one at Yokohama, when the evil spirit was upon her, the end came.

The nimble-fingered Japanese converted her Hong- Kong chair into a bed, which could be carried in and out easily, for there was no moving her from one couch to another now, and she gasped for the open air in the stifling Japanese summer. And thus it was that the ever-increasing number of visitors to the hotel were witnesses of the devotion of Phil and Bryn, which touched them so.

'I'd get a hospital nurse for that cussed woman,' said a lady, who was one of Bryn's principal detractors afterwards. 'I be jiggered if I'd put up with her tantrums.'

For a week or more Mary had not been able to bear even the removal of the couch on which she lay into the verandah, when one day she woke up entirely free from her pain.

She remarked this to them, as soon as they noticed that she was awake. 'But don't move me,' she said. 'I have a feeling that this is the end; and I should like to have you three to myself, not before all the hotel.'

The doctor came as usual in the morning, and shook his head. 'Send for me if you feel that you want me,' he said; 'but I can do nothing. It's a kind of paralysis, which shows that death cannot be far off; nothing can stop it. All I could do is to give her an anæsthetic, if there were any occasion; but she says she is in positively no pain.'

In the afternoon, towards sundown, a hectic spot came into her cheeks, and she looked quite young and pretty again, almost as she had looked when Philip married her, except for a clearness and hollowness in her cheeks, and for the unnatural brilliance of her eyes.

'Give me my baby,' she said; 'I should like to do my last for our little daughter—our daughter, Philip; and tell Kano to get a strong, healthy woman from Kiga or somewhere up in the mountains—not from

Dogashima; there is no air there; it is a hole; and I shall have no air to-night.'

Then, seeing that Phil and Bryn were weeping, she said, 'Don't cry for me; I'm sorry to leave my little motherless baby and you, and the summer, and the mountains, and Japan. I am glad that I was born and have lived nearly all my life in Japan, for it is a little quiet place at the back of the world, and I shall not be forgotten. You will not let our daughter forget me, Phil, when you and Bryn are married. She will call you mother, of course, Bryn —poor little desolate soul. I don't mind that. But when she is old enough, don't forget to tell her of her little mother who lived such a struggle of a life all the time she was with her.'

They dared not look at her or each other. What she took for granted had never entered their loyal minds.

There was a pause before they could find utterance with their choking voices, then they promised that the little Mary should never forget her.

The dying woman took up the thread of her message.

'I am glad that you took me to England, Philip. For I am an Englishwoman, though I was born and lived and died in little Japan. Bryn shall go to England, shan't she? It is nice to me now to feel that we are children of the great nation which covers the earth, though father and mother and I have died away here, and Bryn and I were born here.'

'Bryn shall go to England,' said Philip, first taking the wasted hand in his grasp, and then pressing his lips upon it.

Suddenly a new light seemed to dawn upon her. She spoke with the gentle diplomacy of the dying. ' There is only one way in which I can die happy. Philip is a young man and he will marry again, and if he marries any one but you, Bryn, how can my mind be at rest about baby ? But of course he will marry you, Bryn, when the grass has grown upon my grave. You were made for each other. It is you who should have had him in the beginning, and not I. But you will be married now, and be so happy together, for you have the full knowledge of each other. Don't marry any one but Bryn, Phil. Another wife would want you to forget me.'

Then, with the clear sight of the dying, she saw that Bryn was hanging back. ' Promise me that you will marry each other,' she said suddenly, in a loud, agonised voice.

But before they could promise she was dead.

.   .   .   .   .   .

Down the green valley of Miyanoshita, as soon as a coffin could be brought up from Yokohama, the light body was carried on the shoulders of her own ' bearers.'

Nearly all the people who were at Miyanoshita when Mary died, went down to Yokohama for the day to attend the funeral. In the far East, English customs are neglected or maintained according to fancy. Many ladies were present in the cemetery when Mary was lowered into her grave, with Bryn and Philip standing side by side as chief mourners. As Bryn stood there in her beauty, those who had seen most of her since her sister's marriage were not slow to prophesy her marriage with the man who had had such a humanising influence over her, at no distant date ; and those who had seen most of her since her sister's return as an invalid, especially those who had been at Miyanoshita during the illness, would have been glad to see it.

They observed, with more goodness of heart than good taste, 'She deserves something for being so devoted to her sister.'

There were really few, who thought about it at all, to doubt that, in the light-hearted and self-indulgent East, Philip would be married and happier with Bryn than ever he had been with Mary, before the sward had healed over her grave.

After the funeral he and Bryn (with the baby and its Japanese foster-mother) went down for their much-needed rest among the orange groves of soft Atami.

CHAPTER XIV

FOR the first three months after their return from Atami to Yokohama, which took place in October, sincerely as they mourned Mary, Phil and Bryn found an intense happiness.

In the first place they were able to be, what they had for months known themselves designed to be, all in all to each other, that brother and sister could have been. Their tastes were exactly the same ; and their happiness would have been complete though there had not been another living soul on

the earth. The baby hardly came into their calcula-
tion. Only a mother can love a baby too young to
develop a single idiosyncrasy; though Bryn, like
most women who have been Amazons to men, found
something irresistibly charming in this materialisa-
tion of a man's love for a woman.

And Bryn spent much of her time in the nursery.
She felt that she owed it to Mary to take particular
care of this orphaned little one.

They found a plentiful source of employment and
interest in furnishing and settling into Philip's new
house, which he had occupied such a very few
months before Mary's illness drove them to Miyanoshita, and those so broken with her illness, and
the pressure of work entailed by taking over her
father's business. The necessaries, from the dining-
room table to the drawing-room carpet and the
bedroom suites, Philip had bought in England, and
these had been supplemented to repletion by the
sale of Netheravon. In the heavy items of furniture,
subtraction, not addition, was needed. It was chiefly
in the direction of the distribution of such effects
that they spent time. There was hardly anything
more which they had to buy; but Philip had laid
aside so many hundred dollars for making his house
beautiful with the artistic touches which can be pro-
cured nowhere so cheaply as in Japan.

It was in the planning out and purchasing and
fitting in of these that Phil and Bryn found much
congenial employment. They could hardly have
found a better diversion for the time during which
respect to Mary's memory demanded that they should
withdraw themselves from society. For it gave them

plenty to do, and almost entirely in the company of Asiatics, who did not count for such considerations as mourning.

When Phil came out of his office at four in the afternoon, his *riksha*, with its two smart *kurumayas*, would be waiting, and he would fly off home to get a cup of tea and inquire about his child before going off with Bryn for a two hours' *bric-à-brac* hunt in the curio-shops. And of a Sunday, as being his free day, though they went to church in the morning as a rule, they would go over to Tokyo afterwards to explore the back streets, especially round Shiba.

Some Japanese keep Sunday as a matter of fashion—just as they wear white felt hats or yellow leather boots ; but they chiefly belong to the upper class, or at any rate to some profession in which there would be no commercial profit to be made out of working on the Englishman's Sabbath. The poorer classes have no weekly day of rest in Japan ; there is nothing to mark off one week from another—neither the Friday of the Turk, nor the Saturday of the Jew, nor the Sunday of the Christian. But there are a good many legal and religious holidays in the year, which a good many people seem to be able to observe in the picnicky Japanese fashion.

For the natives whose shops are patronised by foreigners, such as curio-sellers, silk-mercers and the like, Sunday is often one of the busiest and most profitable days, because there are no European shops open to divert patronage.

'O Phil, I wish we hadn't to do our shopping in Tokyo on Sunday. It goes against the grain so with me. As children we were never allowed to go near a shop on Sunday.'

'But you've always been in the habit of making expeditions on Sunday. The banquet at the Maple Club, when I was with you, was not your first visit there on Sunday, nor was the day at Kamakura, on which I asked poor Mary to marry me, the first Sunday expedition you had ever made to the Daibutsu.'

'I know; but somehow or other shopping seems different. Sunday is almost the only day people have time for expeditions. One *can* shop at odd times.'

'But our shopping in Tokyo is a regular expedition.'

'I'm sure it's wicked, and that something will happen to us in consequence.'

She often thought of this afterwards, and felt convinced that she was right.

All the same, those three months were perhaps the happiest she ever had in her life. There seemed to be no particular breakers ahead. And as to restfulness, the languid days they spent for the sole purpose of rest at Atami, just after Mary's death, were not to be compared to these busy, busy days at Yokohama.

The fact was that they had everything off their minds. In spite of what Mary had said on her death-bed they had not given any consideration to the idea of marrying each other. To Bryn it was *ipso facto* impossible, and to Phil it seemed only attainable by the developments of time. It seemed as if they were beginning a pleasant, useful, jog-trot existence which would go on jogging till death did part two such exceedingly healthy young people—a sufficiently remote contingency. They did not see what else could possibly part them.

One day they had an earthquake worse than the usual run in that earthquake-scourged country. Chimney-pots by the stack—even a house or two were thrown down. (The sign of a serious earthquake in Japan is a murrain among the Yokohama chimney-pots.)

But it did not disturb the even tenor of their lives, though there seemed to Phil a good deal in Otori-san's remark that the more you got accustomed to earthquakes the less you liked them.

At another time a typhoon swept the harbour and lifted one of his ships over the *hatoba*, against which it happened to be lying. The ship being insured, and no loss of life incurred, he saw no hand-writing of fate in this, though getting the insurance claims paid involved him in a good deal of extra business.

Neither death, nor earthquake, nor tempest seemed able to strike one whose happiness was so simply and securely founded.

CHAPTER XV

THEY had determined not to break through the isolation of their mourning until after Christmas, partly because they looked forward to enjoying a quiet Christmas together. But during the enforced idleness of the New Year (your Japanese keeps his New Year festival not by his own calendar but the Gregorian) Phil gave a bachelor's dinner party to Mr. Spong, Bob Mathdine, and Charley Dacres.

When they arrived and were received by Philip alone, Mathdine in particular looked very blank, though his admiration for a certain young lady was so very much a matter of history that he felt a delicacy in making any allusion to the subject.

But Mr. Spong, in his rather artificial *rôle* of ' privileged on account of age,' had no such scruples.

' I say, Sandys,' he said, ' you've got us here on false pretences. You never told us that Miss Bryn was not going to be one of the party, and here I've got on a clean shirt and my first-best, top-side suit of evening clothes.'

' By Jove, yes,' said Dacres, whose conversation was mostly at a tangent, though he was pretty clear-headed in business at expressing what he meant to a man who knew what he ought to mean, like his head clerk.

' Is Miss Bryn out ? ' asked Mathdine, plucking up his courage.

' I don't think so.'

' Well, if my young friend is in,' said the older man, who was taking the matter up practically, ' is she prostrated with any kind of illness, which has suddenly made her appearance impossible ? '

' No,' said Philip. ' Why ? '

' Because, otherwise, you owe it to us to ask her to come and explain why she is depriving us in this manner—or, at any rate, to come and say how do you do.'

'But Bryn had only her morning dress on when I saw her two minutes ago, or, to be more precise, I think she had taken off her tight-fitting bodice and slipped into a comfortable silk blouse, before settling down to dinner in her boudoir with a novel.'

'Miss Bryn dining by herself!' cried Mathdine.

'That's the beauty of Japanese servants. They don't consider themselves the least aggrieved at sending in two dinners at the same time. The only difficulty was in persuading them to let Bryn off without going through as many courses as us.'

'You take my message to Miss Bryn, young man, or there will be war between the Clan Spong and the Clan Sandys.'

'Do, Sandys,' said the two younger men simultaneously, Mathdine adding, 'You must give us the satisfaction of shaking hands with Miss Bryn anyway.'

'Well, excuse me a minute, will you?'

'Oh, certainly.'

'Bryn, Bryn,' called Philip, outside her boudoir door.

'Come in, Phil.'

'Will you come downstairs and shake hands with those men? They say I'm a fraud, that I have inveigled them here under false pretences in not letting them know that you wouldn't be there, and that they won't forgive me unless you come down and say how do you do to them. I told them that you had not changed your dress. But they would not take that as an excuse. Will you come and shake hands with them, dear? Of course, if you mind, I'll just say that it is impossible.'

'No, don't say that, Phil,' she said slowly, as if she was thinking what she should do. 'They're old, old friends, all of them. I'll come.' And down she came, though totally unprepared, without so much as a glance at the glass to see that the golden coil, which no one ever remembered ill-ordered or unglossy, was to her satisfaction.

'Remember,' she said, as she shook hands, 'that none of you've seen me in this coloured blouse.' The blouse, than which she could hardly have worn anything more becoming to her brilliant fairness and light figure, was of soft Japanese silk, one of those delicate rainbow blends of pale stripes which you so often see on their counters, and so seldom on their women. 'The bodice of this dress, with its military braidings, and paddings, and stiff military collar, was so black and stuffy.'

'Conditions,' said Mr. Spong. 'Conditions.'

'What conditions?' asked Bryn smiling.

'That you sit down to dinner with us.'

'Yes, do have dinner with us,' begged the others.

'No, I can't,' she replied conciliatorily, but seriously, after a moment's thought. 'Phil wouldn't have asked you so soon, except as a bachelor affair.'

'Do, Miss Bryn,' pleaded Mathdine, his anxiety getting the better of his discretion. 'Philip's an awfully nice fellow, but he isn't quite enough to console us for the loss of such an anticipated pleasure.'

'I'm going to tell on you,' said Mr. Spong. 'I'll tell everybody at the Club how nice you looked in——'

Bryn put on a comical assumption of terror. 'Will you parley, Punch?'

'Certainly, if it keeps you here. Besides, *she* who parleys is lost.'

'I'm going to make my own conditions.'

'Well, let's hear them—perhaps we shall break off negotiations.'

'Well, if you'll keep it—blouse and all—a strict secret, I'll come in like a good little girl, directly dinner is over.'

Of course she knew quite well that neither of them would breathe a word in any case. It was only a light way of discussing with herself what she ought to do.

As she went out Mr. Spong called out, 'We'll see you off as far as the foot of the stairs.' Linking his arms through Mr. Mathdine's and Mr. Dacres's, the three of them marched out solemnly and saluted.

Dinner was announced.

It began with a huge round china tray being handed, which had thirty or more little china dishes fitted into it, containing the queer *hors d'œuvres*, condiments, and sauces popular in the appetiser-craving East. Philip passed it by, but the others helped themselves each to a speck of his particular fancy. Then came oysters, arranged five on a plate, like the holes in a ventilator or the chambers of a revolver.

One with *tabasco*, another with lemon and cayenne, another absolutely alone, they ate their oysters.

Then came delicious-looking clear turtle soup— Japan runs to turtles, so the cooks understand it— the cook, moreover, was one of the Netheravon servants, whom Philip had taken on—a Chinese genius.

'Not for me, thank you,' said Mr. Spong.

'No, thank you,' said Mr. Mathdine.

'No, thanks,' said Mr. Dacres, who got along with
fewer syllables than any one in the settlement.

Philip hurried through his. 'It's awfully good,
you fellows, though I say it as shouldn't—won't you
change your mind, Spong?'

They all shook their heads.

Then came some fried fillets of mullet, that were
a perfect picture.

But Mr. Spong would not be tempted, nor would
either of the others.

'I'm awfully fond of mullet,' said Philip. 'You
fellows won't mind sipping your hock for a minute
or two, while I eat a mouthful; or stay, Kano, you
might open the champagne.'

When the crab came in, taken out of his shell,
and pounded up into a sort of fine paste, in the
American fashion, before it was put back—it was
Mr. Spong's favourite *morceau* which Bryn had put
into the *menu*, to show that she remembered his
weaknesses—

'I won't take any, thank you. I've eaten quite
ufficient,' he said.

'I don't want any more dinner, thank you,' said
Mr. Mathdine.

'Nor I,' said Mr. Dacres.

Philip was flabbergasted. 'Kano,' he called; but
Kano had disappeared. 'You fellows are playing
something off on me,' continued their host, with a
mystified air, while Kano, with quick Japanese wit,
was tapping at the door of his mistress's boudoir.
I think some mistake. Gentlemen no understand,

lady more head — head — more brains in her eyes.'

'What is the matter, Kano?'

He told her what had happened, and added, 'Spong San he look down all the time.'

'Spong San he look down all the time,' repeated Bryn to herself. 'Then it is time that some one lighter-witted than Philip was watching him.' Quick as thought she twisted a lace toilet cover from her bedroom round her shoulders, shook out a few hairpins, and the silver arrow skewered through her coil, and darted down to the dining-room, where she thrust in at the half-opened door an anxious-looking face, thrown into strong relief by the flood of sunny hair flowing down over the toilet cover.

'Is anything the matter?' she gasped, just as the three in chorus were replying to Philip's impatient remark—

'We've done dinner.'

'Punch, I'm ashamed of you,' said Bryn, marching into the room, as she whipped off the toilet cover to show that she was not in *déshabillé*, and with one adroit twist twirled her magnificent hair into a roll, which, with the end of the same motion, she wound into a loose coil, to be pinned by the silver arrow in the left hand, till now kept behind her back. The barb came off and allowed the pin to be thrust through the hair, before it was screwed in again.

'You boys,—for I can't call you anything more,— just deserve to lose your dinner for playing these pranks,' she said, as soon as she could get over the uncontrollable fit of laughter caused by the expression their faces wore at her apparition, at the same time taking the place at the head of the table vacated by Mr. Spong when the gentlemen rose to receive her.

Kano did not require the order she gave him in Japanese to relay the place for her and a fresh one for the chief culprit. The Japanese love a joke, and are always on the *qui vive.*

'I'm going to have the soup and fish and crab brought back,' she said, with admirably assumed severity ; 'and you'll have to eat them cold, just as they are, for being naughty, or else I'll send you home.'

They all were of the opinion that they ought to do penance, and, besides, they were now very hungry ; so they promised.

But the penance did not come off. For the Japanese servants were so delighted with the joke, that they brought everything back almost in the pink of its original condition. They show the same mysterious knack in re-heating food without spoiling it which they show in the adaptation of a garment. A Japanese could make a neat job of taking in or letting out a hard felt hat, though one might not think it, because most of their hats need two or three reefs badly.

'It's too naughty of you, Punch,' said Bryn, in her heart of hearts delighted at being captured, 'and me such a sight.'

They protested quite truly that they had seldom seen her looking so well. The evening was a brimming success almost before the restored crab, the last of the three rejected courses, had disappeared. They lost all count of dishes after the next course of quail, crushed flat in the Japanese style.

'I'm a mere vegetable since I have had to do without your sauce, my young friend,' sighed Mr. Spong. 'I couldn't say a bitey thing to save my life.'

'Poor Punch' said Bryn, showing her white teeth, and with a malicious little dimple in each cheek. 'People will think you horribly old.'

'I feel it.'

'Miss Bryn,' said Mr. Mathdine, 'Yokohama isn't what it was since you gave up Netheravon. There's simply no society left. People have dinners and teas and things, but there's nothing in them. We're getting simply provincial. We don't belong to the world at all now.'

'Don't make me vain,' she said. 'Philip has to have me in the house, so you ought to consider his peace of mind.'

'Philip's a lucky fellow.'

'But he earned his luck,' put in Mr. Spong, 'for he waited for it to come to him.'

This was perhaps not in the best taste, but it passed, because Charley Dacres for once made a remark, 'I'm sure I've waited enough.'

'You've waited so much,' said Mr. Spong, 'that Fate's lost sight of you.'

'What do you think about the matter, Miss Bryn?' asked Mr. Mathdine.

'What is *it* exactly,' asked Bryn. The first part of the conversation had been rather an embarrassing one for her to take part in.

'What do you think about Fate and waiting?'

'Well, I think that if you wait you'll get it, if you're on the look-out to take it when it comes—sometimes ever so easily.'

' Oh, I don't believe in Fate,' said Mathdine. ' A man ought to be able to mould his own fate, if he's worth anything.'

' You try,' said Punch.

' I shouldn't like to cross Fate,' said Philip. ' I'm always almost afraid to try and do a thing until I see it doing itself. I haven't often tried to step in and do Fate's work for her before she was ready ; but whenever I have, it's just been a failure, and I've seen afterwards how beautifully things would have gone if I'd only given them the chance.'

' Fate's a woman,' said Bryn, ' and women dearly love to play the jade at first, so as to relent gracefully afterwards.'

' I hope you won't behave like Fate to me, Bryn,' cried Philip.

' You won't give me the chance. You're not the sort of game Fate shoots at.'

CHAPTER XVI

THE *toute ensemble* of that ultra-superior institution, the Minerva Club, was ultra-Japanese, except in one respect. The ' understandings' of its average members did not admit of their taking off their shoes with *éclat*.

So, instead of having the beautiful inch-thick matting of pale primrose-coloured straw which is the crowning beauty of the Japanese home, they had cocoa-nut matting, which they judged to be of the same ascetic value, if its æsthetic qualities were less obvious.

It was a common one-storied Japanese house, in a quarter for the most part given up to Chinamen, containing more than one public-house of no particular repute, addicted to the drugging and pillaging of sailors, and some other houses of even less repute, which also lived upon sailors, the attraction being that it was near the office of the most accommodating newspaper. The editor of this manufactory of public opinion was expected, with the aid of one reporter and one Japanese translator of the vernacular newspapers, to produce the entire paper every day of the year, except Sunday. All contributions of copy were therefore thankfully received on the responsibility (for libels and thrashings) of the contributors. In this journal the Minerva reported itself very fully, and it cannot be said that its reports were lacking in spirit. The other two papers were more or less closed to its proceedings by the fact that one of them was the subsidised organ of the Japanese Government, to which the Minerva was not invariably respectful, and the other was edited by a man who attributed his domestic jars to the fact of his acknowledged wife being a member of the Club, rather than to the existence of his unmentioned Japanese helpmates.

On this particular afternoon in spring, among the ladies sitting on the floor of the Club—they carried their Japanesity to the extent of having no furniture but *hibachi* (charcoal braziers) and *futon* (flat princess cushions) — were all the female members of Mr. Avon's party at the Maple Club, except Mary, of course, who was dead, and her sister.

'I wish Bryn Avon was a member,' sighed pretty Mrs. Amory. 'We do want a few more of the smart, well-dressed women of the settlement. The men do make such fun of us.'

'Do you think she could get in?' asked the only other pretty young woman in the Club—Mrs. Crosby —entirely without malice, in her thoughtless way.

'What do you mean?' said Mrs. Prince snappishly, 'that we are all jealous of her?'

Mrs. Crosby gave a curious little laugh, which did not sound at all agreeable, though it was not unmusical.

'Haven't you heard that since her poor sister's death she is living with Mr. Sandys as man and wife? I thought it was in everybody's mouth.'

'I don't believe a word of it,' said Mrs. Amory indignantly, her fair cheeks flushing scarlet at the imputation cast on womanhood in the person of Bryn Avon.

'Nor I,' said Mrs. Prince tartly. 'Bryn Avon is a minx; but she's much too artful and designing to give herself away like that. Such a poor creature of a man too. No! that is impossible.'

'Oh, I don't suppose there's anything in it,' rejoined Mrs. Crosby; 'only everybody is talking about it; and what's that proverb, "There's no fire without a smoke."'

'There's no smoke without a fire,' said Mrs. Prince, and she added *sotto voce*, 'that idiot can't even repeat a proverb without mangling it. I wonder what the story was like when she first heard it?'

'I've never had any opinion of the younger Miss Avon,' put in Mrs. Phelps. 'I've always considered her bold and unprincipled.'

'This is really serious,' said Mrs. Sparling, whom the frumps of the settlement always spoke of as *such a jolly little woman, the life and soul of the place,* as she showed her teeth in what was intended to be a sickly smile, but suggested a sickly horse.

'But people do say such awful things,' protested poor Mrs. Crosby, beginning to get thoroughly frightened at the storm she seemed to have raised. 'Why, it was only last year, when I was staying at Miyano-shita, that a lady, who was peeping into the Japanese part of the Fujiya Hotel, recognised her husband's boots and portmanteau a week after he had left her "to go back to his business in Yokohama."'

As the lady in question was Mrs. Phelps—Mrs. Crosby had forgotten who it was—this did not mend matters much.

'If there weren't women like Miss Avon about, the men would behave themselves better,' Mrs. Phelps simply snorted out.

'Aren't we here to discuss " *Women. What are we to do for them?*"' mildly suggested good-hearted Mrs. Amory. 'It was down in my notice.'

'Yes,' answered Mrs. Prince; 'I think Mrs. Phelps has something to say upon the subject.'

Mrs. Prince was not to be repressed. The Commander was absolutely devoted, and she was so sour-looking that a scandal positively curdled the moment it was applied to her. So Mrs. Phelps poured out the vials of her indignation on Bryn.

'To think that I've allowed myself to associate with that girl : to make an intimate of her.'

'The secrecy, too ; that's the most compromising part,' said Mrs. Prince.

Mrs. Phelps affected to consider that these last remarks applied to the new scandal, while her tormentor continued in a *sotto voce* voice that might have been heard in the street, 'Fancy Bryn Avon the intimate of that Mother Fawkes. Mr. Phelps ought to keep her in his *godown* all the year round, as the Japs do their treasures, and only bring her out on special occasions, like the English Fifth of November.'

'I've suspected something of the kind for a long time,' continued Mrs. Phelps, still working herself up.

'I'd believe it of any woman in this room before Bryn Avon,' said Mrs. Amory hotly.

'Americans do not understand the sacredness of domestic relations just as we do, perhaps,' answered Mrs. Phelps loftily.

Mrs. Prince laughed out rudely, and said, 'Perhaps you will tell us about English domestic relations, Mrs. Phelps—as you have found them.'

'This girl is a disgrace to the community,' emphasised Mrs. Phelps, feeling that she must say something strong. 'Unless a firm stand is made, who knows which of us may go next?'

This appealed to frivolous Mrs. Crosby as so funny that she giggled uncontrollably, and every one thought that she was presuming on her youth and good looks so far as to believe that she would be the next, which made them very angry.

The jolly little woman, having the reputation for

steam and energy, had felt all through this rather typical Minerva debate that she must do something ; she had been waiting for an inspiration, or to see which way the cat jumped.

'I shall make arrangements,' she observed sententiously, 'that Mr. Sparling shall see nothing of her. He is just the kind of good-natured man that——'

At this untoward moment, Mrs. Prince, who was far from willing to see a girl whom she felt to be incapable of anything of the kind hounded down by slander, cordially as she disliked her personally, gave another of her maddening derisive laughs, and observed to Mrs. Amory in an aside, which the outraged Mrs. Sparling overheard, 'Christopher Columbus ! Bryn and Mr. Sparling ! Hold me up !' and the 'jolly little woman' went over, horse, foot, and artillery, to the enemy.

And Mrs. Sparling was perfectly sincere. Granted that Bryn was justly accused, to a woman of her narrow mind it was impossible to recognise any of the extenuating circumstances. Such a woman could make no allowance for the temptation to which Bryn had been subjected in being kept by her sister's illness in constant contact with the only man she had ever loved, both of them in riotous health and confined so much to the house ; nor for the graciousness and dog-like fidelity with which Bryn had devoted herself to the happiness of the sister who, in her last year, had so many dark hours of inconsolable madness. And, being angered by Mrs. Prince, Mrs. Sparling took it for granted that Bryn was guilty, though the girl was absolutely innocent.

Further, a woman of Mrs. Sparling's 'steam'
could never be satisfied with minding her own
business, and merely guarding the vacuous Sparling
from any insidious designs on the part of Bryn.
She said she would take the advice of all her friends,
which meant that she would worry them into taking
her advice.

There was also a sort of house-to-house visitation
against Bryn by certain members of the Minerva,
who were shocked by the editor of the *Japan Sun*
refusing for once the copy offered in such generous
quantities by the Club.

In the first place, he liked Philip, who, attracted
by his brains, had made a friend of him as none of
the other leading men in the settlement had. In the
second, he had a shrewd sort of idea of the kind of
man that Philip would be where his beautiful sister-
in-law was concerned, and, having an office on an
upper floor, had no desire to leave it by the window,
or by whole flights of stairs at a time; and in the
third place, a libel action spelt ruin to the paper.

CHAPTER XVII

THE slander on Bryn soon spread all over the
settlement. There were so many opportunities or
temptations for such a thing that it obtained ready
credence. But what mortified Mrs. Phelps and Mrs.
Sparling, neither of whom really had any particular
grievance against Bryn when they went into the

Club that afternoon, was that the two principals
lived in such absolute retirement during their mourning that they heard nothing of it.

Mrs. Prince thought they should know, and
appointed herself the legate to carry the intelligence
to Bryn. She felt no repugnance to taking Bryn
down a peg, but to salve her own feelings, for she
was a good-hearted woman at the bottom, she determined to conclude the interview by asking her and
Philip to meet the Amorys and others at a small
party to dinner, as the Commander was on his way
up from Kobe. Mrs. Amory heartily approved of
the invitation; she knew nothing of her friend's other
purpose in calling on Bryn.

Bryn could not help a feeling of wonder, even of
uneasiness, when Mrs. Prince's name was announced.
She did not call so often that she was likely to have
come without an object. But want of courage was
by no means one of her faults, so she walked into
the drawing-room — with her eyes raised rather
inquiringly perhaps.

'I have come to ask you, my dear, if you and
Mr. Sandys are enough out of mourning to come to
a little dinner party. We should like to show you
that we do not believe the rumour.'

'What rumour?' asked Bryn, with flashing eyes.

'That you and Mr. Sandys—you know.'

'Leave the house,' said Bryn, white and stern,
holding herself like a queen, glancing at the door
with steely eyes.

Mrs. Prince went out without another word
to Bryn, quite uncharacteristically. She was very
philosophical in her acid, lemonish way, only she said

to herself as she left the house, 'She turned me out like a dog. But I'll forgive her for her spirit. What wouldn't I give to have looked like that! But she was a fool, as all the English are.'

So Bryn was, in one way. With a very little tact and the smallest morsel of humble pie she might have had all the Americans behind her. To unite on a cry that vexed the English was the most toothsome chew for men and women alike in the Yankee community, conscious of its inferiority in wealth and numbers.

When she was summoned to receive Mrs. Prince she had been giving Philip tea in her boudoir, the little room made so exquisite and homelike with the trophies of their expeditions among little curio-shops.

He was standing by the mantelpiece, toying with some of the hundred and one *netsukes* and other tiny treasures with which it was strewn—each one simply laid where there was room for it.

As he heard her light step he laid them down and turned to meet her. How often for a year afterwards she remembered that honest, kindly brown face, with its ever-fresh look of welcome.

'What shall we——?' he began, when he noticed Bryn's horror-struck look.

'Oh, Philip,' she cried, stumbling towards him. 'They say that I am your——' She never finished the sentence, but buried a scarlet face against his shoulder.

'Don't listen,' he said. Then he stiffened his huge muscles, and hissed out through his clenched teeth, 'But I'll find out who they are, and shake the life out of some of them.'

But his muscles soon relaxed, for Bryn was sobbing against his heart.

'Never mind, Bryn dear,' he pleaded. 'None who really know you would allow themselves to think of it, let alone believe it.'

'But, Philip, how can we disprove it?'

'It does not need disproving.'

'Oh,' she sobbed, 'we cannot live together this dear, dear life any more.'

'You must marry me,' he said simply. 'It was Mary's last wish.'

'Oh, Phil,' she said, 'but it is impossible. The Church forbids it. Poor Mary's mind was so weak in those days that she forgot this.'

'Say rather,' he said, 'that she saw with the clearness of vision which God's finger gives when it touches us to transfer us to another sphere. At these moments we are apt to distinguish between essentials and accidentals. There is nothing divine about the rubrics.'

'To me all the prayer-book is sacred,' said Bryn gently, but firmly—at the same time disengaging herself. She had had her outburst of misery, and now was about to look things in the face, as her wont was.

'Will you marry me, Bryn?'

She allowed herself to be drawn to him without resistance; and her lips were his. She could give herself to him body and mind. She could love him, honour him, and obey him in every iota if her religion would allow. But her soul was fettered, and could not struggle to him.

'I could not marry you, Philip; almost rather the other thing.'

This told him that her answer was final, but the next day he went to enlist the aid of the Bishop of Kamakura. Human happiness did not appeal to the Bishop. In fact, he thought it was wrong, though he was rather shockingly utilitarian.

When Philip, who knew him well, explained the circumstances which made it so desirable that Bryn should marry him, and that there was absolutely nothing in the way except her rigid adherence to the rubric, the Bishop looked grave. But when Philip went on to entreat the prelate to go beyond granting absolution and persuade Bryn into accepting it, he could get no sympathy.

' I need not ask if the charge is false—I know Miss Avon. The guilt is on the head of those who started such a rumour. But I do not see why you should marry. It is quite customary for sisters-in-law to live with a sister's widower, especially where there is a child to be taken care of. Your wife left a child, I believe?'

'Yes ; a little daughter.'

'All the more reason why your sister-in-law should be in the house.'

'But she refuses to——'

'Absurd,' said the Bishop. 'I never heard of such a thing. Have you any idea what started the rumour?'

'None whatever.'

'You have, I daresay, indulged in—h'm—mild anacreontics, shall we say?'

Philip looked at him stiffly. 'I *have* kissed her ; but I have not been in the habit of doing so.'

'Perfectly natural,' said the Bishop. 'Your sister-in-law is a very beautiful woman, and, besides, it's a recognised thing. I should never censure my clergy for doing so—within bounds of course ; so that the thing was not a scandal. You have not been caught in compr——' He suddenly remembered Bryn, and his tongue clove to the roof of his mouth. 'But to be serious, my dear Sandys, I will certainly see your sister-in-law and do my poor best to persuade her to do the right thing—to do nothing—to go on living with you. It would be very wrong of you to marry —in fact you could not marry—it would not be a marriage—but I cannot see the faintest objection to your living in the same house, as you have done.'

'But Bryn is so young and beautiful, sir, that perhaps for her good name——'

'Tut,' said the Bishop. 'No, I don't mean that. You're not the first man who has had a beautiful young sister-in-law to take care of his children. If you have sufficient control over yourself to behave like a gentleman to her, why, that's all about it ; there's nothing so very much in a kiss between such near relations.'

'Then you do look upon us as relations ?'

'Certainly ; I was saying that there is nothing so very much in a kiss between such near relations, provided that'——Philip raised his eyes—'that there is nothing in the kiss. But if, as might be natural under the circumstances—being both so young—you doubt yourself, there is nothing to do but——'

'But—— ?'

'But engage Mrs. Plumtree.'

Mrs. Plumtree was a lady of uncertain age, whose zeal for good works rather embarrassed the Church of England in Japan. She was also short-sighted. Did this occur to his Lordship?

'Well then, we shall expect you to-morrow, sir,' said Philip, as he went away with his mind tolerably relieved.

'Yes.'

'To lunch?'

'Well, I think it had better be.'

CHAPTER XVIII

PHILIP naturally did not allude to the Bishop's object in coming to lunch when he announced it to Bryn, nor did he think it wise to make any reference to the event of yesterday in the interval, and she was so smiling and composed during the meal that he augured well.

But the Bishop found her adamant. As he went out, he drew Philip into the library. 'My poor fellow, you must prepare yourself for a shock. She has made up her mind to leave you and go to live with her cousins in England, if they will have her. He is a clergyman, I believe ; she can hear if they will have her in three months. In the interval, I offered to ask Mrs. Plumtree to stay with you. But she did not meet the proposal as I expected— she——'

The good Bishop's prattle was stopped by Philip's groaning ' Oh, my God ! ' as he covered his face with his hands.

'It's a very sad case,' said the Bishop to himself.
It doesn't do to be peculiar.'

.   .   .   .

'The Bishop tells me that you are going to
England,' said Phil to Bryn, when he joined her.

'Yes,' she answered almost fiercely, 'and he
insulted me by suggesting that we should have old
Mother Plumtree here till I go. I told him that
there had never been anything objectionable between
us, and never could be — that I wasn't going to
England because I feared people's tongues, but
because I could not prevent myself from marrying
you if I stayed here.'

'But, Bryn, why can't we stay as we are? It
would break my heart to lose you.'

'And mine too, Phil, as near as hearts can be
broken.'

'Then why are you going?'

'Because, like our first weak parents, I have eaten
of the fruit of the tree of the knowledge of good and
evil. It would never have occurred to me till those
lewd - minded women forced it on my attention,
that we could not have gone on living for ever
exactly as we were. But now that it has been
uttered, it is different.'

'Why not start a little house of your own out here,
with some old lady as a companion? You'll have
money enough for that of your own in a year or two,
and in the interval you can use some of the principal
which the curios have fetched.'

'Philip, if I stayed out here, I should be for ever
thinking of you, and leading a life without an object,
because I could not have you. If I go to England,

especially in the house of a clergyman, I hope to
find some work in life which has been, as it were,
laid down for me. I shall never marry, dear, dear
Phil. I couldn't marry any one but you.'

.   .   .   .   .   .

As the Bishop was returning to the station he
met Mrs. Sparling, whose respect for a bishop
amounted to adoration.

'You have heard of the rumour about Miss
Avon?' he said.

Mrs. Sparling's heart gave a little leap of satisfaction, but it was as suddenly checked.

'In my humble opinion,' he continued, 'those who
are responsible for it have come very near breaking
the Seventh Commandment as well as the Ninth.'

CHAPTER XIX

THE last month before the few days which had to
be spent in Yokohama in preparation for the voyage
they decided to spend at Kyoto—the ancient capital
of Japan. Phil had never seen it; and Bryn wished
to drink in Japaneseness from Japan's most typical
city, that she might remember as much as possible
of her country during her life-long exile. They
stayed, of course, at Yaami's, on the brow of Maru-
yama, the only haunt of Europeans in Kyoto in those
days. To have stayed anywhere else would have
been to confirm the lying rumours which had been
spread about them.

It was rather disheartening work, for all that month, with rare intervals, the rain streamed down to match their fortunes. Not that it kept them at home. For twenty *sen* Bryn bought a huge oiled-paper rain-umbrella, the last she ever expected to use, and Phil turned up the collar of his waterproof. Their enjoyment was a little spoiled by the inopportune arrival of the Mikado a few days after themselves, which prevented them seeing the imperial palace or gardens, though fortunately they had on their very first day gone over the Castle of Nijo, built by his feudatory *daimios* for Iyeyasu's reception, whenever he rode down the Tokaido with a feudal retinue that amounted to an army, to pay a visit of state to his puppet sovereign. Exquisite were the paintings on the *shoji* — the paper screens which broke up into rooms the castle of the great Tokugawa.

Kyoto is the paradise of the sightseer. They soon found it to be a city of temples, and shows and curio-shops and native art factories, such as they had never seen before. It was only since she had known Phil that Bryn took an interest in such matters. In her former visits to Kyoto she had been satisfied with the *miyako-dori*, or cherry dance, shooting the rapids of the Katsura-Gawa, and driving out to Lake Biwa or over to Nara. It was new to her to spend day after day of eager sight-seeing in the potteries, where they were making the delicate, cream-coloured Kyoto *faience*, or among the silk weavers, or in taking her *riksha* up one quaint back street after another in search of Japanese picture-books, and battered *bric-à-brac*, which received its exquisite form or colour a

century possibly before the taint of the foreign
market corrupted Japan.

Their hotel accommodation was a dream to Bryn
for many a month afterwards. Their suite lay at
one end of the hotel, commanding, with its verandahs,
three different aspects—the dark grove on the mountain behind ; the garden of the hotel and the Japanese
tea-house beyond, on the side ; and in front, the
great city of three or four hundred thousand inhabitants, resting in a plain girdled by mountains.
The side view was entrancing. No hotel in Japan
has such a garden as Yaami's—in its prime when
they were there. It is a garden of many elevations,
united by winding stairways of mossy stone, em-
bosomed in clusters of scarlet and yellow azalea—a
blaze of blossom, through which velvety black butterflies as large as humming-birds sailed in the lazy
consciousness that no Japanese would wantonly disturb them. When the tropical rains lashed down,
the bushes in full bloom were protected by huge
umbrellas—a coolie being on duty day and night to
ship or unship these *parapluies.* In the middle of
the smooth lawn at the top was a tiny scarlet shrine
to Inari, the rice goddess—guarded by her faithful
stone foxes. Inari is supposed to live at Kyoto,
where a whole mountain is abandoned to her foxes.
The successive tiers of garden below, with their irises,
azaleas, and camellias, were dotted with tiny pools
full of six-tailed gold-fish, the pools being connected
by a miniature river six inches deep, which in one
place fell over a waterfall quite six feet high. And
the wonders did not end here, for through the hotel,
under the low, heavy-browed gateway which had

once adorned a temple, was the little stone garden in which the finest of the irises and azaleas grew in sunken beds in a little white, white court with an exquisite green bronze fountain in the centre, and tall green bronze storks, marching or stooping in every attitude of nature on the flagged pathways. The Japanese tea-house beyond was full of life, night and day. The tinkle of the *guecha's samisen* was hardly ever silent, and there was a waving of gay draperies by day, and of lamps by night.

The view, in front, of the low, one-storied city of unpainted wood would have been monotonous but for the huge masses of the two Hongwanji temples, looming up black against the sky—ancient Nishi Hongwanji saved from fire by its miraculous *gingko* tree, and huge Higashi Hongwanji rising from its ashes by the efforts of the faithful, typified in its huge cables of human hair.

'We must go to the *miyako-dori*, Phil.'

'The cherry-dance business. What is it?'

'A sort of a ballet and panorama combined—a Japanese ballet.'

'I think I've finished with Japanese ballets, Bryn.'

'You must go to this one. All the best dancers in Japan are gathered together for it. And it's such a typically Japanese thing.'

'Very well, Bryn San. Order the *rikshas* for to-night, will you? I'm not putting the ordering off on to you for laziness, dear, but with these boys, who only know a word or two of English, you get so much forwarder than I do. You can get out of them exactly the right time to go, and so on.'

Bryn came back saying that they must start directly after dinner.

Luckily it was dark as they rattled past the interminable Gion Temple—half peepshows—and turned sharp to the left and then to the right, for otherwise they would have missed the effects of the cressets, whose tall flames shot high above the low roofs of the native street. They dashed up through a perfect avenue of *jinrikshas*, and sat down a moment on the steps of the theatre for their own *jinriksha*-boys to slip over their feet the white linen bags which enabled them to dispense with the tiresome and undignified process of disbooting—one good result at any rate of having somebody who could give orders in Japanese.

Phil found the theatre more than most Japanese theatres the adjunct of a tea-house, and the prettiest Japanese theatre he had ever been in. For they passed through a carpeted corridor to a large room, open on one side to the stage, full of little tables and chairs for the use of Europeans refreshing themselves. They had paid a shilling or two each at the door, and this included not only the spectacle, but tea and sweetmeats and other Japanese delicacies, offered by delicious little *mousmees* in most brilliant and tasteful costumes, who flittered about like so many gentle little butterflies.

Bryn, who was Jap enough to partake of their victuals with impunity, and as a matter of habit (and probably not forgetful of how soon 'things Japanese' would be things of the past for her), partook freely and chattered Japanese to the *mousmees*, who were immensely delighted ; while Phil took stock of the arrangements of the theatre, which was built round a hollow square, packed with poor Japanese families who had brought half their culinary apparatus with them. The wealthier ones went into the tea-house with the Europeans.

The tea-house in which they were seated formed one side of the square ; the front stage was opposite them, and the two flank stages formed the other two sides.

These flank stages were occupied by the orchestra —a drum and string band dressed in the full dress of the olden times, with huge, stiff shoulder flaps like elephant's ears. Their dresses were of scarlet.

Amid a vast tum-tumming from the drums, which were held on their left shoulders, and an inordinate squeaking from *koto, biwa*, and *samisen*, the Cherry Dance began. The costumes justified the name, for as the maple-leaf predominates in every portion of the costume at the Koyo-Kwan in Tokyo, so the cherry blossom pervades everything in the *miyako-dori* at Kyoto.

The ballet was like any other Japanese ballet, largely made up of posturing and fan-play—pretty enough. On this particular occasion the effect was doubtless as much enhanced to the Japanese as it was spoiled to foreigners by having panorama'd for its background scenes from suburban life in England, of which Battersea Park and the Crystal Palace were the most notable.

Philip wondered where he was going to escape seeing the cloven foot of despair. Here, at any rate, he had hoped to be in the midst of surroundings so purely Japanese that he might forget Bryn's departure, when, lo and behold, he was confronted by the most sordid reminder of the British middle-class life, in which beautiful Bryn, his eastern flower, was so soon to be lost.

'Come away, Bryn; it makes me sick. These graceful little Japanese, the finest dancers in their country, in their exquisite cherry-blossom costumes, with Battersea and the Crystal Palace for a background, remind me too bitterly of that other thing.'

Then a few days' golden weather made their hearts lighter, as they did the temples—no light task in that city of magnificent distances and unnumbered shrines. So many of the principal temples, moreover, are in parks on the outskirts—miles from each other.

Bryn enjoyed doing the Kyoto temples with Phil much more than she had enjoyed the Golden Shrines of Nikko. For one thing, she was so soon to turn her back on the heathen temples, with their picturesque ceremonials, which had been her environment all her life—for another, the Kyoto temples are much less stereotyped.

Only less than Ise is Kyoto the sacred city of Japan. The two great Hongwanji sects have their chief temples there; so has Inari, the Rice Goddess, the most popular of Japanese deities. Half the most important temples in Japan, both Shinto and Buddhist, are at Kyoto.

How they revelled in these temples! The shady groves of the Tionin Temple, whose mighty eighty-ton bell, eighteen feet high, shook them in their rooms at the hotel two or three hundred yards away, when it tolled a sort of curfew every night, were almost as retired for lovers' rambles as their own garden on the Bluff.

Whenever they wanted to see anything typically Japanese, they sauntered down to the Gion Temple, almost touching the hotel grounds on the other side, to watch the crowd having a sort of merry-go-round on real horses, indulging in the ancient pastime of horse archery, or ordinary archery at thirty shots a *sen*—in its depreciated condition worth somewhere between a farthing and a halfpenny ; or teasing the savage red-buttocked monkeys, caught on the mountains between Kyoto and Kobe; or playing a kind of Aunt Sally by firing big balls at the Seven Gods of Wealth, who beat even the Rice Goddess in popularity, but are content with humble shrines in the house instead of a regular temple.

One of the chief charms of the Kyoto temples lies in the great, famous, and ancient monasteries attached to them ; for instance, at Nishi Hongwanji, the vast temple which is a city in itself, with all the fair-booths which have grown up in its interminable precincts, or the temples of the Gold and Silver Pavilions. All three of these contain the masterpieces of the great Japanese painters on *kakemonos,* or on the paper *shoji* which divide their interiors. They had an ideal day for Kinkakuji, the temple of the Golden Pavilion, which nestles in an exquisite bamboo grove at the foot of a mountain. The rain had gone off to the hills, leaving a clear blue sky and the soft balmy air of the Japanese May ; and the recent heavy wet showed all the foliage at its best. The Kinkaku, or Golden Pavilion, a sort of wooden pagoda, with the gilded *shoji,* from which it derives its name, so

perished since the disestablishment of Buddhism that
the priest no longer demands unshod feet for admis-
sion, was poor enough, apart from its quaint shape
and the tip-tilted eaves of its roof. But the old
Chinese garden over which it towered retained its
unrivalled beauty, the climax being the lake with its
stone tortoise islands, its innumerable little stone
pagodas, lighthouses, *torii*, votive lanterns and shrines,
its immemorial fir-tree cunningly trained to the pre-
sentment of a junk in full sail.

'In the groves there is a dear little *cha-no-ma*,'
said Bryn, 'which the priests use for the solemn
tea-ceremony. It was built by Yoshimitsu, whose
priests invented the solemn tea-ceremony. I believe
it *was* he who introduced tea into Japan. I'll
ask the priests.' Gliding across the smooth lawn,
she went into the monastery.

'No,' she said, when she came out; 'it wasn't
Yoshimitsu who invented the tea-ceremony, but
Yoshimasa. It is Ginkakuji, the temple of the Silver
Pavilion, once the country palace of Yoshimasa,
which has the oldest tea-room in Japan, where he
and his friend Yoami and the monk Shuko started
the tea-drinking mania. We can't go there this
afternoon, because it's right the other side of the city.
But this was the country palace of Yoshimitsu, and
the priests invite you to come and have tea with
them and look at their famous *kakemonos*.'

'I don't think we will, Bryn. Things take so
long in Japan.'

'It's rather fun. They have a little square hole
sunk in the matting floor—lined with stone, I think
—and the kettle is hung by an iron chain from the

ceiling. That's the way Yoshimitsu made his tea.
I think everything is Yoshimitsu here, as everything
is Yoshimasa at Ginkakuji.'

'We'll have tea if you want it, Bryn; but I'd just
like to sit with you on the steps of the little *cha-no-
ma* and look over the sunny lake, and this wonderful
bric-à-brac garden, which looks like a bit out of the
Arabian Nights.'

'Oh, I don't want any tea. See what the priests
gave me,' she said. She had come back carrying
her hat upside down; but he had not noticed that it
was full of the tiny pipless oranges hardly bigger
than cherries. 'A woman gets awfully spoilt by the
Japs,' she said, 'if she can speak Japanese, and
doesn't look like the devil.'

'What do you call looking like the devil?'

'Looking like a missionary's womenkind. They're
almost as bad as Christian Japs.'

'Why, is there any difference in Japanese girls
after they become Christians?'

'Certainly. They wear pigtails for one thing, and
boots for another, along with their native dress.'

They sat on and on outside the little *cha-no-ma*
(the Japanese always choose the finest views for their
tea-ceremony chambers) until they had watched the
sun down the sky over the placid lake with its dainty
stone *bric-à-brac*, while outside their *riksha*-boys
chatted and smoked innumerable *kiserus*, reflecting
probably on the folly of Europeans who wasted a
whole five *sen* (twopence) an hour on retaining them
while they mooned about the gardens of a temple
that had fallen from its high estate.

They did not talk much. In such a scene, on

such an afternoon, sitting by each other, it was sufficient joy to live.

'Bryn, do you remember that poor old woman who was found ripped up in the temple of Iyeyasu while we were at Nikko, with a paper in her hand, which said, " At this happiest moment of my life I take leave of it "?'

'Yes.'

'I feel sorely tempted to commit *hara-kiri* myself. I don't see how I can ever be so happy again as I am now. For you will soon be gone, and afternoons like this come only once in a spring.'

'How can you be so wicked, Philip! A man has no right to raise his hand against himself.'

'Oh! I shan't do it. I'm not the sort which ever despairs, though I look forward to dead months of misery. Besides, I am not my own. I have a child to provide for, and I owe it to my father and sisters not to leave Japan, alive or dead, till I have made the money my father advanced me to take up your father's business secure. I shall just pray, until your heart is turned.'

'It is wrong to pray for what is wrong. Besides, do you think that such prayers are ever granted?'

'He is Lord of the Sabbath also!'

'Oh, Phil, it is wrong to think that a thing can be made right only because you so earnestly wish it.'

'Ears of corn for the hungry, Bryn.'

'Oh, but that was a physical necessity.'

'For the Son of God.'

'It was for the physical necessity of the men who were with Him.'

'Is not the moral necessity greater than the physical?'

'But you have not proved the moral necessity.'

'That is what I shall pray you may see.'

'I don't wonder at the poor Japs committing suicide,' said Bryn, to change the subject, 'with only *hibachis* (charcoal braziers) for fires; they are never warmed beyond the tips of their fingers. They live on the waste of the world, such as seaweed. They often have to keep body and soul together on a few *sen* a day——'

'And on the other hand, the religion in which they all choose to die,' said Phil, 'promises them a happy release from everything, the winters and starvation of this world, on the one hand, and the fires of the Christian hell on the other.

'I really don't know why any of the poor Japanese go on living. They don't fear death; and they don't have hope. What life can there be for a population of forty million people, nearly all of them crowded between the mountains and the sea of the island we are on? And yet they go on living bravely, unless honour demands their death. It's much braver for a poor Jap to live than it is to die. Their poverty is certainly appalling. The compradore says that an English sovereign would often buy a house, the ground it stands on, and everything in it.

'Don't you see the moral of all this, Phil?'

'What is it?' he asked, knowing too well.

'That if they can live and toil dumbly on with no hope, how much more you, with every hope but one.'

'Bryn, I told you that I had never contemplated

such a thing as suicide ; I only meant that it seemed almost attractive.'

'I don't mean suicide. Of course you wouldn't do anything so absurd. I mean that you ought to be able—not to forget me—but to give up all ideas of our living together again, and do your duty in the very prosperous state of life into which it has pleased God to call you. I'm not worth it all.'

'Oh, Bryn, don't torture me. I shall live for nothing but the hope of being with you again.'

'Perhaps you will see me again some day, in a few years' time ; when you have established our affairs satisfactorily out here you may have to come to England on business. By that time I ought to be a deaconess or matron in a reformatory, or something, and you will see me once in a way.'

'Don't say that. I would almost rather see you married to some one else than doing menial work. I couldn't bear to think of you drudging for your living.'

'I could never marry any one but you, Phil,' said the girl, leaning towards him to hold up her lips to be kissed. 'And that is impossible ; and I shall have to work for my living.'

'I don't think so,' he said ; 'you will have enough to live on.'

'Besides, I must have something to fill in my time and thoughts. I am really as miserable as you, Phil.'

'Then why do you trample on both our hearts ? '

'Because it's right, Phil.'

'We Christians will not let the poor heathen derive hope of salvation from letting the car of

Juggernaut roll over their bodies, but we have our own juggernauts, and the crushing sometimes lasts a lifetime.'

Bryn gave a little shiver. 'The sun is going down,' she said ; 'we must be getting home. Besides, look at that hornet.'

Phil sighed. 'As it was in the beginning,' he said to himself, 'just when life seems all afternoon, with the stir and stress of the morning over—all a garden full of stately trees to be under—smooth turf to be on—sweet flowers to your eye and nostril—all a sunny lake full of quaint islands—down goes the sun, and with a little shiver everything passes away. Later on the friendly night brings oblivion.'

CHAPTER XX

'WE must go to Nara, Phil,' said Bryn, in their last days at Kyoto ; 'I want to take a distinct image of Nara to England with me. I have always thought it one of the most beautiful places in Japan ; besides, the way there is so beautiful.'

Provisions were accordingly packed, and they decided to start off to Nara next day. Their journey was a gloomy one, however, for it rained the whole way there, and as they were passing through Fushimi, the first town of any consequence between Kyoto and Nara, an accident happened which gave their nerves a heavy shock. Halting for lunch just outside the town, Phil discovered that they had not brought any beer with them. He accordingly was on the look-out for a shop where they sold beer all the way through the streets of Fushimi, though he had not mentioned the circumstance to Bryn. At last he saw some in a window he had just passed, and called out very suddenly to his *riksha*-boy. The latter stopped dead, and Bryn's *riksha*-boy, who was following with his nose almost touching the *riksha* in front of him (a position dear to the soul of the *riksha*-boy), had to pull up so short that he shot Bryn over the back of the *riksha* right out into the middle of the road. Her forehead struck something hard, not in the direct fall, but as she rolled over, and a terrifying bump was the result—terrifying to Philip. Bryn could not see it, of course, and did not complain much of the pain.

This threw a shadow over the journey, apart from the fact that it was so wet that they had to have the hoods and aprons of the *rikshas* up, a stuffy and disagreeable proceeding always. But, whether for reassuring Philip or what not, Bryn showed great animation during the last part of the journey. It was night, and raining hard, before they pulled up at the slender bamboo paling of the lonely little tea-house in a grove on the outskirts of Nara. But the little *mousmees* ran out on their clogs to welcome them ; and in a minute, by the dim light of an oiled paper lantern, they were picking their way across the broad, flat stepping-stones, which served an obvious purpose in the mud of the little garden.

They were installed in a room which seemed to swallow up nearly the whole of the tiny native inn. At the north end there was the narrow recess usual in guest chambers, divided into the *toko-noma* for the Mikado's bed, and the *chigai-dana*, with its rack for the guests' swords, and its queer little cupboard and zigzag shelves. Over the *toko-noma* hung a rather handsome *kakemono*, and at its foot was a bamboo jar containing a spray of fruit-tree blossom—quite a large cutting, with only a few blossoms, and those half-way up it. The room was lit only by paper *shoji*, but it was too dark for this to signify.

'You must take off your boots, Phil,' said Bryn, starting to unlace her own slim feet, a task in which one of the *mousmees* insisted on relieving her. 'This is a real native inn—look at the beautiful yellow matting;' and, seeing that he did not seem to relish it, she added, 'It's all for the best, Phil, it will reconcile you to there being no tables or chairs. You'll want to sit on your feet in a few minutes to keep them warm.'

No. 17 came in and said something to her in Japanese.

'It's lucky we have brought some grub of our own, Philip. They have nothing here but rice, and eggs, and chickens, which are not killed yet—no milk, no bread, no beer. We shall have to go back to Kyoto to-morrow night. We haven't got more than one day's supply with us.'

'I'd like to wash before I sit down to eat.'

'Well, so would I, of course.'

This caused quite a harangue in Japanese with the *mousmee*, and then Bryn said—

'I thought so; we shall have to take turns and wash in the verandah at the back. The room we are in is to be our bedrooms presently. They will divide it up with *shoji*, where you see the long grooves; if there were more of us they would make it into more rooms by putting up more *shoji* in the cross grooves.

In the verandah there was only a queer little brass basin and a flimsy cotton towel, such as the natives use; but there was a tiny bit of soap, left behind by some English traveller, cherished in a little cheap bronze soap-box, with a hole in the bottom and a white metal crescent moon let into the top. Soap-boxes are commoner than soap in Japan; just as children often have purses before they have any money to put in them.

Under the circumstances ablution did not take them long; but by the time that Philip had finished, he found that queer little tables about a foot high had been brought in, and No. 17, as clean as a new pin in spite of his thirty-mile run, was arranging the food they had brought with them in what he imagined to be European style, to the great admiration of the *mousmees*. With the good breeding characteristic of the lower-class Japanese, he had brought a change of clothes with him on purpose to wait on them, and had bathed as soon as ever he arrived.

After supper mine hostess came in herself to put up the *ama-do*, or wooden outer shutters, which fitted into grooves about a yard outside the *shoji* to keep out nightly intruders. Each succeeding one fitted into, and was the only fastening for, its predecessor, and the last one of all was secured by a flimsy wooden bolt.

'Why, a drunken man couldn't lean against it

without bringing the whole thing down,' said Philip.

'That's nothing to the *shoji*; our bedrooms will only be divided by a sheet of paper.'

The hostess caught the word *shoji*.

'How soon shall I put them up and bring the *futon*?' she asked in Japanese.

'I will clap my hands,' said Bryn. (In a paper house this is quite sufficient by way of a bell.)

'She wants to know when she shall put up our bedrooms, Phil.'

'I don't think it will be very long. Sitting on these flat cushions, with my feet cramped under me, tires me more than if I had walked the whole way from Kyoto. Are you any the worse for your fall, Bryn?'

'Not a bit.'

'I wish you hadn't fallen.'

'Why?'

'It's so unlucky.'

'At your superstitions again.'

'Your being thrown out, especially when it was caused by my pulling up so suddenly, seems a sort of omen that you are to be thrown right out of my life for good and all, just when I was beginning to hope against hope that——'

'Please don't, Phil. It's hard enough for me without that. I'm glad I'm not superstitious. I should not attach that meaning to it if I was, perhaps, but it is rather a nerve-shaking thing to happen on the eve of such a momentous journey.'

Fate never makes favourites of those who are not superstitious.

'Shall we clap hands now, Bryn?' said Philip.

Both his feet were asleep.

Bryn clapped, and the hostess and all her *mousmees* came in. To put up the shutters was only an affair of a minute or two, and then they began bringing in the great *futon* or quilts, some of which were for lying on, and one each for bed-clothes. Bryn knew from experience what sleeping on the floors of Japanese inns meant, and she had told them to bring in every *futon* they could spare and pile them up. Nor did she feel inclined for a Japanese pillow. These were replaced with rolled-up *futon*. Before the *mousmees* retired she bade good-night to Phil, and told them to fix the last *shoji* between them.

They were a good deal puzzled; they could have seen at a glance that Phil and Bryn were not brother and sister, even if they had not been previously acquainted with the Avon family. And even they knew that it is not usual for a young English gentleman and a young English lady to travel about *tête-à-tête* when they are neither brother and sister, nor husband and wife. They would probably have gone off into peals of their delightful childish laughter at the idea of a make-believe brother and sister, except for an improper purpose. So the only thing they could do was to fall back on the reflection that the English were very mad.

The hostess's face was a study when Bryn asked for the *shoji* and separate *futon*.

'Are you not his wife?' she said in Japanese.

'No, his sister.'

'I did not know you had a brother, Bryn San.'

Bryn explained that he was her brother-in-law,

and that Mary San was dead, and Avon San himself. However, she could not help the presentiment that the hostess thought it very wrong that Philip should not be treated like a husband. She had hardly felt more shame when Mrs. Prince first broke the news to her.

'Good-night, dear Bryn,' called Philip, almost directly. He thought it more delicate to sleep in his clothes, as if they had been in a sleeping-car crossing the Rockies, as he and Mary had crossed them not two years ago.

'Good-night, Phil.'

She soon fell asleep, while Philip luxuriated in lying awake. Before he turned in he had stealthily drawn his *futon*—soft, silky, noiseless things—as near as possible to the *shoji*, that he might hear Bryn's soft breathings in her sleep. And there he lay, half in gentle sadness at the might-have-beens, half in gentle rapture at spending one night so near the well-beloved. Not a thought came into his mind which he would have blushed to tell Bryn in the morning. He had never given her one caress that was not pure and worshipping, and even those caresses he would gladly have given up to have had her loveliness and fine rare spirit for ever in his company, as they had been during this never-to-be-forgotten year. Not a thought did he give that night, as he lay awake, thinking of her and nothing but her, that was not purely romantic. He loved her so much that he could not think of her sensually. As the hours rolled on he could hear her breathing grow less regular ; followed by tossings in the bed ; followed by low sobs. Bryn too was lying awake, more thoroughly frightened and miserable than ever she had been in her life. Her mind harked back to their conversation about superstitions, and she wove fresh fancies round it, till her nerves were so over-strung that she longed to creep in beside Philip.

Here was she in an agony of nervousness, with the only man she had ever loved in the world lying within a few feet of her, with nothing but a sheet of paper between them, and shuttered off from the rest of the world till the morning by the *ama-do* bolted round the room. She yearned to lie in his arms— without one ill desire — simply for the mesmeric effect on her nerves of contact with the strong man —the only man on whom she had relied.

She, too, slipped out of bed, and stealthily drew the *futon* as close to the *shoji* as they would go. And she—Bryn Avon—acknowledged to herself that if Philip Sandys should belie all she had ever thought of him and pull down that flimsy paper barrier, she could refuse him nothing. In her present state of nervousness her moral power of resistance was at vanishing point. At that moment she would have done anything to feel the magnetism of his touch.

At last she could stand it no longer.

'Phil,' she called, in a sweet, low voice.

She said only 'Phil.' She could not be sure that she did not mean it for an invitation—not a lover's invitation, though if he had taken it as a lover, her nerves were too unstrung for her to have gainsaid him.

If he had torn down the piece of paper that divided them, when she called the rest of this history

would never have been written. They might have
lived happily and unhappily together, but cut off
from the rest of the community, till death called one
of them to the Happy Valley. But though it would
have been all the same to Philip if no paper shutter
had been there, that sheet of paper represented to
him all the law and the prophets. So he did not
stir, as he answered softly—

'Yes, Bryn.'

His voice in his wonted respectful tones recalled
her to herself, and her power of resistance returned ;
but she was still in a state of nervousness which she
had never known before.

'Talk to me, Phil, will you? The loneliness of
this place frightens me.'

Honest, chivalrous Phil! He felt it would be
unkind to talk to her of the wish nearest his heart,
just at the moment when she would have listened to
him. And the opportunity passed.

As soon as the morning light began to send long
shafts through the joints of the *ama-do*, one after the
other, in a shamefaced manner, they stole out of bed
and moved the *futon* back to their original position,
and when mine hostess stepped in to undo the
ama-do and peeped through a pinhole in the *shoji* of
Bryn's room, half expecting a surprise, there was
Bryn's tired golden head slumbering peacefully,
while the regular breathing of sleep could be heard
from Philip's chamber also.

CHAPTER XXI

EXCEPT during the agonised nervousness of the pre-
ceding night, Bryn had seldom been so much in
love with Philip as she was that morning. She felt
so grateful to him.

And the sun shone out in sympathy. Nothing
could be lovelier than May in Japan, when the rain
keeps off.

No sooner was breakfast over than they rambled
off to the most beautiful of all the Shinto temples of
Japan, the *Kasuga-no-miya*. But they did not linger
in the long scarlet colonnades of the temple itself,
nor gazing at the dancing for which it is famous.
On a day like this, when she needed a nerve tonic,
it was so much more soothing to Bryn to wander
down the long avenue of lanterns, and stand in the
shady walk by the bronze deer, commemorative of
the milk-white deer on which the god came to
Nara, watching the clear spring water gush from its
mouth, or feeding the roe deer which throng to
visitors for tit-bits ;—to roam through the acres of
glorious scarlet azaleas for which the world has no
match. Beautiful as the temple is in itself, it is its
park which is its crowning glory.

'When you are in England, Bryn,' said Philip,
'remember that I told you that the only park
approaching this for ancient culture running wild
again is Richmond Park. There you will see just
such a mound with just such a sweeping view as

that on which we are standing. A king stood on that mound once to see the signal which should tell him that his beautiful young queen, so lately idolised, was beheaded.'

'Poor Anne Boleyn!' said Bryn. It was one for Anne Boleyn and two for herself perhaps. At this moment the idea flashed into her head that Henry VIII. was responsible for the difficulties in the way of deceased brothers' wives and deceased wives' sisters, and she did not feel altogether amiable towards him. A still more awful corollary flashed across her; what if the Church of England's adoption of this part of the Romish Church laws rested entirely upon the Divorce Court episodes of King Henry VIII.? Certainly Philip had everything in his favour. If he had only known that, he might have renewed his solicitations! But he respected Bryn's oft-expressed desires, and the opportunity passed.

'Come along, Philip,' cried Bryn, who was beginning to grow afraid of her thoughts; 'let's go and see the Daibutsu, if you have never seen it, and then we can be working our way homewards. Remember that we've no provisions for staying a second night,' she added, suddenly recalling the circumstance with devout thankfulness. She did not feel nervous now, but she could not have faced a second night in that lonely tea-house.

The temple in which the great Buddha, fully sixty feet high (the greatest of all the world's idols, except the brick and plaster Buddha of Bangkok), was lodged, looked dilapidated enough to have been the oldest in Japan.

'What an old, old temple, Phil.'

'It isn't really — not more than two hundred years, I believe. But I suspect that it may not have been put up with the care and patience the Japanese generally bestow on their temples. What is it you said that *Nure-botoke* meant?'

'The Wet God.'

'Yes, that's a neat way of putting it, that the god was exposed to the elements for some time— one hundred and thirty years, I believe — the Japanese are so very chummy with Heaven. Finally they got anxious and rattled a temple up round the image, without reflecting that a few years more without a roof over his head could not make much difference to an image which had proved so hardy.'

They went into the temple.

'This is not the same Buddha as the Buddha of Kamakura,' said Philip. 'He may be six feet or sixty feet higher, but he is not god-like with his coarse, black head—or is it that I am changed since the old days at Kamakura?'

'No, Phil, you have not changed,' said Bryn softly. 'If you returned to Kamakura you would draw the same comfort from the peace and mercy in the face of the great Daibutsu there.'

'Has his message never come to you, Bryn?'

Bryn was silent.

And Philip was silent too.

Outside the temple of the great Buddha stood their *riksha*-boys—the bronze statues of listlessness that *riksha*-boys always are till they see an employer or possible employer—smiling, blinking at the sun, tapping their little *kiseru* against the wheels of their *jinrikshas.*

'No. 17,' called Philip, and all four boys, the two *jinriksha-men* and their outrunners, sprang to attention. 'We start now. Go see Ko-buku-ji first.'

'Number one temple,' said 17, 'very old.'

Presently, as they drew near, he pointed out south of the temple, under the hill on which it stood, a small lake.

'Lovers' Pond,' said 17, who was very proud of his English. '*Sarusawa-no-ike*—lady very beautiful. Five—ten—thirty, so many say I marry her. Lady say no marry only Mikado. Mikado no love her—drown.'

Bryn sighed; the cap so nearly fitted; and on bowled the *rikshas* to Uji, where the world's most famous vintage of tea is grown. Tea-picking was in full swing. Between what looked like close rows of low privet hedges were scores and scores of neat little, sun-blacked peasant women, some of them ever so pretty, each of them with a pale blue coolie's head-towel arranged almost in the form of a sun-bonnet, and most of them with a dash of scarlet about them. They hardly appeared to be doing anything, but they were really transferring choice tea-leaves with astonishing rapidity from the plants to peculiar baskets. Here and there a tree was left, and on the windy side of the plantation there was always a tall screen of matting. On the uplands especially choice gardens were roofed over with a coarse matting. And everywhere there were long, narrow matting-sheds used in connection with the preparation of the tea.

'Did you know, Phil, that some kinds of Uji tea fetch as much as five or ten dollars a pound?'

'Yes; but except as a merchant to sell them again to somebody else I should be sorry to give five or ten cents a pound. I have never been able to cultivate a respect for Japanese tea.'

'Phil, that's not worthy of you; you take such an intelligent interest in most of the things which belong to our country. I can't help sometimes looking upon myself as a Jap, as poor Mary used to do.'

What Philip might have replied was interrupted by No. 17, who suddenly turned round in the shafts and said, 'You see number one temple—Biodoin—old as the sea.'

Old as the sea sounded so original that they agreed, and their *rikshas* deflected from the main road a little along the river, past the bridge of Uji.

'That's our Thermopylæ,' exclaimed Bryn, 'where Yoshimasa fought his last fight. With only 300 men he held the bridge against 20,000, while his prince effected his flight. When this was done he retired to the temple where we are going to, and while his last few followers kept the enemy at bay committed *hara-kiri*. But the Japs as usual have spoilt the story by painting the lily—Yoshimasa at the time was a young man of seventy-five!'

'But the river is superb,' said Phil, 'with its swirling blue-green waters. Why, the Limmat at Zurich is not finer than this.'

And his rapture increased at every minute. It is difficult to conceive anything much more impressive than Biodoin, the Phœnix Temple. Built of wood before our Norman Conquest, it is to-day more perfect than the majority of Oxford colleges untouched by the hand of the restorer. And for quaint beauty of design and situation the whole East has not its superior.

'Is this the Phœnix Temple?' asked Bryn, as it rose up from the marshes before them on the banks of a placid mere.

He nodded.

'I don't see where the phœnix comes in?'

'It's conventionalised.'

'Away——?'

'Well, typified or indicated. The two-storied central part is the head and body; the colonnades right and left, with raised roofs at the ends, are the outspread wings; and there is a long corridor behind for the tail.'

'Rather far-fetched.'

'Well, it is rather far-timed. You must remember that, though it is built of wood, it has been standing ever since 1052, before the very foundations of Westminster Abbey were laid. And think how its inimitable grace—the centre tower I suppose I ought to call it, and the two side towers connected by the roofs of these colonnades, all melted into the curves of ancient woodwork, would suffer by being worked up into a caricature of a phœnix!'

'O! I see the phœnix—two of them.' She pointed to two quaint bronze effigies of the fabled bird, about three feet high, which did duty for weathercocks.

'Thoroughly Jappy,' he said. 'A thousand years cannot radically change the Oriental mind. The good Jap built a phœnix temple, typifying, with

due regard to his architectural etiquette, the bird.
But lest the name should be " misunderstanded of the
people "——'

' That's me.'

' Yes—you come in on this count—he added, in
a small detail, representations of the bird so exquisite
that the whole temple might worthily be called after
them.'

' Oh, I understand well enough, Phil. I was
only talking to amuse myself. Let's sit down in
this little arbour by the water's edge. I love these
wistaria arbours ; I like swishing the water with the
long tails of the flowers. How long is this one I
have in my hand ? '

' Quite four feet, I should think.'

' And isn't it a lovely delicate lilac ? I like it
better than the white.'

' Take care, Bryn. You'll have the whole swarm
of bees on us. There seems a bee for every petal
in this arbour ; and you can hardly see the sky for
the thickness of these tails, as you call them.',

' Oh, the bees won't touch us ; they know we
don't want to hurt them. The Japanese educates
his bees as well as his trees, till they do all sorts of
things not dreamt of in your gardener's philosophy.'

' Bryn, you've been reading up.'

' Don't be unkind, Phil. I've done quite a course
of reading ever since I lived with you and had the
run of the library you brought out with you. I've
been so cruelly conscious of my deficiencies—I never
had a book in my hand except a circulating library
book before then—that whenever you've said a lot
about a book at table, or when we were out together,

I've always hunted it up, if you had it, and—at any rate cut its leaves.'

Phil took off his hat.

' To use a vulgar colonial expression you "had me on toast" that time, my pretty sister. The fact is that I did all my reading with books borrowed from the libraries when I was at school and Oxford, and bought the books I wished to have with me in Japan while Mary and I were at home. We made a list of them on the voyage from that catalogue book of somebody or other's.'

' That's all very fine, my brother,' laughed Bryn, only to lay a light hand on his arm the next moment, and take back the remark, lest she should seem to doubt him.

' Can you picture Yoshimasa in his absurd lacquer armour fighting his way back inch by inch along this tall bank, between the still mere and the rushing river, till his men made a stand at the temple door while he cheated his enemies of the pleasure of killing him by committing *hara-kiri* ? '

' I don't think I can picture that armour out of a curio-shop. But it was worth while having it, for I think the lacquered armour boxes too beautiful for words.'

' Don't chaff, Philip ; remember that I'm a Jap. Do you want to go into the temple ? '

' Not particularly. I suppose it's full of the clumsy wooden images one always gets in old Buddhist temples.'

' Yes ; but there's rather an interesting image of Yoshimasa, by which they set great store, in one of the back buildings.'

'Let's go and see that.'

When they were ushered into the room where the image was kept, the young priest who showed it assured them that it had been there ever since the time of Yoshimasa, who committed *hara-kiri* on this very spot in 1180—in the face of the fact that the image was obviously some centuries later. Further, he went on to state that it had never been moved from its present position. He could not speak English, but Bryn interpreted, and added—

'To show you what a magnificent liar this man is, I will tell you a little story. This very priest—I know him by his harelip—told us the same story three or four years ago, when I was here with Punch and Bob Mathdine. Father and Mary were sitting in that wistaria arbour. We had been having lunch there, and they couldn't be bothered coming on. That was in the first days of kodaks, you know, and of course Bob Mathdine had one. The Japs mastered the science of developing kodak films directly. It was such a fertile source of revenue from globe-trotters. Well, when he trotted out this story Punch asked me to offer him ten *sen*[1] if he would bring the image out into the sun where Bob could kodak it.'

'And did he?'

'Of course. It's rather odd his not remembering me ; there are not many Europeans come here—especially as I speak Japanese. But there are many Japanese to whom all Europeans seem alike, just as all Chinamen seem much the same to us.' Then she added in Japanese to the priest, 'You are telling us what is not true. I was myself here when you took

[1] About threepence halfpenny.

that image out in the sun for the gentleman to make a picture.'

'I was telling you for the other gentleman,' said the priest, with a knowing smile. 'He does not know. You would not tell him.'

'Now, Bryn, you mustn't stand there all day chattering your native language. We've got to get home to Kyoto before dark—that is, before dinner.'

'O wise young man! A Daniel——'

'Surely I never recommended you to read Shakespeare.'

'Does that come from Shakespeare? I got it out of a birthday book.'

'Where shall we stop next? Do you want to see O-Baku-San?'

'Oh, the great Chinese monastery founded by In-gen. You know best. Do we?'

'I don't think so. It has a very fine red *sammon* (front gateway), but we pass that on the road. Well, the roofs of the Kai-san-do (founder's hall) and the other buildings are more strictly Chinese than usual, so you might just skip off your *riksha* and peep in through the gate. The *tout-ensemble* is the best thing about it, unless one has time to do it thoroughly. I believe it is rather interesting if one does go into it, because the temple is still a sort of university—of the old school. But there is one thing we must not miss. I'm sure it is somewhere about here, "The Empress Jingo's Fishing Rod"— a beautiful kind of bamboo which has all its leaves at the top like a palm. It's rather a rare tree.'

Presently, as they sped along for Kyoto, they saw little clusters of these trees from time to time, especially by graveyards, rivalling Areca nuts in their slender grace.

As they were on the point of entering Kyoto, 'We might go into the temple of Inari,' she said. 'It is one of the principal in Japan—the head temple of all the thousands of Inari temples and shrines that one meets at every turn throughout the country with foxes sitting on their doorsteps.'

'All right,' cried Phil, springing from his *jinriksha*. He was rather anxious to examine the avenue of poor little scarlet *torii*, which wound up the hillside till it was out of sight. As they passed under the huge scarlet *torii* at the main entrance and up the flight of steps, a priest came out of the *honden*. He was all smiles when Bryn addressed him in idiomatic Japanese, and extremely voluble.

'He says that his temple is very well off for gods. I don't know where Inari herself comes in, unless she is the same as U-ga-no-mi-tama, the food goddess, but the others are the harvest-god, and the monkey-faced god, and the personification of the Mikado's palace, and the islands of Japan.'

'What a kettle of gods!'

'Hush! you must be serious. This priest is not like the harelipped priest. He is very much in earnest. He says that we have come at the wrong time; that the gods are away.'

'I will be serious, Bryn; but it does sound a little. . thin, doesn't it?'

'Let me finish what I've got to say. The gods are away on their annual visit to the temples of Ise, which, as you know, is the Mecca of Shinto. He means their images, of course; they go in great state

in grand *mi-koshi*, like we saw in the temple of
Iyeyasu at Nikko. They left about the end of
April, and will be back just before the end of May.'

'Do look at our old friends—the lion and the
unicorn—Ama-Inu and Koma-Inu, don't you call
them? They have gilt faces and bright blue manes,
and emerald green fringes to their legs.'

'You must remember that this is a very grand
temple, Phil.'

They shook the priest off as soon as they could,
and rambled away from the temples up the avenue
of little *torii*.

'The priest says that this mountain is full of
wild foxes; that no one has ever been allowed to kill
them since Inari appeared to Kobo-Daishi in the
guise of an old man carrying a sheaf of rice on his
back, and took up her quarters on that great boulder
the priest showed us in one of the temples.'

'What a useful man that Kobo-Daishi was,' said
Philip, relapsing into irreverence now that they were
alone again. What year was that in?'

'711, the priest says.'

'That shows that Europeans don't come here
much. When Europeans first came to Japan, everything, from the Mikado-ate downwards, was 2000
years old, then it got to 1200, and now, in places
frequented by white men, they don't go beyond 600
if they wish to be believed.'

'Oh, Phil, drop it; I do want to take my country
seriously—to England.'

As they left the temple, Bryn pointed out the
other entrance, only used by the gods on their
annual visit to Ise, though the bearers who staggered

under their *mi-koshi*, loaded with splendid ornaments of gold and silver, and copper and iron, had necessarily to accompany them.

She paused, too, to spend a *sen* on one of the rough wooden *torii*, painted scarlet, which the poor Japanese, making a pilgrimage to the abode of the beneficent goddess to whom he looks for food and drink, loves to carry away with him.

'I don't want to lose touch of Inari Sama when I am in England.'

'There's no fear of that in an English parson's family,' said Philip grimly—'they're death on rice-pudding.'

'How you do go on about parsons, Phil. You seem to have quite a personal dislike to my cousin.'

'So will you, perhaps, before you've done with him. My only objection to him at present is that he is taking you away from me.'

'It isn't him ; it's my conscience.'

'Well, he's the outward and visible sign of your conscience.'

'That's pretty good. James Penthorne the outward and visible sign of my conscience! I wonder if he looks the character?'

CHAPTER XXII

BRYN'S last day but one in Japan was a glorious summer day, with a light breeze and a dancing sea.

Bryn, who dreaded being with him except when they had something to keep their thoughts from the one absorbing subject, had dragged Philip to sight after sight, and even now she insisted on going somewhere.

Without exactly knowing why, except that it was improbable that they would have any European passengers, Philip suggested that they should take the little steamer which ran down the bay to Yokosuka, the Japanese arsenal, which by the sarcasm of events is close to Uraga, where Commodore Perry dictated the opening up of Japan to the hated and despised foreigner. It did not take so very long to get there, and when they got there they wasted no time in going over the arsenal, but, taking *rikshas*, drove a mile or two out to the little village of Hemi-mura, which contains the graveyard where Will Adams lies in his long sleep, so far from the white cliffs of his beloved Kent.

'Ask the boys if they know the English *anjin's* tomb, Bryn, will you?' said Philip. It had not so very long been rediscovered in those days.

Oh yes, they knew it well, and soon set their 'fares' down before quite a handsome tomb of the cushion-topped pattern, enclosed with iron railings by a patriotic Englishman, yearning like Will for the home which his children had never seen.

'You know all about Will Adams, I suppose, Bryn?'

'Not really; though his name has always been a household word.'

'Well, Will was the English pilot of a Dutch fleet, thrown by stress of weather or something of the kind on the coasts of Japan. The name of the ship in which he came to grief was the *Charity*. He was brought to Iyeyasu, the first of the Tokugawa Shoguns, who made the discovery that the Kentish pilot could also build sea-going ships such as had never been known in Japan. So he made him constructor-in-chief of the Japanese navy, and gave him all he could want except the one thing he wanted, the liberty to go to England to those he loved best. He ennobled him, and gave him the lordship of Hemi. And the inhabitants of the street in Tokyo, in which he lived when he was in attendance upon Iyeyasu, made a god of the man who had such godlike skill in building ships. But we know by the god-pilot's letters, which by one chance in ten thousand have survived, that there never was a time in his long exile in which he would not have given his lordship and his godship to be with the wife and little children whom he had left behind in Kent.'

'I think they published his letters in the *Japan Gazette*,' said Bryn.

There was a look in Philip's eyes, though he was not in the merriest of moods, which made her hasten to explain that she referred to a republication.

'Poor Will!' he said, 'they could not have chosen a better place for his tomb.'

'No, isn't it lovely? On this green hill, with all the little bays and islands spread out like a map below.'

'So it is, Bryn, superlatively lovely; but I wasn't exactly referring to that—look as far as you can to the left.'

She shaded her eyes and looked.

'What do you see?'

'A whole lot of big ships—steamers, I think—why, it's Yokohama!'

'Exactly. Don't you see that his tomb on one side commands a view of the great commercial port of Japan, with the flag of the England he loved so well flying from nearly every stern; and on the other looks down on Yokosuka, the arsenal of the Japanese navy, of which he was the creator?'

'I see; it couldn't be more appropriate. And the Japs do not forget the god—or shall we call him the patron saint?—for a Shinto god doesn't amount to much more, of their navy. There are two offerings of fresh flowers on his tomb; and the people of the *Anjin Cho* in Tokyo, which was named the "Pilot Street" in his honour, still give him an annual festival. I am not sure that they could not point out the house in which he lived, though every house in the street has probably been burnt down a dozen times since.'

'How like I shall feel to Will, Bryn, when you are in England—with ten thousand miles of sea between me and all that is dearest to me, except her baby that cannot speak.'

'Don't talk like that, Phil. You'll get over it before I leave the steamer at Plymouth.'

He shook his head.

'Will lived to be an old man without getting over it. I am a prisoner in Japan,' he added, 'just like him. I could not stay here without you if I was not bound in honour and duty to my father to stay and make a success with his money, which I have invested in taking over your father's business. I wish from the bottom of my heart that I had never touched it.'

'Don't talk like that, Phil. You know that it is to avoid you that I am going to England. If I stayed here I should marry you; and I must not. If you could go to England, England would be no place for me. But don't bring this up at our last picnic.'

'I'll try not to,' he said, in the bitterness of his heart; 'but you're all the world to me.'

Then by a strong effort he brightened up.

'Let's eat our lunch by Will's tomb—he can be our patron saint too, and then I've a good idea. Let's take the *riksha*-boys right on to Yokohama instead of going back to Yokosuka to catch the steamer; the woods will be delightful, and your own favourite Negishi——'

'Lovely! how many miles is it?'

'I haven't the least idea. Not too far to get back by dinner-time; and you've got everything packed, haven't you?'

'Everything that could be packed if I was there.'

'Ask the boys if they can do it. I shall never be able to make them understand such a mad suggestion, as I can't speak Japanese. Probably no foreigner has ever been by *riksha* between the two places, it is so hilly.'

He distinguished the words *yoroshi—dekimas—* (good—can do) in the voluble reply.

'They say that they could do it if the woman at the cottage down below will lend them lanterns, and take a message back to their wives. They have not brought their lanterns, as they did not expect to be out so late, and the police of Yokohama are very strict, if they should happen to get there after dark. And they say they cannot go for less than eighty *sen* each.'

'Oh, I think it's worth a dollar. Say all right, eighty *sen*, and that we will give them a dollar if we are pleased.'

While one 'boy' had gone for the lanterns, Phil asked the other how it was that Will Adams had two tombs, for there were two monuments on the tomb. The man could talk a little English.

'No 1 Will Adams, No. 2 Will Adams's Japanee wife.'

Japanee wife has a special significance to the English dweller in Japan, and Bryn could not repress a smile, in which Philip thought he recognised a silent request.

'Bryn, you don't think that, do you?'

'No, Phil, honestly I don't, and I hope for my sake you won't.'

The 'boy' could not follow this enigmatical conversation in English, and wondered if the pressure of the hand with which they ratified the bargain was some new kind of worship which they were paying to the spirit of Will Adams.

But just then his mate arrived, and they started on their rather heavy journey.

'I'll just love having a long *riksha*-ride, as it will be almost my last; and between this and Tomioka is a part of the country that Europeans go through so little that I shall see all kinds of typical little things to carry in my memory when I am in Japan no more. And the lilies ought to be out in the woods.'

' Lilies ? '

' The *Lilium auratum*. Don't you know the Japanese tiger-lily—a big, white spotted thing with a scent like fifty narcissuses ? That little copse at Netheravon was full of them.'

' Oh, I remember. I didn't know they grew wild. How glorious it would be to gather a great bunch of them for you to take on board.'

They were not long in coming upon the lilies, where the road ran through the wood, with a steep bank on one side high enough to catch the sun over the tops of the trees on the other side. At first they could only find buds, pale green affairs something like minute vegetable marrows, but Philip looking up saw far above them a great white star full-blown, and, scrambling up to it, they found themselves in a veritable garden of lilies, which sent forth scent a hundred yards or more.

They gathered an armful, and not having, as they thought, too much time, hurried back to their *rikshas*. Phil took the *puggaree* of fine white silk crepe three or four yards long, deftly plaited round the crown of his broad, gray *Terai* felt, and gave it to Bryn to tie round the lilies. Bryn had deft fingers, and, giving him the lilies to hold while she smoothed out the *puggaree*, tied them into quite a Boulevards-looking bouquet with a huge creamy bow. Many a tear she dropped on that *puggaree* in England.

Then they started on homewards, up hill and down dale ; now round narrow cliff paths hanging most uncomfortably over the sea ; now along the

little raised causeways between interminable rice-
fields ; now through meek little Japanese villages,
where the only shops were the tea-houses, and perhaps a stall or two of sandals or sweetmeats and red
and white syrup in queer little thin bottles for the
children.

Philip walked nearly all the way, except for the
short stretches when they were on a dead level high
road in passing through a village or the like.   He
was a heavy man for a single *kurumaya* (*riksha*-boy)
to pull so far over a bad road.   He walked behind
Bryn's *riksha*, feasting his eyes on the queenly way
in which that exquisite golden head rose from neck
and shoulders, and when she turned round to speak
or to listen, on the beautiful face which had become
part of his life, and which he was so soon to see no
more.

' I'm going to ride every step of the way,' she
said.   ' It will very likely be my last ride, and I'll
give the boy something extra.   Besides, I am lighter
than you.'

After many rice-fields, with round wooded bluffs
rising out of the paddy, they came to Tomioka,
beautiful Tomioka, consecrated to Bryn by many a
picnic with the father and sister laid in premature
sleep on the hillside at Yokohama.   She could not
remember, of course, the high-bred mother, whose
fiery life burnt itself out so early in exile, and from
whom she inherited the thoroughbredness in her
beauty.   The beauty itself, perhaps, she owed more
to her father.   Latimer Avon had been a singularly
handsome man in a blonde Dundrearyish way —
Latimer Avon, whom his high-spirited daughter had

always more or less despised, till the tragic sudden-
ness of his death effaced every thought except the
memory of his unvarying and prodigal kindness to
his children.

Then came a *twinge*. All her people were dead
—father, mother, sister—except a baby, too young
to speak, and yet she could not help acknowledging
to herself in ruthless self-examination that she would
be parted from them all with less pain than from her
dead sister's husband.

, Never had Tomioka looked more lovely than
upon this summer evening, with the low sun orange-
ing the little temple on the point overhanging the
sea. Round the point at that moment shot a
graceful Japanese barge, a huge *sampan* serving out
the net, the end of which was held by a crowd of
sun-blacked, almost nude coolies on the sands,
standing now stolid as statues, to be transformed into
jabbering, howling monkeys as soon as the net was
drawn in far enough to disclose the finny prey—
no matter how humble.

'We must stop at the old friendly tea-house for a
last cup of tea, Bryn; the boys too will be glad of a
meal.'

They did not go upstairs, because they did not
want the bother of taking off their boots, but ordered
tea in the little garden, where they sat watching the
riksha-boys flinging bowl after bowl of rice down
their throats with chop-sticks.

'If I did not know my countrymen,' said Bryn,
with a little sigh, 'so well, I should doubt our ever
getting to Yokohama to-night.'

'I should like to stay here for ever,' he cried, and

when she gave him a little pleading look, explained,
'I think this spot, with its sweet little bay, and its
sweet little temples, and its groves right down to the
sea, and its quaint fishermen, in this summer sunset,
the most beautiful thing that could be imagined.'
But—he would fain have added—'with you beside
me.'

Philip was never going to forget her, as she sat
there in her *riksha* (the 'boy' was standing balancing
the shafts ready to start) with the rich Japanese
sunset behind her, and her fair beauty rising as it
were from the glorious bunch of pure white wild
lilies.   In Japan the lily is the emblem of purity.

'Sunsets don't last,' said Bryn sadly ; 'we must be
hurrying on.'

There was still daylight enough when they
reached Negishi, the little village with steeple-
crowned roofs of thatch, almost like Hakone, which
nestles under the cliffs not far from Yokohama ; so
Bryn was able to have a parting look at her favourite
little graveyard in the bamboo brake, half-way up the
cliff, with its rows of little gray Buddhas, with
pitiful faces, peeping out of the tall grass.

'Oh, how I shall miss these,' she cried ; 'these
are Japan—you and Japan, Phil !'

All Negishi seemed to be taken up with drying
the newly-threshed grain ; in front of every house
were long mats covered with grain, evenly spread
out like the sand in a canary's cage.

The *kurumayas'* hearts rose when they saw
Negishi.   They knew exactly where they were now,
and that they had a high-road all the way before
them.   For the last mile or two they had been a

little anxious and unwilling to slacken down for Bryn and Philip to look at anything.

In the village right below the Bluff, less than a mile from Philip's house, they were carrying a poor little Japanese harvest. There were no waggons or trucks ; the beasts of burden were men, each carrying two huge sheaves balanced, like pedlar's boxes or anything else in Japan, one at each end of a shoulder-piece.

Here, too, the mats were spread out for the grain-drying. The harvest field was hardly bigger than a good-sized backyard. And dear little children were playing at a miniature harvest in one corner of it— the little girls with still smaller children on their backs in *haori*. And on these and the queer willow-pattern hills of the Bluff, which rose behind them, was beginning to shine the splendour of a glorious full moon, which had just slain the feeble daylight.

'O Japan, Japan!' cried Bryn, almost in a moan.

'I suppose we may call this the harvest moon— though it is only July,' said Phil, with more than one meaning.

And amid the chorus of the frogs in the paddy they climbed the hill up to the Bluff, for Bryn's last night but one in Japan.

The heavy-footed *riksha*-boys trailed with light hearts down into Yokohama, where they said they were going to pass the night, for over and above their promised dollars Bryn had given each of them a crisp blue dollar note, that she might carry with her the remembrance of the look which came into their faces.

CHAPTER XXIII

SAD, sad was Bryn's last day in Japan. In the morning they visited the hillside cemetery overlooking the sea, where Mary had so recently been laid beside her father and mother.

One of the few romantic traits in the practical English who wander away the width of the world to found new Englands in its waste places, is their desire to sleep their long sleep in a spot overlooking the sea, which is their link with the old England, where they would not or could not stay.

'Whenever I am by the sea in England,' said Bryn, 'I shall feel that something might be wafted to my feet from within sight of where they lie—and where you live, Phil.'

He and she had divided their lilies into three parts. One for Mary's grave, one for Bryn's cabin, and one for his lonely house.

'When they are faded on her grave, Phil, just put them into a box and send them home to me.'

On her father's and mother's graves she laid bouquets from Philip's garden; she had been up since daylight gathering flowers to arrange in all the rooms where he would see them after she had gone.

CHAPTER XXIV

'Is it true that you're going to England, Miss Bryn?'
he asked with an air of sympathetic respect, which
went straight to her heart, and pacified the rebellious-
ness which she felt against the world.

'Yes, Bob,' she replied, hanging her head.

'Oh, why are you going?'

'You've heard what they say of me, haven't
you?' she asked bitterly.

'But who are they?—not half-a-dozen people at
the outside who know you.'

'Enough to blast my character and drive me out
of the only home I have here.'

'Why not brave it out, Miss Bryn? You were
never wanting in pluck; the untruth of it is sure to
be exposed in a few weeks.'

'Thank you for that, Bob,' she said, with a grateful thrill in her voice; 'but it cannot be. I owe it
to poor Mary's memory to leave Philip's house when
they can insinuate such things.'

'Oh, Bryn,' he said, 'I can't keep up the Miss
when my heart is so full. You remember the day on
which you gave me a kind of leave to call you Bryn
if I liked, but let me understand, I thought, that you
would rather I did not?'

She nodded her head mournfully. Those dear
old days at Nikko!

'Do you remember the circumstances?'

She gave one of the swift glances, in which she

A JAPANESE MARRIAGE

seemed to look right through any one—almost the
old imperious glance.

'Yes,' she replied, wofully ill at ease.

'I may as well come to the point at once,' he
said, rather despairingly.   There was an ill omen for
his hopes in her manner.

'Bryn, I've come again to ask you to marry me.'

'But how can I?—you, the heir of an ancient
and honourable house — the future Sir Robert.
Don't you know what they say of me?' she asked
savagely.   'They say that I am Philip's——'

'Not that word, please, darling.'

Bryn softened.   'It will never be proved that I
am not; oh, why did I not give one of those old cats
five hundred dollars a year to play Mrs. Grundy in
the house!   I'm sure it's a Trades Union business
among the old maids, because we did not make a
place for one of them.   But Phil and I were so
happy; we did not want to share the memory of
Mary, or her baby, with any one, and we got into
each other's ways so.'

'If it were proved that you were, Bryn, I'd ask
you all the same.'

'But I'm not, Bob — O Bob, you will believe
me?'

'How can you ask one who knows you?   I could
never believe that, until I saw it with my own eyes.'

She said nothing, but took his hand and held it
with her own hands, drooped almost into the position
in which a soldier's hand is before he raises his sword
to salute.

Her touch sent the blood surging through his
veins

261

'Will you marry me, Bryn, and set all these wagging tongues at rest?'

'Please, Bob, don't ask me.'

'Oh—why, darling?'

'Because I love Philip, and he asked me to marry him; and I'd give all the world to marry him, if it only wasn't wicked.'

'Poor Bryn,' he said softly. Then he spoke out vehemently. 'You must marry Philip. What does it matter what they say at the end of the prayer-book? The Scotch, the Irish, the Welsh, and a good part of the English attach no more value to the prayer-book than they do to a dictionary.'

'But it's law too, Bob.'

'Is it? Yes, I suppose what's law in England is law in H.B.M.'s Consular Court in Japan.'

'But I don't so much care about the law.'

'Then, *why* don't you marry him?'

'Because it isn't right.'

Bob Mathdine was silent; he was Scotch.

CHAPTER XXV

SAD indeed was Bryn's last day in Japan. She was sacrificing all the happiness she looked to have in the world for an idea, which she felt in her heart of hearts to be a bogey, though she would not let herself believe that any other course was right or possible.

She loved Philip so, that she knew she could not

stay in Japan without marrying him. And to marry her dead sister's husband was, by the creed she had cherished from childhood, a sin, though that sister had besought her to do so on her deathbed. But the wrench was awful.

Philip did not go to the *godown* that day. He felt that he had so much to say to Bryn. And yet they did. not speak for an hour at a time. They simply sat together, as a wife and a soldier-husband might sit, when the husband was under orders to go to the front.

On that day Bryn and he knew that, though they had never been married, nor contemplated the act of marriage, they had been husband and wife for many months in the companionship for better or worse, which is the pure and beautiful side of the sacrament the prayer-book declares to be primarily intended for the procreation of children.

'You will write to me, Phil, and send me papers from dear old Japan, and *kodaks* of the quaint characteristic things one sees here, to bring back the flavour of my home to me, in my long exile.'

He did not ask her to write ; he believed in her. She felt doubtful of a man's memory, when he has been long parted.

'Oh—why are you going, Bryn?' was all he said.

'Phil, you need not ask me.'

'Bryn, Bryn, change your mind before you make a purgatory of my life.'

'And my life too,' she moaned. 'You know why I am going; oh, please, don't talk of it any more, dear Phil.'

A JAPANESE MARRIAGE

He knew what it cost her to say it; for she kissed and kissed him as if her heart was going to break.

'Why won't you go and stay with my people in England?'

'Because your ways must not be my ways, and your people must not be my people. I am going because some divine law which I do not understand says that we two must not be as one flesh. I have not the strength to be near your people. My resolution would fail. I am going to stay with my father's cousin, a clergyman, in the hope that I may forget in a life of usefulness the life I should have chosen —with you. Perhaps I shall be able to become a hospital nurse or a matron in a reformatory.'

'Don't, Bryn, it seems such profanation. It is almost like becoming a nun, dead to the world.'

'From the bottom of my heart I wish that I was a Roman Catholic, that I might become a nun, to put an inexorable barrier between myself and my longing.'

'Thank God you are not!' was all he could say. Presently he went on—

'About this money, Bryn. It was wicked of your father to make you an executor, so that nothing can be done without your consent. Do you know that if we adhere to the agreement, as you insisted on its being drawn out before you would sign it, you will not have twenty pounds to spend in the whole year after you have paid your passage home and have paid your cousin his pound of flesh—the hundred a year which that clerical Shylock demands to let you live with them? That's all that the sale of Nether-

264

avon yields, and I'm afraid that there'll be nothing at
all coming from the business this year.   It has only
escaped bankruptcy by a miracle.'

'This is what killed my father,' said Bryn, with
a sudden inspiration.

'Of course there are the curios.   I sold that *Lapis
lazuli* lacquer cabinet yesterday for six hundred
dollars. Three hundred dollars of this belongs to you.'

'Three hundred dollars of that is not mine to
spend.   The interest of three hundred dollars is.
But what is the interest of three hundred dollars?
It must just wait until the end of the year—when,
perhaps, it may amount to a little something.'

'Bryn, dear, you must gang your own gate, as the
Scotch say.   I can only pray God unceasingly, night
and day, to turn your heart, and let you look at
things from the common-sense point of view, instead
of entailing all this misery upon us both.'

'Oh, if He would!' groaned Bryn.

'Perhaps Buddha may do something for us.   Poor
Mary had great comfort from the gods of her country,
though she knew them to be false.   And I have
faith in this Buddha, though he is only a graven
image,' he said, taking from a box an exquisite copy
about a foot high of the great Daibutsu at Kamakura.
I don't mean in the religious sense, Bryn, dear,' he
said, noticing the shocked look on her face, but in
giving you the *heim-weh*. He is very old, as old
perhaps as the Daibutsu himself.   I commissioned
your father's old compradore, who bought all his
curios for him, to buy me the finest he could hear of
in a moderate size, as a parting present for you;
because I told myself that when you looked on his

merciful beauty, with the whole genius of the immemorial and immortal East typified in his repose,
you would feel a mandate that you could not resist
to return to me—to Japan. Promise me that the
Daibutsu shall stand in your room where your eye
will fall upon it, and that once a day, if it is for ever
so little a time, you will look at it steadily and think
of Japan, and those who love you in Japan.'

And Bryn promised.

CHAPTER XXVI

To us—who have been down to the sea in ships
many a time in stormy weather and fair ; who have
trailed from end to end of an ocean without ever
seeing a sail ; who could to-morrow, without any
wrench, pack our portmanteaus and go back and live
the lotus-life in the beloved East, which we 'have
heard a-calling' ever since we quitted its fantastic
quays for London, where all things come—to us it
is but a little thing to start round the world.   But
every time we scramble into our temporary home—
the great snorting ship, which is to take us to live in
some new land—happy and excited, comparing new
and old surroundings, we see tragedies sadder than
any on the stage.

Now it is the only son of a widow going out, 'it
may be for years, and it may be for ever,' to win the
fortune that home cannot offer him ; or for a change
it is a lover.

A JAPANESE MARRIAGE

While we, who have lived in greater Britains, where people have no abiding city, buzz and laugh, there are always pocket-handkerchiefs in plenty, and white grief too deep for tears.

Under the clear sub-tropical blue, with the glittering seas round it just crisped with white by the light landward breeze, lay the mail steamer. The Blue Peter at her fore pointed to England, before the east wind, which carries so many sighs to one little island.

The decks were cleared, the companion hoisted, and the beautiful young girl, who, a few minutes before, had, down in her cabin, been clinging in a passionate embrace to the man from whom she was wilfully separating herself, was leaning against the taffrail, dry-eyed, but a very statue of wild grief, gazing at that sad sight, a man abandoned to tears, who was holding up in his arms a little child.

Nor was he the only man with eyes misted.

'Phil, old man,' said Robert Mathdine, when Bryn was out of earshot and eyesight, and the lessening masts of the tall ship were beginning to lie over the slightest bit, as the gulf opened, 'she'll be back with us some day, and marry you!'

Phil shook his head in dumb despair.

BOOK III

CHAPTER I

SUFFICIENTLY gloomy was Bryn's introduction to England. The steamer had literally crawled into Plymouth ; for some hours before the fog-horn had been wailing straight on end. The Sound, as beautiful in its way as Sydney Harbour, might have been the Regent's Park Canal for the fog that concealed it, and the soft Devonshire rain, in an unassuming way, soaked all the passengers and their bundles of wraps. When at last she got away from Plymouth and the tiresome attentions of the Custom House, the old-world aspect of the placid pool of Teignmouth, with its battered brown-sailed schooners, and its battered oyster-catchers' cottages on the islands in the mud, might have beguiled the loneliness from her heart, as might the red rocks of Dawlish, the lake-like expanse of the Exe's mouth, and the towers of Powderham and Exeter. But they were all enveloped in a wet blanket of mist, and there was nothing to notice except the oscillations of the train as it tore from Plymouth to Bristol and Bristol to the sluggish Wiltshire town where she had

to disembark for the second time. On board ship a
girl of such beauty, coming from a place where she
had lived her whole life, was bound to receive all, or
more than all, the attention she wanted; and this
made the loneliness of the railway journey after the
leave-taking on the tender all the more lonesome.
But it was nothing to the drive from the railway
station to her future home at Dunstanbury. The
Rev. James Penthorne, the cousin with whom she
was going to live, had sent the town fly to meet her;
it was more respectable. Bryn would have to pay
six shillings for this. She could have gone by the
omnibus for a shilling, and had a fellow-passenger
to talk to during the six long miles. It rained so
heavily that she could not see whether the scenery
offered any compensation for the half-hour's crawl
up-hill and the momentary risk of having her neck
broken through the slippery mud of the descent. It
was just pure misery.

And when Dunstanbury was reached at last, one
of the dull old market-towns left behind the door
in the march of *progress*—which is another way
of saying *railways*—her cup was full. Anything
drearier than the main street of Dunstanbury on a
fine day it was impossible to conceive, except the
main street of Dunstanbury on a wet day; it had
three grocers' and drapers' shops combined, all of
whom sold boots and smelt of them, and a post
office, which was also a stationer's; the doctor was
his own chemist, and the blacksmith was too far off
to count. There were no other shops, though there
were a good many other inhabitants; the butchers and
bakers came round, and so did the kerosene man,

which made the three grocers and drapers, who sold oil, Radicals. There were no other public people in the town except the sexton, and he complained that the people didn't die as often as they ought.

'You see, sir,' he would say, 'the doctor's such a very old man.'

Bryn had no time to look at the exterior or garden of the Vicarage; she was occupied with trying to get herself and her wraps into the house undrenched. The Vicar did not allow hired conveyances on the cherished gravel drive from the front gate round the garden, especially in wet weather, when the gravel was soft, though the Squire, patron of the living, might have ridden into the drawing-room with his hounds if he paid for the damages. The Squire had wasted a good many fat cheques on snob-baiting since the installation of the present incumbent, whose life was embittered by the fact that he did not care for hunting. In the Dunstanbury country, nobody was considered a gentleman who did not keep half-a-dozen grooms, and a proportionate number of hunters. The clergy were pitied as a kind of caretakers, unless they imitated the vices of their patrons, when they were called 'good fellows,' and pitied still more.

All this of course Bryn had to find out; perhaps if she had known what a hell a grass country is for any one between a lord and a serf, she might even have preferred to face her conscience and stay in Japan.

The door was opened by an immaculate parlour-maid; the Penthornes were by way of being immaculate. She rather despised Bryn, though neither she

nor Bryn knew why; she felt that it was expected
of her. Then Mrs. Penthorne came forward, a little
dark, rather prepossessing woman, with a pathetic
face, which looked as if it ought to have been full of
fun, and a figure which suggested neatness in disguise.
She was just a little bit dowdy; perhaps the Rev.
James felt that he would have to tell the truth to
the Income Tax collector if his wife's clothes fitted
her properly. She had nice teeth, and expressive,
dark eyes, and on the rare occasions when the Rev.
James was away, and she had a girl friend staying
with her, she was ready for any joke which a lady
need not be ashamed of. She needed some anti-
dote; for the rule of life devised by the Rev. James,
with its compromises between canters and canterers,
was so very like walking on the tight rope. When
Bryn arrived the Rev. James did not come into the
hall; he thought it would be more impressive if he
received her in his library, sitting at the twenty-six
guinea escritoire with a patent shutter, presented to
him with a purse and an illuminated address by his
former parishioners. They had given him a silver
tea-service as well, so elated were they at their de-
livery, and so impressed by what he would expect of
them.

The Rev. James was of a good height, and had
had a good figure, which was growing a little plump.
He never played games now, though he had been in
the eleven at Oxford. For the same reason the jaws
of his clean-shaven Napoleonic face were growing a
little fleshy. He had greenish, unsympathetic eyes,
and a measured metallic voice; everything about
him was measured. He had no saving sense of

humour, but an excellent set of false teeth, which he displayed so freely that the fox-hunters he toadied to always referred to him as Ivory. To Bryn, when she was introduced to him, he showed the whites of his eyes and the whites of his teeth. He wore an air of resignation, because he expected all those over whom he had any power to be resigned; and he called the seventeenth-century house in which he lived *fifteenth*, because it would not want so much furniture, and the decorations would be more within the scope of the village carpenter.

They were at tea in the drawing-room, although he was sitting in his study when Bryn arrived; and he set to work at a half-finished cup of tea and a bitten piece of bread and butter with an injudicious familiarity, when she had given the servant money for the fly and joined the tea-table.

The Curate was there. He had a weak, red face, liable to eruptions, which made his yellowy moustache and whiskers poor. James Penthorne chose his curates for their weak faces; he wished a curate to know his place. Mrs. Penthorne received Bryn affectionately; Mr. Penthorne with a restrained unctuousness, and the Curate as was expected of him. In the Vicarage it needed more than ordinary qualities not to do things as it was expected of you. It was Wednesday evening, and though it was pouring with rain, Bryn noticed that Mrs. Penthorne had her hat on and her gloves beside her. She nerved herself as she drew them on, and said to Bryn, who had had nothing since breakfast, and whose tea was not yet cool enough to drink—

'I suppose you'd rather stay and finish your tea

than come with us to church; but we have supper at nine, if you'd rather not miss the service?'

'Oh, tea for me; I'm dead beat!'

Mr. and Mrs. Penthorne exchanged glances; and the Curate keeked out of the corner of his eye to ascertain if they were doing so. Perhaps he promised himself a livelier time.

They went to church; Bryn finished the miserable remains of the tea, and sat on thinking. She fancied that they would be back in an hour at the latest, but eight o'clock came without any sign of them. She rang the bell for the lamp. In Japan she had always been accustomed to the electric light; here in England, in an ancient town, they had not even gas.

'They won't be back from the church, miss, until close on nine; there's a meeting after the service.'

'*Yoroshi.* Just bring me the lamp.'

'Master don't allow the lamp to be lit while he's at the church.'

For economy, wondered Bryn, or to advertise that he was doing something for his living?

'Bring me a candle, then,' she said.

'The bedroom candles are not put out till the family comes home.'

Bryn groaned in her spirit, but with her observant eyes she had noticed a couple of red candles in the churchy-looking brass candlesticks in her bedroom, and she always carried Bob Mathdine's favourite silver match-box, which he had given her as a personal keepsake, when he said good-bye. It looked like a tiny drinking flask, till you examined it closely.

So she walked upstairs and illuminated; then, feeling hot and travel-stained, commenced unpacking. It was heartrending to her to find how a long ocean voyage crushes dresses. In her despair she turned out her whole wardrobe to start getting rid of the creases. The room was fortunately large, and by no means overfurnished, but she covered every available inch. 'What dress shall I wear to-night?' she said to herself—'Oh, that little white; I'm sure to want it the first time we go out to a garden party; and there's nothing takes out creases like wearing,— besides, I'd like to look nice for them the first night.'

The costume might have been simple from Bryn's point of view, accustomed as she was to seeing so much society in a land where light gossamery fabrics are a necessity in summer; but it would have been too grand for a wedding dress according to the Vicarage standard.

When the Vicarage party got home, there was Bryn standing in the doorway like a young queen. It was too dark to see the creases by the hall lamp, which had been lit as soon as Bailey heard the saintly footsteps on the gravel. The Curate always came to supper on Wednesday nights, and Mr. Penthorne had brought the mistress of the voluntary church school, so as to impress upon Bryn, from the very beginning, the officious life which she was to lead.

As soon as they were in the dining-room, where the only decent lamp in the house was standing (it was James's study lamp except when he was eating), noticing how very conspicuous her dress looked in the company, Bryn said—

'You were so long in coming that I thought I'd
smarten up a bit and make a good first impression.
How do you like my frock ? is it awfully old-fashioned,
Isabel ? I shall call you Bell.'

Isabel said nothing; she had caught her husband's eye, while he said in his church voice, 'For
what we are going to receive, may the Lord make
us truly thankful.'

The others apparently were not going to receive
anything except bread and cheese and toast and
water ; but a fragrant little stew on a hot-water plate
was put in front of the Vicar.

'James has to take great care of himself,' said
his wife, feeling that some explanation was due to
Bryn, who was offered nothing but the bread and
cheese.

There was a jug of claret, too, at his elbow, from
which he helped himself.

Bryn loathed cheese. 'I won't have any cheese,
thank you, just bread and butter,' she said, though
she was dying of hunger ; 'but I'll take a little claret,
please.'

James telegraphed to his wife.

'We generally keep the claret for James. He
has to be careful about the strain on his voice.'

Bryn looked so bewildered that she felt constrained to add—'Two services, you know.'

The Curate was simply astonished with Bryn's
audacity when she said—

'I'm feeling very knocked up to-night; I have
been travelling all day, and have had nothing to eat
since breakfast.'

The idea of an afternoon tea with three pieces of

bread and butter not counting, made Mr. Lancing almost forget that he had been James Penthorne's curate for six months. Presently, after an interval of parish conversation, Bryn said—

'I think I must ask for some meat; I'm just fainting with hunger. I suppose you have some cold meat in the house?'

'Of course,' said Isabel, 'er-er, we don't generally have meat for supper, though I insist upon James swallowing some; but to-night of course——' She was waiting for James to telegraph consent.

'Meat, Bailey,' growled the Vicar.

'We think it so bad to eat meat more than once a day,' continued his wife, 'though I always make James take something with his breakfast.'

'I don't think Jim—is that what you call him when you are alone?—looks bad, you know,' said Bryn, growing a little tired of his dieting.

'Jim!' The Curate and the schoolmistress expected the earth, or, at any rate, the dining-room floor, to open.

Mrs. Penthorne's eyes twinkled, when she found that no one was looking at her. She said, as good-naturedly as she dared, 'I call my husband James.'

'I shall call him Jim.'

The Vicar thought it was time to change the subject. 'Lancing,' he said in a severe voice.

'Yes sir,' said the Curate.

'We must not have "Lead Kindly Light" again. I did not like the way the congregation sang it. They seemed really to enjoy it, which is not what church services are intended for. I am thoroughly in favour of congregational singing, but I think it should be sung with a feeling of where you are, and not with high spirits.'

'I think it is a lovely hymn,' said Bryn.

'That is exactly what we have to guard against,' said the Vicar, 'the sensuous enjoyment which is the besetting sin of High Churches ; sensuous is but one degree removed from sensual.'

'What is the difference ? ' asked Bryn.

'Too little, I'm afraid, my dear Brynhild ; sensuous is only a gentlemanly version of sensual.'

'I am afraid I don't follow you. Do you get many to your Wednesday services ? '

'Oh yes, we get from twelve to twenty people now, including the Vicar and myself,' said the Curate, quite jubilantly.

'And the organist and pew-opener and the bell-ringer and Mrs. Penthorne,' put in Bryn. 'That is a parson's dozen ! '

CHAPTER II

BRYN'S nose was on the wheel by the very first morning. 'Church is at eight,' Mrs. Penthorne had said. 'What time would you like to be called ? '

Bryn was not a girl who took so very long to dress, except in the morning ; but she dearly loved her bath, and liked to linger over washing and brushing away the traces of sleep. James Penthorne, in his most censorious days, derived satisfaction from her well-groomed appearance, though he

considered that a decent Vicarage lady ought to
screw her hair tighter.

After early service came breakfast, an egg or
herring meal, and then Isabel disappeared to do her
housekeeping and parish work.

Before she went out she said, ' Brynhild——'

' Oh, call me Bryn, please.'

' Well, Bryn, about half the people who come
won't be satisfied unless they see some one, so will
you see them, please ? Bailey can tell you what to
say to most of them, and the others you can ask to
call again, or use your discretion. I can see by your
face that you have discretion, though perhaps not
much enthusiasm.'

Enthusiasm is not easily inspired by an egg and
herring meal after a P. and O. breakfast, with its
score of substantial alternatives ; but Bryn—she was
a small eater like most people born in hot climates
—did not explain this. While giving her instructions Mrs. Penthorne had begun to dust the drawing-
room. Bryn came up to her and laid a hand on the
duster——

' I'm very light-fingered ; please let me do this.
I really want to be useful, and may I call you Bell ?
I should never be able to manage the Isabel with
the dignity which *Jim* puts into it.'

' Jim ! ' Bell could not resist a merry laugh—
merry laughs had been far too infrequent with her
of late ; but it seemed so exquisitely funny for any
one to call the headmaster ' Jim.' His nurse could
hardly have taken such a liberty when he was a
child.

' Yes, call me Bell,' she said, suddenly remember-

A JAPANESE MARRIAGE

ing that Bryn had asked her a question. She anticipated storms while Bryn was being broken in to
the iron rule of the Vicarage, but it was a perfect
godsend to her to have a woman in the house.
James was not a man to make up for the want of
woman's society. As Bryn said afterwards, he ought
to have been kept in the vestry between the services.

'And now you must excuse me, Bryn dear; I
have to go to a *home.*'

'Can't I go with you?'

Bell did not feel quite certain what her cousin
might do or say till she was broken in, so she
replied—

'You're a little too fashionably dressed, dear, for
visiting poor people's homes. I shouldn't be able to
get them to attend to anything but your clothes.'

'May I come when my clothes are old enough?'

Bell remembered the story about the man who
was going to be beheaded by a certain caliph, and
got a reprieve of three years by promising to teach the
caliph's donkey how to speak within that time; and
when asked how he could promise such an impossible
thing, replied that one of three things might happen,
either the caliph might die, or he might die, or the
donkey might die,—so she said, " Oh yes.'

Bryn dusted everything about twice, so fearful
was she of being left alone with her thoughts. She
had never seen the black shadow of Despair so large.
This was the England of which she had dreamt, as a
land with the towns half like Regent Street and
Piccadilly, and the other half like Downing Street,
full of brilliant equipages and smart people; whereas
she found it more stunted than Japan.

Like many colonial women, Bryn had never done
any sewing. She sat and chewed the bitter cud of
her reflections. So silent was she that she heard
the knock at the kitchen door, followed, a minute
later, by a knock at the drawing-room door.

'Please, miss, Mr. Lancing says that Mrs. Peters
of Paradise Row is to have a pint of beef-tea; shall
I give it to her? Here is the paper.'

'I suppose so, Bailey.'

The woman applying for parish relief brought
home to Bryn her own poverty. The thought
dinned into her head like the harsh church bell
which had hurried them from their scanty breakfast
in the morning, that when she had paid the Penthornes the sum agreed for her board she would have
only a few shillings a week to spend; while a few
months back she had been living with dear old
Philip, not indeed in her former extravagance, but
indulging every reasonable taste without a thought
as to how many cents went to the dollar.

Had she done wisely to lay such violent hands
on hope?

.   .   .   .   .   .

'Please, miss, Mrs. Johns wants a ticket for a
bag.'

'What on earth's a *bag*, Bailey?'

'Oh well, miss, about two pounds of beef for
beef-tea, and tickets for the next four days on the
parish accounts, and wine for the mother, and——'
Bailey was almost blushing; she hummed and
hawed a minute and then made a desperate bolt,
and got out—'and clothes for the baby, miss.'

'Oh, I see,' said Bryn.

Having broken the ice, Bailey grew voluble.

'I don't think she ought to have it, miss; it's her ninth baby; and there never was a Mr. Johns, miss, as I knows of; you'd better not give it till the mistress comes.'

'What will you do then, Bailey?'

'Tell her to wait till the mistress comes, or to *call* again.'

Mrs. Johns turned the current of Bryn's thoughts. She had had nine children without marriage, and probably without love. And she looked to the Church for support!

Marriage meant the universe of love to Bryn. She had denied herself. And James Penthorne, the mirror of orthodoxy in Wiltshire, evidently looked upon her as little better than Mrs. Johns.

In the agony of her heart she almost groaned, '*Cui bono?*'

.　　　.　　　.　　　.　　　.　　　.

'Here's a woman brought a girl that is at last willing to go to a *home*, and she wants to see Mrs. Penthorne very particular.'

'Perhaps I'd better see her, Bailey; if Mrs. Penthorne is long she might change her mind.'

'She don't look boltish; she's got the almighty fit of repentance on, if I might say so, miss. I think the mistress wouldn't like you to see her; them young women are generally put in the study, miss.'

'For Mr. Penthorne to see?' Bryn asked with almost a smile.

'Oh no, miss; gentlemen don't do that; only missus and the missionary sees them,' said Bailey, with a faint hint of pity for Bryn's ignorance.

'Missus never lets them wait in the kitchen a minute; only her and the missionary sees them.'

'Aren't missionaries gentlemen?'

'No, miss; Miss Skeet's the missionary.'

'Well, show her into the study to wait for Mrs. Penthorne.'

'She's there already, miss,' said Bailey, with the air of a person who understood her duty.

Rescue? If she had married the man she loved best in the world, and lived in all purity and godly life, in the opinion of the Vicar, perhaps of herself, she would be a firebrand to be plucked from the burning, like the worst of the wild women who lived by profligacy. What good was she in the world?

. . . . . .

'Please, miss, can Mrs. Sparks have some help? Her baby's dying of diphtheria.'

'Of course, Bailey.'

'She doesn't belong to our parish,' said the servant doubtfully.

Bryn felt quite sick, and, going upstairs, took five shillings from her own light purse and sent it to the woman.

Bailey of course had no idea how light the purse was, but from that moment she loved Bryn.

Bryn was thankful when Bell came in; for the papers did not come till the afternoon.

Lunch was really dinner, beautifully served; Bailey's demeanour, like her cap and apron, was perfection. The china was costly; the soup was brought on in a silver tureen which shone like a mirror, though the soup itself reminded Bryn of the 'Forgotten Soup' of the old days at Nikko. Silver dishes followed. Bryn soon learned to be glad when the dish in front of James contained a skinny little cutlet for each, for if it was a joint it came back and back, and was carved as beautifully as if it had been real ivory. James prided himself on his symmetrical shavings of beef.

The puddings were poor little moulds of corn-flour, beautifully tinted and turned out in the daintiest shapes, or fascinatingly *petites* fruit-tarts. There was never enough of anything except bread and salt. Even the mustard in the lovely antique silver mustard-pot hardly covered the bottom. ' It is so much nicer to have it fresh,' Bell had to explain.

Why the servants stayed with them was a mystery to Bryn, till she found out that a servant who left the Penthornes with a character could get a place in any of the great houses round for the asking.

When Bailey left the room, ' Why do you drink toast and water, Bell ? ' she inquired, in the desperate hope of getting something better.

' For the example, dear. How can we expect the poor to abstain if we do not set them the example ? '

' But it looks just like sherry in these sherry decanters and little goblets.'

' James thinks they look better on a gentleman's table.'

' Then I don't see where the example comes in,' said Bryn bluntly.

' Why of course we can tell them we abstain ourselves when we are asking them to take the pledge.'

'But James doesn't abstain.'

'He only takes wine medicinally.'

'Oh,' said Bryn, 'that reminds me of the local agent of the Phœnix in Yokohama. He wanted the Bishop of Kamakura to join; but the Bishop said, "I understand that the motto of the Society is *Touch not, taste not, handle not.* I am a teetotaller, Mr. Lymph, but if I were ill I could not promise to die rather than to take spirits, and if I were at a friend's dinner-table I could not refuse to pass the decanters."—"Oh, you needn't be so strict as all that," Mr. Lymph explained, "your name is the principal thing we want, my lord."—"Do you mean to say, Mr. Lymph, that you expect me to sign a declaration which I do not intend to keep?"'

'I think, Brynhild, that these scurrilous stories of Church dignitaries are in very bad taste,' observed James.

'I must let the steam off, Jim.'

'Ladies ought not to have any steam, Brynhild.'

She often wondered afterwards how he expected them to go.

Lunch was hardly over before Bell said, 'I'm going to a Parish Committee Meeting at the Dowager Lady ffolliott's; you might come there, Bryn.'

James raised his eyes at the familiarity of the diminutive. But his wife took care not to see, and said hurriedly, 'You had better get into the parish work as soon as possible.'

'Very well,' said Bryn cheerfully. 'How are we going to Lady ffolliott's; are you going to have the fly? Why don't you keep a pony chaise, Jim? You could afford it, couldn't you?'

'There are some expenses which the clergy have no business to incur,' said James, with official humility.

Judging by the contents of the Vicarage, Bryn thought there must be a special dispensation in favour of old oak and rare china. The house was quite a museum, exquisitely arranged.

'Lady ffolliott's is just opposite,' said Bell.

'That red brick cottage?'

'You might call it so, perhaps; the old-fashioned red brick house with a magnolia over its front.'

'Oh,' said Bryn.

'Lady ffolliott is not rich, you know. Her son— Sir Briggs ffolliott—a very bad man, has pauperised the estate on the Turf.'

The meeting was principally taken up with voting and deciding what should be voted on at the next meeting, and it was characterised by common sense. Most people who can be got to attend a meeting so unpleasantly close upon the top of lunch take more or less real interest in the affairs under discussion.

But the meeting of the Zenana Mission Committee, to which they went on afterwards, was of a very different order. It was held at Mrs. Hogg-Smith's, almost half-way between Dunstanbury and Tole. James was Vicar of the united parish of Dunstanbury-cum-Tole, two places some five miles apart. The church and all the conveniences were at Dunstanbury, and the population was at Tole, which had large butter and bacon factories. Wiltshire is nothing if not a dairy county, and Mr. Hogg-Smith as a customer for cream and Mr. Herbert as a pur-

chaser of pigs were the two greatest benefactors the
county had ever known. Very different men they
were. Mr. Hogg-Smith looked like an old farmer,
for the great butter factory had grown out of a small
dairy farm ; and Mr. Herbert, who was a young
man, was so smart as well as wealthy, that strangers
invariably asked him what relation he was to Lord
Pembroke, with whom he had no more connection
than the man in the moon, being an Irishman from
Waterford. Bryn got very sick of the Zenana
mission. She was introduced to all the ladies, but
they were most of them stiff or *gauche*, and a more
incapable lot of women she never set eyes on. The
fact was that, it being of no earthly consequence to
Dunstanbury - cum - Tole or its Vicar what happened
to the Zenanas, he always asked weak-minded ladies
whose purses were useful to his parish, and who
wished for office of some kind, to join his Zenana
Committee.

To Bryn, who knew something of the East, the
idiocy of the proposals of most of the members of
the committee was more than usually apparent.
While they talked they sewed little red and yellow
coats, such as are worn by organ-grinders' monkeys.

Mrs. Hogg-Smith disliked the example set by
owners of Zenanas to Mr. Hogg-Smith. Lady
Whewell thought that Mr. Penthorne looked so
delightfully like a Roman Catholic priest, and
wished he would start a confessional. Pretty Mrs.
Herbert thought it an unmitigated bore, but her
husband wished her not to be left behind by the
Hogg-Smiths in anything. Mrs. Maskelyne went
there because Pope Maskelyne was always talking of

starting a Zenana, and she wished to find out what the special attraction was. And the others were church-hacks, who talked more nonsense than any of the rest because they imagined that they only had to agree among themselves about the form which the reform or abolition of Zenanas should take for it to be adopted without hesitation throughout India.

And this kind of thing went on till nearly six o'clock. There was no afternoon tea, because Mrs. Hogg-Smith, though she lived in a gray stone house which would have done for the principal hotel at Ilfracombe, had not moved in the sphere penetrated by afternoon tea until the last few years, and she was very conservative. She was a decent body. She dressed like a monthly nurse, but she was worthy of presiding over something nearer home than Zenana missions. They dragged through the long walk home almost in silence. Bryn was wondering how she could school herself to endure a lifetime made up of days like this; and Bell, good little soul that she was, was puzzling out a report, not absolutely at variance with facts, of the Zenana meeting which would satisfy James. When they got home Bryn felt sure that she would be offered some tea; but James considered all meals not at the regular hours demoralising, so she was left to worry herself over the headache provided by emptiness and tiredness, while Bell saw a fresh batch of parish people. On their way home they had called in at one or two cottages, and been received with the usual category of ailments. In backward agricultural districts the poor wish to see a doctor, not to get his advice but that he may hear their complaints. For

this purpose the Vicarage people do equally well and
are cheaper. After supper, at which no one, except
James, was offered anything but a piece of fish,
which was no fresher than it often is in remote
inland places, James went to sleep amid a hush
made for the purpose, and Bell knitted or sat with
folded hands watching the apostle. It made little
odds to her ; she was too tired to desire anything.

'You cannot go out,' she said to Bryn ; 'the paths
of the river and the woods are full of the butter and
bacon factory people—the young men and the young
girls,—and we should only see how powerless we
are to prevent immorality. I am afraid that it
always increases in proportion to the lack of interests
and amusements.'

How Bryn longed to say, 'What price me ?'

'But we don't always do nothing in the evening,
Bryn,' she continued. 'You see on Sundays, Wed-
nesdays, and Fridays we have evening services, and
on Saturdays I have a Girls' Friendly Class because
James is busy with his sermon.'

'What do you do at the Girls' Friendly Classes ?'
asked Bryn, with a ray of hope though she really did
not know why.

'Oh, we sing a few hymns, and the girls sew,
and I read a book aloud to them.'

'What book ?' asked Bryn eagerly. 'I didn't
know you had any in the house.'

'Oh,—James's books are all theological. I get
one out from the Hogg-Smith Institute at Tole,
one of Miss Yonge's generally.'

'Have they got a good library ?'

'I think so. James chooses the books himself.'

Bryn felt at that moment as if she would like to wring James's neck ; but promised to come to the next meeting.

When the Saturday evening came she sat patiently among them listening to their harsh voices singing hymns which they rendered still more excruciating by verbal alterations such as ghostess for Ghost. She watched them cutting out ugly aprons and uglier other garments ; she even read them an improving story. But when she got to her bedroom she would have liked to have shouted. She said to herself that they looked so ' beastly good ' that she couldn't stand them. She would have liked the bad ones, who came to incarcerate themselves in the *home*, much better. They, at any rate, had lived, while the others had had hardly as much experience as vegetables. But Bell would not hear of her speaking to the 'rescued.' Perhaps she was right after all. For it might have been a great shock to Bryn, brought up to consider herself as belonging to a superior race, to find out how much lower white women can go than Japanese. When Bell knew her much better she approached the matter with much hesitation and delicacy, and was shocked by Bryn's callousness, till the latter explained that morality is merely a matter of property in Japan.

' Well, I always thought Dunstanbury was about as bad as a place could be. It was Mr. Harraden, our squire, who said that morality was a matter of amusement. Of course he did not say it to me but to James. He gave James the living, and is always trying to horrify him, because James did not turn out so much a man of the world as he had hoped.

You see Mr. Harraden, not being a hunting man, is
rather more dependent for society on his vicar than
most of the surrounding squires. When he comes
in of a night he makes James sit up dreadfully late,
which doesn't agree with him, and drink a lot of
whisky, of which James hates the smell, though I
believe he keeps very good whisky. Well, one
night he started the question of morality, and said
that it was merely a matter of amusement. James
was very shocked, and said he did not see how. Mr.
Harraden shrugged his shoulders. " I'll tell you
what it is, Penthorne. You have—how many people
in your parish ?—twelve thousand, I daresay, including the factories at Tole, and they have no amusement at all, except the society of the opposite sex
or the lowest of the low travelling shows. Nothing
better would pay, apart from the county people, who
live a long way out, most of them. You haven't
one gentleman per thousand souls in your parish.
But the thing reacts. Having no elevating amusements, people are satisfied with the most unelevating
of all forms of pleasure." '

' I think I should like to meet Mr. Harraden.'

Bell was a good deal shocked.

' You see, life is so very dull without its little
paradoxes.'

' Don't think me a meddlesome Matty, Bryn, if I
ask you not to air these paradoxes quite so often at
meals. James thinks your conversation most unfit
for a vicarage.'

' I should like to put some homœopathic doses
of dynamite in James's pockets ; but as you ask me,
Bell, I'll try and sit like a statue at meals.'

' I didn't say that.'

' I know you didn't. But if I have to go to that place, I'd rather not go for hypocrisy. I can't do the " brethren " business. I wasn't brought up to roll my tongue in my cheek.'

' Hush, Bryn. Oh, and one other thing——'

' I do mean to try and be good, if it isn't too desperately uninteresting. What is it, Bell ? ' she asked wearily.

' James doesn't like your clothes. He does not think they are seemly for a vicar's family. To start with, he objects to light colours. He never lets me wear anything but black and dark blue, with a very little white sometimes, such as a bird's-eye spot or a fine stripe.'

' Perhaps I ought to dress as he wishes. I'll go into Bath and get some plain frocks.'

' And he hates big hats. I have to wear a very plain bonnet, though I am allowed a black mushroom for the garden.'

' All right ; bonnets too while I'm about it.'

' I am afraid you're making rather a martyr of yourself.'

' My dear Bell,' said Bryn rather enigmatically, ' I came to England to make a martyr of myself.'

CHAPTER III

BEFORE the flowers were dead in the vases in which Bryn had arranged them, Phil had left his pleasant house on the Bluff and was installed in the spacious suite over the *godown* in which Latimer Avon had lived, while he was laying the foundations of his fortune in the good old days when merchants were accustomed to live over their *godowns* in the infant settlement. He left the house almost entirely as it stood when Bryn quitted it, with the exception of the nursery and the servants' part of the house, which were not identified with her presence. He even went so far as to buy a new writing-table and transfer his papers so as to leave his study as Bryn remembered it.

The suite was furnished. When Mr. Avon's circumstances had warranted his moving to Netheravon, he had kept the furniture in the *godown* so that he might be able to extend hospitalities to visitors whose business relations with him gave them claims on him, but whom he did not wish to introduce into his aristocratically-conducted home.

Several things decided Philip in making the change. In the first place, it was martyrdom for him to be in a house which was so permeated with the sunshine of her presence, now that it was to be for ever bleak. In the second place, it was misery to him to alter a single thing from the position or condition in which she had left it; he wished to make a Bryn memorial museum of it. And in the third place, he was on the horns of a dilemma. The whole time that he was down at the Settlement, while the baby—all he had left to his devotion— was on the Bluff, he was in agony lest it should have some mysterious malady which might carry it off before any one thought of summoning him.

And yet it was imperative that he should devote his whole time to his businesses. Ever since his marriage, nearly two years before, his time had been broken up, first by the trip to England, then by Mary's being ordered off to the mountains, and her death, and lastly by his trouble over Bryn and the month they had spent in Kyoto, which should have been one of the busiest months in the year.

In his original business, as agent for his father's ships, matters could take care of themselves pretty well, for he had the help of the experienced chief clerk, who had been in charge of the agency till he came out from England.

But the business which he had taken over from his late father-in-law was in a very different state. There, too, he had the help of an honest, experienced, and, as far as he went, competent chief clerk, his fellow-executor; but the business itself, instead of being plain sailing and sure small earnings, was the hollow shell of what had been a great business, but had been brought to the verge of a crash by the depletion of capital to pay for Mr. Avon's ruinous private establishment, and the consequent recourse to risky operations. To rehabilitate such a business, to give it the 'life' which would alone divert bankruptcy, was beyond the capacity of any of the late Mr. Avon's employés, even when the drain had ceased and fresh capital been introduced. Philip had foreseen that this would be the case when he took it over, but he had not anticipated the succession of troubles which overtook him and kept him from attending to it.

Had he known how bad things were, how near

her father's affairs were to involving him in bankruptcy, how imperatively they demanded his undisturbed attention, he could have addressed to Bryn the one argument which would have induced her to remain with him—the taking household worries off his hands while he saved himself from being ruined by her father. In his transactions with his son-in-law, Latimer Avon had not kept too far within the rather elastic boundaries of commercial morality. But even if Philip had known, that was exactly the kind of pressure which he would have been too generous to apply.

It may be that his business troubles saved his brain when Bryn's departure left his life such a howling wilderness. In bodily health he rapidly became a mere wreck, for while he lost all appetite for food, he worked day and night, hardly allowing himself or desiring any exercise. For one thing, all through that steaming summer he never left Yokohama for the mountains. The baby was well, and while the baby was well he dreaded going into the country where he would be at the mercy of his thoughts. In Yokohama he could give every minute of the day to the thousand and one arrears of business.

Soon it seemed quite providential that he had shifted his establishment from his house on the Bluff to the *godown*, because anguish of mind, want of nourishment and sleep, and overwork, brought his system down so low that he suffered from intermittent fever, which made moving about, or even standing upright, almost impossible. But at first he managed to crawl down into his office; and when he got too bad for that, it was almost as easy for the clerks to go up and see him as he lay on the couch in his room.

All this was kept a strict secret from Bryn. He alluded to no troubles of any sort but the one trouble—the misery of separation from her—in the letters which he wrote to her at every leisure hour, and posted regardless of mails, thinking that she would enjoy receiving them separately more than in one accumulated budget.

But through all his mental and bodily anguish he preserved two things,—unfailing attentiveness to his employés and a clear faculty for business. It was quite a pleasure for any of the clerks to go up and see one who could be so considerate, instead of gouty, in his agony ; and it was the gratification of a lifetime to Mr. Avon's old chief clerk to see genius for the first time applied to a business which had hitherto owed its success to the start it had received in the times when a log could have made money.

With the cooler days of autumn, when the great rains were past, and day after day of cloudless blue was tempered with pleasant breezes (unbroken that year by the dreaded typhoon), and his friends came back from the mountains, Philip gradually shook off his malady and began to crawl about again. Bob Mathdine had been down to see him more than once, from Nikko, when he heard how ill he was, and passed a night or two with him.

The first time he came after Philip could get about again, he was taken up to the house on the Bluff, to see if Otori-san (who, not being needed any longer by her mistress, had married Bryn's *riksha*-boy Taro, out of employ for the same reason) had

answered expectations as a caretaker. When Phil
had made up his mind to go and live in the *godown*,
and the information had filtered through Kano that
the Bluff house was going to be left exactly as it
stood in charge of a caretaker, Otori-san entreated
that she might have the post. Bryn San's things at
any rate she considered that she had a right to take
care of until Bryn San returned. She had a firm
faith that Bryn San would return, which predisposed
Philip in her favour ; and when he mentioned that he
thought he would have to leave the house with a
married couple, with true Japanese adaptability she
offered to marry Taro on the spot. Being questioned
if Taro had asked her, she said No, but that she
knew he would have her, to meet the case. And as
it got Philip out of the difficulty of letting Bryn's
own personal servants leave him, he was glad to fall
in with the arrangement.

Everything was spotlessly clean, and everything,
as far as Philip's exacting eye could discern, put
back after dusting into exactly the position it occupied when Bryn was there. When Bob Mathdine
noticed the dead flowers in the vases he caught
Otori-san's eye. She glanced at Philip in a way
which made Bob feel a lump in his throat when he
suddenly remembered the incident on his way home
from the Club quite a month later.

' Poor old Phil !' he said, as they strolled down
the avenue to the gate, where they had left the
rikshas in case the boys should be curious, ' I am
glad you are keeping the place sacred to Miss Bryn's
memory.'

' Call her Bryn, Bob.'

'Not to you, Phil; I would rather not; she is yours. I'd hate to have our remembrance of what she used to do here and what she used to do there obliterated by the everyday life of other people. Bryn Avon was such a woman as our little Japan will never see again unless she comes back. She had all the honours and nearly every trump in the pack.'

This was a few weeks before most people came back to town, but Bob did not go up to the mountains again.

'You want looking after, Phil, old boy. I'm going to stay in Yokohama and keep you company. I'll stay at the Club till Dacres comes back. It'll be nearer you than our "Bachelor's Hall" on the Bluff. I want to tool you out in my dog-cart to see the autumn leaves—maples I believe they are—at the various places within a drive. You can't refuse. You never went in a dog-cart with her, did you, old boy?'

CHAPTER IV

BRYN had gone home by the long P. and O. route, so Phil did not get a letter from her from England till the beginning of October, though she telegraphed her safe arrival at the beginning of September.

Her letter made him heart-broken and furious. After she had made him laugh over her cheerless journey and reception, and the fly, and her first day's round at the Vicarage, she wrote :—

' I have been here a week now and nothing I do seems right. James treats me as if he was a headmaster and I was a recalcitrant boy. I feel quite surprised that he hasn't whipped me. He simply ordered me to attend every service while I was at the Vicarage, and I have not missed one, though we have a service every morning, and on Sunday, Wednesday, and Friday evenings, besides Sunday afternoon children's services and the Sunday School.

' Yet he sent the servant—I beg her pardon, the parlour-maid, Bailey, a most immaculate and righteous young person, your regular model English servant, who looks upon me as a sort of " rescued woman " —that's their cant word here,—he sent for me, I say, on Saturday night. When I got to his study I felt so frightened that I almost called him " Sir."

' " I have sent for you, Brynhild," he began, " to talk to you about the services."

' " I've been to church every time the bell has rung," I said.

' " Yes, you have. You have sat there in your well-fitting clothes with about as much expression as one of the images in papist places of worship."

' " I can't help my want of expression, James."

' " But you can help wearing clothes that are a scandal in a vicarage. That large white hat of yours with its assertive trimmings takes up the whole attention of the Sunday School. Those light dresses of yours with their elaborate fashions, which I have no doubt admirably suited the fast, godless society in which you have had the misfortune to have spent so much of your life,—they might do for a music hall, though I've never been in one, but I must say they are entirely unsuited to a vicarage pew."

'These were my brown-holland-coloured Chinese silks, Philip, which I had picked out as the soberest cool dresses in my whole wardrobe. I never opened my lips in reply. And then he went on to speak about my stereotyped manners, which he said were unchristian and I don't know what—though he says that Mrs. Norman, who would give her top hat to have them, and would kill you with laughter at her attempts to imitate me, is such good style, because she is a pew-holder, and takes sittings for herself and family and half her servants. He did have some people in to meet me one day, but I could see him glaring at me when I laughed a little in trying to introduce one ray of ease into that arctic drawing-room ; and as soon as they had gone he said, " Don't you think you could do without that giggle, cousin ? " Just fancy a man that calls you cousin !

'We hardly ever say a word at meals ; I can't talk before him unless I feel desperate ; his silence terrifies me ; he sits at table and simply breathes. It's more depressing than any amount of scolding to have to watch the man, on whom your entire day depends, simply breathing.

'This Wednesday night the trouble was that, when I came back from church so dead beat with all the work I'd done for the Lord in the day that I could not eat the miserable supper (they hardly give you enough food to keep a Jap alive, though it's served on real silver plate and such lovely old china)— well, when I came back from church I felt dead beat, and I just took up a novel that some one had given me on board ship, and I had forgotten to read ; it was *Robert Elsmere* or something of that sort. He came right up to me, and blew me sky high for taking up a work of fiction so soon after I had come back from worship.

'If only some one had the courage to tell him that he was the Pharisee alluded to in the New Testament ; but I am frightened to tell him—like every one else—he is so oppressively good.

'And oh ! the creepy Christians he introduces to me, that he may talk to me about my inferiority afterwards, and pray that I may grow more like them. There were some there that afternoon he spoke to me about my laughing. I was mad when I heard him explaining me away to one of them.

'But his crowning impudence is that he will never leave me alone five minutes with Isabel—that's his wife—if he can help it. I think she might be a nice little thing if I could see anything of her ; I'm sure she was cheery, and merry, and broadminded once, whereas now she hasn't a soul to call her own, and has to dress her body like an ascetic. He says the reason why he does not leave us together is that he objects to his wife having friends ; that it is quite enough for a vicar's wife to have acquaintances ; that there is nothing leads to so much trouble as romantic friendships between women. But, of course, his real reason is that I should corrupt her—polite of him, isn't it ?

'I talked of his crowning impudence just now, I hardly know what his crowning impudence is ; for after he had been harping back to the subject of dress, and letting me almost understand in so many words that I looked like "a Shanghai woman," he went on to say that he would not tell me these things unless he loved me (spiritually, of course), that some people would be hypocrites enough to let these little things pass unnoticed. "You'll forgive me, won't you?" he said quite briskly, with the air of a man apologising for paying cash!

Bob Mathdine coming in at that minute was surprised with an expression on Philip's face which he had never seen there before, and which in certain classes of society would be described as 'ugly' or 'wicked' — not in the classical sense of these words.

CHAPTER V

SPRING had come at last—the soft caressing spring of the warm west of England, which Britain's Roman conquerors loved.

Bryn had now been three-parts of a year with the Penthornes, and outwardly was pretty well drilled. She wore the plainest dresses of black and dark blue (the making of which in Bath nearly drained her purse), attended all the innumerable services, and the Sunday School (though she was only allowed to sit by Isabel's side at the latter, lest she should corrupt the impressionable youth of Wiltshire), and cultivated the habits of a mute (before the Vicar), and generally tried to win happiness in the world to come by excluding it from the earth we inhabit.

But when the Vicar went fishing—he was a famous angler, and had the run of all the famous trout streams in Wiltshire—Bryn and Bell played at being human beings again.

Isabel Penthorne had long since fallen as deeply in love with Bryn as any of her male admirers.

'Come along, Bryn,' she would say, when James had had to catch an early train for the other end of the county; and, having been up to give him his breakfast, she was well ahead with her work—'Come along, Bryn, do let me see you in some of your pretty frocks.' And once, when he was away for the night, she made Bryn put on one of her smartest low-cut dresses after supper to revel in the girl's loveliness.

Bryn, in the self-sacrificing mood she had been cultivating for the past nine months in her endeavour to fit herself for a life of church work, was what the Americans call lovely, meaning lovable, as everybody recognised except James, to whom she could never be acceptable till her spirit was broken. Bailey, the parlour-maid, who had begun by thinking that cavalier treatment of Bryn was doing her master's service, had become her absolute slave. Nothing that attention could do on her part to minimise the effect of James's pharisaic bullying was omitted.

To Isabel, the one bright spot in her life since the first year of her marriage was Bryn's companionship. She found a new zest in doing her duties like a steam-engine, that she might get them finished and run up to Bryn's bedroom for a chat.

A JAPANESE MARRIAGE

Bryn spent most of her spare time in her bed-room, which was the only place sacred from James's canting voice. Here she could sit and gaze on the merciful countenance of her Buddha, drawing comparisons, and write the letters to Philip which gave him such pain because she now limited him to a letter a month. James had said that she was causing a scandal in the neighbourhood by receiving such a number of letters in the same gentleman's handwriting.

After a while, it was true, Philip evaded his vigilance by getting all the ladies in his acquaintance to direct envelopes to Bryn on one pretext or another. And she had no such pleasure as when she discovered the well-beloved's writing under a stranger's envelope.

Bailey used to leave the morning's letters on her writing-table while the family were at church—and the other post's too whenever she could manage it unobserved, as soon as she noticed that her master extended his bullying to the very letters that Bryn received.

'Bryn,' said Isabel one afternoon, 'would you like to drive over with me to Landguard Manor? I'm having the fly from the King's Arms. I owe a call at the Manor, and James wants me to leave that splendid brace of trout he caught yesterday.'

James never sent his fish to his own by no means overstocked larder when they were good enough to send elsewhere. He bestowed them partly on the people who took the greatest number of sittings at his church, and partly on the people who had given him shooting or fishing ; which latter was excusable enough, as in such matters one has to be just before one gets the opportunity of being generous.

Bryn, being a stranger, did not know to whom Landguard Manor belonged. Indeed, she took studiously little interest in county affairs when she discovered that her cousin was only recognised in a patronising or pitying way by the fox-hunting grass-shire squires. She went the drive for the pure pleasure of accompanying and obliging Bell. It was not until she heard Bell inquire if her Ladyship was at home, and the footman replying in the negative, that she thought of asking whom they were calling on.

'Fancy your never having heard—the Dowager Lady Romney and her son.'

'Is Lord Romney at home?' asked Bryn of the footman—rather abruptly, and not in particularly good taste, as it seemed to the wondering Bell.

'No, miss. He's in London; the House of Lords is sitting.'

Bryn said no more; but Bell said to the footman—

'I may show Miss Avon the reception rooms and the gardens?'

'Certainly, Mrs. Penthorne,' said the man civilly. 'Shall you want me?'

'No, Robert, thank you.'

Bryn was a little distrait as they wandered through the house; and Bell thought she was not duly impressed with the hot-houses and green-houses, which were very fine, and regarded by the country people as the eighth wonder of the world. Many of their treasures Bryn had seen growing in the open.

air, and the glass-houses at Nethcravon, with their skilful Japanese gardeners, had produced all kinds of marvels.

But when Bell had taken her down into the combe to see the effect of the house from below, she could hardly find words for her delight.

The combe, one side of which was grassy, the other covered with woods, had a clear brimming river meandering through it, with an old-fashioned mill at the end—a river full of stately trout, and with clusters of orange marsh marigolds, springing from rich, dark, fleshy, shield-shaped foliage at intervals along its brim. The primroses, huge as undisturbed primroses will grow, were ubiquitous, nodding just over the water, starring the grassy hill and firing the woods. The woods, too, were white with anemones, and here and there out of a bank of dead leaves rose a forest of lilac hyacinths, the blue-bells of England.

Bryn was wild with enthusiasm over the primroses.

'I think this the most beautiful thing I ever saw in my life,' she cried. 'We never had anything like this in Japan. I like this better than all the hot-house flowers in the world.'

'I'm glad you like my beloved "primmies." To me the primrose has a charm no other flower possesses; for it means that our long wet winter is over—the primrose is the New Year's first smile. But I did not bring you down here to look at primroses, Bryn: all the combe is carpeted with them. Climb a little way up the grassy side of the combe—now sit on this bank and look at that.'

Out of the woods opposite, which were almost as
white as a cherry orchard in flower, with their first
pale buds, rose one of the stately homes of England,
almost the only country in Europe where antique
unfortified mansions have escaped the torch of war.
There seemed to be no end of it, wing after wing
and gable beyond gable roofed with rich red,
clustered round a tall central tower, looking with its
steep pitched cowl like a bit of old Lucerne.

Landguard Manor—the vast palace (one could call
it no less) built of Bath stone, hoary with age, but
sharp as if chiselled yesterday, which rose out of the
magic woods of Spring, as quaint in outline as one of
Albert Dürer's castles—owed its name and its splendour to the same circumstance.   The first Wiltshire
Romney, the builder of its oldest part, was a man of
Kent that had won the regard of Henry VIII., who,
whatever his faults may have been, was very jealous
of England's prestige, by the manner in which he
had repulsed the French from Seaguard, the ancient
stronghold of his family in the marshes, from which
they took their name.   Seaguard, which occupied
one of those Acropolis-like hills that occur at
intervals in the Kent and Sussex marshes, was an
imposing enough place from below; though when
once you were within its walls, you found it consisted
of hardly anything else, for the keep was of the most
modest proportions — the explanation being, that
the lords of Seaguard, deriving their sustenance in
piratical days from wool, had to have a place of
refuge into which they could drive their flocks from
the rich grazing grounds of the marsh when
threatening sails appeared on the horizon.

Such a fortress victualling itself fell in well, moreover, with Henry's vast schemes of coast defence ; so, having plenty of confiscated monastery lands in his treasury, he bestowed a rich Wiltshire Abbey on Sir George Romney in return for Seaguard's becoming a royal castle, of which Sir George and his heirs were to be castellans, owners in all but name, compelled to keep up a posse of a certain strength for coast defence.

Sir George lived to an unconscionable age, and his eldest son having married an heiress of the ancient house of Hungerford, it was natural that he should live on the new Wiltshire estate, converting the dismantled Abbey into a home.

Being a Romney, moreover, he knew the value of sheep, and the men who understand them, so he kept on the farm servants of the Abbey, which had been famous for its wool.

When his father was carried, full of years, from the watch-tower to his death-bed, the son preferred to stay in the statelier home he had been forming for so many years, which his father had always called the Landguard, leaving a younger brother to rule at Seaguard, until his own heir was old enough.

And succeeding Romneys, one of whom was raised to the peerage half a century later, had grown to despise their rude Kentish seat, with its risk of a visit to France in the hold of a privateer.

Such was the history of Landguard Manor, which rose before Bryn's eyes with the added interest that she might at this moment have been its mistress had she so chosen.

'It's glorious,' she said, with sparkling eyes. 'I never dreamt of such a place.'

'And weren't the pictures and armour superb?'

'Living in a place like that is life; living as we do is only preparation for another life.'

'Hush, Bryn.'

'You know it is, Bell. You—and I, I suppose,' she added with a weary sigh, 'when James has broken me in, I shall be just like you—have not a moment to think. The mistress of a place like that could get up as late as she liked, and think all day if she wanted to, except when she chose to be entertaining. I often think I should like to go into a convent. You do get time to think there. James doesn't believe that a Christian has any business to waste time on thought. He thinks they ought to be worrying about something. Besides, if I was in a convent I should be a prisoner without chance of escape, and could not marry Philip. Now, though it seems unkind to say it to you, I always feel like a prisoner who could escape by summoning up the courage for a dash.'

'Do you still love Philip, Bryn?'

'Do I still love Philip? Do you think that Hans Andersen's mermaid loved the man who gave her a soul? Philip gave me a mind.'

'What a pity it is that it's wrong to marry a deceased sister's husband. It's against the law too; but they're always trying to repeal the law. It would be repealed, only the Lords stop it, and it's about the only thing they do that they don't get blamed for. People say that it would be a blow at the whole family system — that a man would no longer be able to have his wife's sister, their natural guardian, looking after his children and keeping house for him, if it was possible for her to contemplate him as a husband.'

'I don't think they need trouble themselves about the law,' said Bryn bitterly, 'when the whole business tumbles like a house of cards before the first breath of scandal.'

'It's a scandal we never contemplate in England, and yet I'm sure that it must often exist. When you come to think of it, there really is more risk of a sister-in-law than any other woman doing what she ought not with a man, for the chances are that she knows him so intimately that only the last line of defence remains to be carried ; while with another woman, equally modest and suitable to take the head of his table, there would be barrier after barrier to break down. I am afraid that if she sees enough of a man, almost every woman will let him caress her eventually, provided that he plays the game and does not try to take two moves at once. Most of us in our heart of hearts yearn for it so much that if only a man will take the trouble to break us in, as he breaks a horse, and pause when he sees that we are scared, he can lead us right up to the brink of the Rubicon.'

'I was never broken in,' said Bryn. 'Philip wasn't that sort of man.'

'Hasn't Philip ever kissed you ?' said Bell. She called him Philip, the two women had so often spoken of him.

'Why, of course ; he was my brother in every-thing, and I love him better than any one else in the world ; but he did not do it in your second way, Bell.'

' If you were never " broken in," as you call it, Bryn, how did Philip, who seems to have been a shy man, break the ice ? '

' I broke it,' said Bryn proudly. ' When he was going away to England for his honeymoon with poor Mary, I kissed him on the steamer's deck, as we were seeing them off, before everybody, to show him and the other men how I appreciated a resolute masterful man, who could be so alert and so able in business, but so diffident with a sister-in-law, except in defence of his wife. I used to be such a beast to Mary in the old days—all my life, until she was engaged to Phil, and he wouldn't have it. He was the first person who ever disputed my will, because he never hoped to please me, he told me afterwards, and I just liked him awfully for it. After that, till they got married and went away to England, I was just nice to her so as to win his good opinion. And he never noticed that I cared, and that's the reason why I kissed him when we said good-bye on board the steamer. But when they came back and we all lived together—that was after her accident, you know—I was just as nice to her as anything ; and she was—what shall I say ?—*cussed*, you know, when her spine troubled her. I can't recall any one thing I did not do which would have made her happier. And I did it, why ? Because Philip was so gentle that it was impossible to live in contact with him without catching it. To live with him was a liberal education.'

' I do wish it was right for you to marry your

Philip, Bryn. I don't believe you'd ever marry any-body else. And it's a sin for such a beautiful woman not to marry and continue the race. I am one of those who think that a woman has not fulfilled her destiny until she is married, though there is such a ghastly percentage of failures,' she added with a little sigh. ' But, Bryn, we must be getting home. James will be cross at our being so long, as Lady Romney was not in.'

' I wish James was more like I am at the present moment. I'm in terror of treading on a violet. You can hardly move without, here.'

' I'm afraid James doesn't notice the violets of life,' replied his wife. ' To do him justice, he doesn't mind handling a nettle.'

They walked up the combe to one of the numerous grass roads running through tall, dark, fir plantations. It was full of squirrels, and wood-pigeons kept flying out with a swish above, while rabbits scampered into their burrows below. But it was the sight of the pheasants that enchanted Bryn, for they brought back Japan.

' Are these bamboo-pheasants ? ' she asked.

' I don't expect so. But I really don't know much about game. Why ? '

' Because we stick their tails in the Fujiyama vases, and they look ever so nice.'

Bryn was very silent till they got back to the hired fly at the front of the house. She was hankering after the flesh-pots of Netheravon. The sight of the super-annuated trap and weedy horse aggravated the feeling.

' I could have enjoyed this place,' she said to herself. ' But oh, I'd rather have Philip.'

CHAPTER VI

MRS. PENTHORNE showed very much more courage on Bryn's behalf than she ever had shown on her own. On the point of church James was obdurate. Every service Bryn must attend, and the Sunday School at which she was not allowed to teach. He would like to have insisted on the other drudging items in Bell's common round of trivial tasks ; but Bell said—

'Can't you see, James, the only parish work she takes the slightest real interest in is the rescue work ? In a pure young girl of her age this is not a healthy sign. It implies a morbidity which might culminate in mental trouble. She gets terrible head-aches on the top of her head that last for days, and she sometimes doesn't sleep for a week together. You must be a little more human (she ought to have said humane) to her, or we shall have her going out of her mind, or having brain fever, or leaving us for God knows what.'

'Isabel, I must ask you to leave me. To hear a minister of the Gospel's wife using language such as that in which you have just indulged is such a shock that——'

She was so glad to get off that the last part of the sentence was lost.

Bryn did not know whether she would not just as soon have gone to meetings, it was sometimes so deadly dull sitting alone at the Vicarage while

Bell was busy over parish work. She had never done any sewing; and of literature at the Vicarage there was nil. The only papers they took in were the *Standard*, the *Church Missionary Gleaner*, and *Church Bells*. She did not understand enough about English affairs to care about the first, and though she read the other two so as to be able to take her part in the conversation at table, which was almost exclusively church 'shop,' they did not feed her mind. The food it required was woman's gossip, not scandal; not reports of society and would-be society functions, but chatter about dress, artistic furniture, table decoration, the home lives of the people of the hour, men, books, and what not. There was no reading-room in the village, and after she had bought the plain black and blue dresses in Bath, because none of her own were suitable 'for vicarage people,' she had no pocket money left for buying papers or books—Bryn to whom money had been as water.

Often and often she wished that she was dead. She wrote to poor Philip: 'It is heartrending to feel that though I am only two-and-twenty, and gifted with such perfect health, I am no more use in the world—I have no hope—life is one long misery. I do feel so awfully low, when I think over everything, that I would gladly . . . if it would relieve me of the responsibility of my own life, as I really don't know what to make of it. . . . To deliberately kill myself mentally by becoming a vicarage drudge seems hard lines after my life of perpetual interest. . . . I can't write, Philip, I'm sick in mind and at heart. It's a horrid feeling that one has lived too long, and only twenty-two at that. . . .'

More especially did she need it now when she had exchanged a life full of colour for a life of hodden gray, when she had to do without Philip's conversation, kaleidoscopic in the range it covered. Almost her only relaxations, except when she could get Bell for a long natural talk, were to go to her bedroom and, leaning back in the one harsh easy-chair, gaze with half-closed eyes like an artist at the gentle Buddha ; or to follow the road across a lofty sort of common, till it rose with a very sharp incline, and halt, just below the summit, to look at its yellow rim against the sky, and tell herself that if she climbed it she would see Fujiyama rising before her as she had seen it on that memorable walk from Miyanoshita to Hakone.

This illusion she preserved. She never climbed that last bit to behold, not Fujiyama, but miles and miles of rolling Wiltshire downs—blue in the distance, blotched with the dark green of fir plantations, when they were near enough for large objects to be distinguishable. The one anchor of life she had was Philip, the memory of those happy months with him, the thought of how he would feel her death.

It is probable that had James not bullied her into going to church, she would have gone none the less often, and found the same comfort as Philip found in the exquisite and peace-giving liturgy of the Church of England. But as things were, the Church was the very emblem of the iron bonds in which she had allowed herself to be fettered. She wondered why she did not rebel ; her tongue sometimes did. One night, for instance, when James was at supper after a day's fishing, to which he had gone away at daylight, leaving Bell such mountains of parish work to get through that she had not been able to get to early service, Bryn said in her meekest voice—

'I wish to consult you on a question of propriety, James.'

He pricked his ears and, metaphorically, preened his feathers.

'Do you think people would talk if they knew I was in the church alone with Mr. Lancing this morning?'

'I think you cannot be too careful about that kind of thing, Brynhild.'

'Well, I won't go to early service again then, when you're away, unless there is some one to chaperone me.'

'What do you mean?' he asked unpleasantly.

'I mean,' she said, 'that it seems something like a solemn farce, when the congregation consists of one person driven there against her will.'

'No one can remain in my house who sets the bad example of not going.'

The very next time that the Vicar went away fishing and Bell was unable to go, when Bryn reached the church just as the clock was on the strike, there was no curate there, so she started walking down towards his lodgings. In a minute or two he made his appearance, flying up the street with his tall hat —James insisted on tall hats—unbrushed, and his coat-tails flying.

Bell and the servants were her slaves. Mr. Lancing might almost be said to worship her. Twice or thrice his sermons had got quite mixed as his eye happened to fall on the beautiful sad face in the Vicarage pew.

'Oh, Miss Avon,' he gasped, 'please don't tell the Vicar I was late.'

'I will if you have the service. I was going to be Irish and say that there is no one there but me.'

'But the bell-ringer?'

'He never stays to service when James is not there to see.'

'And the pew-opener?'

'Oh, she has left her little baby at home all by itself; her husband is at work on week-days. I'll just tell her she can run back to her baby, and that I'll take the keys up to the Vicarage when we are ready—I always do when James is away—and if you won't be offended at my offering, I'll darn your socks for you.'

'Very well, Miss Avon,' said the curate, who would have given her his head on a charger if she had asked for it. 'But may I ask one thing?'

Bryn nodded.

'When you've taken the trouble to get up in time, and are actually at the church, what difference can twenty minutes' service make?'

'It would make me feel so good to have one day without penance.'

'You shock me, Miss Avon.'

'I wish I dared speak to Penthorne about it,' he added to himself thoughtfully; 'what a beautiful character he is blunting.'

Bryn was not afraid of speaking out her mind to James on occasion.

As there was only a chapel of ease at Tole, where

nearly all the population of his parish lay, James was
building a large new church there, at which he meant
to officiate, with the sanction of the Bishop, instead
of at Dunstanbury. He was very anxious that this
church should act as a beacon to draw attention to
what he had done for the diocese. And as the
diocese contains hardly any steeples except the
beautiful spire of its Cathedral, he decided that there
was no better way of drawing attention to the church
than by setting it on a hill, from which it could be
seen by three or four counties, and giving it a most
ambitious steeple. People noticed that he had been
a great deal oftener in Tole since the new church
was building.

'Isabel, love,' he said one day on his return from
Tole, 'the steeple is all but finished. I went up to
the top of the scaffolding to-day and held a beautiful
service of praise.'

'Are you insured, James?' asked Bryn.

'No.'

'Then you ought to be ashamed of yourself.'

This was a new way of regarding the matter, and
he could not but admit that there was something to
be said for it. But in the matter of church-singing,
though he was a far better musician than Bryn in
every way—he had a beautiful ear—she could not
shake him from his adherence to the most unattrac-
tive church-music.

She was a good reader of character, and she saw
at a glance that it would be a fatal error of tactics
for her to take any notice of the mood he was in.
He was the kind of man who not only treads on

worms, but chops them up with a hoe, to show how he would like to treat a snake.

So one Sunday at midday dinner, quietly ignoring the fact that he was looking as black as thunder, she began—

'I have never heard such good singing since I have been here as you had in church this morning.'

'I was perfectly shocked with it,' he replied severely; 'I did not hear a single voice except the choir's. I call that singing for the glory of the organist, and not for the glory of God.'

'Well, I can't help saying that I always feel more religious in a High Church than in a Low Church, though I have no patience with incense or processions or candles on the altar. The music carries me away more, especially the anthem, if it has a fine tenor or treble solo.'

'Such religion is purely sensuous, if not sensual, to use the old expression again.'

'Perhaps you are right. I know I have often felt more reverent when a service was going on at a temple than when I was in church—that must be appealing to the senses.'

'I have no hesitation in calling that idolatry. And that reminds me, Brynhild, that I've had it in my mind for some time to speak to you most seriously on the subject of the idol you keep in your bedroom. I don't mind telling you that Isabel was so disturbed about it, that she made me take a step I had the strongest objection to taking—that of going into your bedroom. There in a most conspicuous position, such as a Roman Catholic would choose for a crucifix, I saw a great idol, and in front of it two little brass candlesticks, two little brass vases with silver flowers in them, and a censer, standing on a very flat table of a very peculiar shape which had apparently been recently used. Your heart cannot be so far darkened, I hope, that you worship an idol.'

Bryn burst out into a fit of delicious merry laughter.

'My poor old Daibutsu, to think of my worshipping you! No, Mr. Inquisitor, I don't worship the Buddha, but he is my link with home and happiness, and I like to keep his temple furniture in front of him, just as it is in front of his original, the most wonderful image in the whole world; and I occasionally burn a little incense in front of him, not to make him feel good, as the Americans would say, but to make me feel as if I was back in dear old Japan. James, if you ever read the works of such a limb of the Evil One as Rudyard Kipling, you would probably not understand what he meant when he wrote—

> If you've heard the East a-calling,
> You won't 'eed nothing else
> But them tinkling temple bells
> And them spicy garlic smells. . . .

But it's desperately real to me. Oh, how often have I groaned—

> Take me somewhere East of Suez. . . .

I won't finish that quotation.'

CHAPTER VII

ONE day a Missionary Bishop arrived at the Vicarage. His coming was rather an event. He was of course to address a meeting on behalf of the Spiritual Necessities of the Solomon Islanders, and with his aid James Penthorne hoped to make a record collection for a country parish. On the one hand, Wiltshire was, as every one knows, a county of great territorial magnates, and moreover they were not a very churchy lot, therefore their pockets had not been tapped to any extent for ecclesiastical purposes; and on the other hand, the fame of the Bishop of New Guinea was of the kind most likely to draw them to the meeting. No living member of the Church of England had made such a mark or done such good work 'in the parts of the unfaithful' as this hero of the school of Kingsley.

A man needed to be a better judge of character than James Penthorne to gauge the Right Rev. Robert Moresby at first sight—a tall, loosely-made man, with a large good-natured nose, and with a ready grin, accompanied by a jolly laugh, which suggested weakness. He was ungainly in his motions, too, and had legs which for their leanness and slight bowedness might have belonged to an Australian bushman—an effect of course heightened by the episcopal gaiters. But there was something in the straightness with which his iron-gray coat hung from square, moderately broad shoulders, indicative of well-trained muscles.

When the Bishop arrived, Isabel, to the Vicar's great annoyance, was out, engaged on some parish business, for, tell it not in Gath, the Bishop had arrived on a bicycle, in company with a travelling tinker whom he had overtaken riding a rusty tricycle (with his paraphernalia for tinkering in an iron box tinkered on to the saddle). The Vicar, too, was busy with the proofs of some printed matter that was to circulate at the meeting, so there was nothing to do but to introduce the Bishop to 'my cousin, a most worldly-minded girl, I am afraid, my Lord.'

'A missionary has to meet all sorts,' replied the Bishop cheerily. He feared neither a fair woman nor a Papuan head-hunter.

The Vicar rang the bell. 'Ask Miss Avon to come here, Bailey.'

'Miss Avon,' said the Bishop. 'I have heard of a Miss Avon; if she is that Miss Avon, what you say may have special significance. My work, you know, Mr. Penthorne, throws me much in the way of men-of-war. When there has been an outrage in New Guinea or the neighbouring islands, a missionary inwardly digested by cannibals or a boat's crew from a labour schooner surprised and murdered, I make it a practice to accompany the man-of-war sent to exact punishment or reparation. The present Admiral never lets a ship go without me. The natives know me and trust me, and if the outrage is the work of their bad men, and not with the authority of the chief, they will generally give the

A JAPANESE MARRIAGE

murderers up ; and thus the wholesale destruction of
life and property and the creation of a universal
hostility to white men is prevented.   On these
expeditions I not only went in the ship, but messed
with the officers in the ward-room, so my acquaintance with naval officers is very large.   Many of
them had been on the Japan station, and few of
these but had something to say about this Miss
Avon—her beauty and her pride, her utter heartless-
ness and her scornful wit.'

'H'm,' said the Vicar, and inwardly congratu-
lated himself on his condemnation of Bryn, who
entered just at that minute, rather 'with her tail
between her legs,' as she would have put it in the
old days.   She never remembered James having
anything nice to say to her when he sent for her.
These summonses were for the most part of the
head-magisterial order.

'The Lord Bishop of New Guinea,' said James,
in his loftiest manner.   'Miss Avon.'

'From Japan?' inquired the Bishop.

Bryn gave him one of her rare old smiles, which
was, however, lost on James, who added, 'Perhaps
his Lordship would like a cup of tea, Brynhild.'

Bryn took it for granted that he had been in
Japan, and was vexed at being caught in one of her
Vicarage frocks.   She did like to look nice before
people who had been to her home, so she made up
her mind to shake off her Vicarage deportment.

So as soon as they were in the drawing-room she
began—

'I'm sure you'd rather have a whisky and
soda.'

323

'Tea, please,' said the Bishop, with a twinkle in his eye. 'I've seen too many people go to the "Happy Valley" before their time to want any whiskies between meals.'

Bryn caught the twinkle in his eye. This and the little bit of Far East slang acted as passwords. She felt that they would be friends.

'I've often heard of you,' he continued. 'When the *Orlando* came down from Hong-Kong, she brought more than one officer wounded by you.'

'I was a beast in those days,' said the girl.

'Beauty and the Beast should be two people,' observed the Bishop.

'I don't know about the beauty,' she replied, rather sadly, 'but I know now that no one has a right to be a beast.'

This much Christianity had taught her.

'Solomon might have said that,' was the Prelate's comment. He made a wild attempt to drink his tea. He only scalded himself. He dreaded hot tea more than a shower of spears. Then he approached what might prove a hostile force with a skilful flank movement.

'I won't ask you about the Church in Japan. I daresay it did not interest you much?'

'Indeed, yes.' She did not tell him how much she had given up for the Church, or he might have regarded all his own achievements in risking his life among the cannibals as of small moment compared with her self-denial.

'We knew the Bishop very well, that is to say the Bishop of Kamakura; we often stayed at each other's houses. He stayed with us when he had to

spend the night in Yokohama, and we girls sometimes went to stay with him at Kamakura.'

'You have a sister then?'

'She is dead. She had not been married much
more than a year.'

'Had she a child?'

'Yes,' said Bryn briefly, rather fearful of what he
might say next.

'She has a good *amah* probably. Eastern women
are good to motherless children. Baby won't need
your care for a year or two yet.'

The Bishop, though a master of homely eloquence,
had preached many a sermon with less effect on
humanity. He proceeded, 'Well, tell me about the
Church in Japan.'

Bryn told him about the compact little congrega-
tions of English at Yokohama and Kobe; how faithfully they kept up Church traditions and festivals;
how people enjoyed the ministrations of the religion
of their forefathers in that distant land. She told
him so naïvely that he said—

'You're a native of Japan, or were taken there
very young?'

'Yes. I am a Jap. How do you know?'

'Because you talk of the Church as people talk
of a foreign land. We have only one eye for what
is familiar to us. I am so interested in what you
tell me. I don't know that any one has ever told me
about the spiritual life of the English themselves in
Japan. Missionary as I am, it is almost more
interesting to me than the conversion of the
Japanese.'

Bryn smiled.

'Why are you smiling? Don't you take any interest in the conversion of the Japanese?'

'I know them too well. What is the good of trying to convert a Japanese? He has two natural religions to start with, and generally uses both.'

'Really?'

'Yes, the poor ones. The educated ones are as irreligious as they say educated Italians are.'

'Well, how do the poor ones manage?'

'We always say that they live *Shinto* and die *Buddha*, which means practically that they have hardly any religion at all till they die, for *Shinto* doesn't amount to much more than a canonisation of the living Emperor and their dead ancestors, though they generally have a little shrine to one or more of the gods of Wealth; the *Shinto* priests hardly worry their flocks at all.'

'That's rather an odd expression to apply to the ministers of a religion, is it not? We are taught to look at the priest as the shepherd who keeps the wolves from worrying the flock,' said the Bishop, with one of his really rather silly grins, which belied the strong man so.

'I suppose it depends whether the flock belongs to yourself or to the enemy, though I think the flock sometimes hates the dog almost as much as the wolf.'

'I'm sure of it, though we of the Church of England have the name of being less dictatorial to our flocks than some ministers, the Roman Catholic or the Calvinist, for instance.'

It was Bryn's turn to say 'H'm' now, but she did not.

'And the Buddhists?' said the Bishop.

'Oh, that's largely a matter of politics. The adherents of the *Shogun*, who was overthrown in the revolution, make a good deal of fuss over Buddhism, and the Buddhist Church, which was disestablished by the triumphant Mikado, makes a good deal of fuss over the Tokugawa anniversaries. With the average Jap, Buddhism begins and ends with cremation.'

'Christianity might come in very well, then?'

'In at one ear and out of the other, I'm afraid. People talk of the unretentive American mind, but that's a joke to the butterfly attention of the Japanese. Do you play chess, Dr. Moresby?'

'Not a D.D., I'm afraid. My naval chums always call me simply "Bishop."'

'Then, Bishop, do you play chess?'

'I just know the moves.'

'Well, that's just about as much as the Japanese wishes to know of anything except the warlike and scientific appliances of the West.'

'Am I to draw a deduction?'

'I think there are more or less earnest believers among the two hundred and fifty thousand alleged Christians.'

'It is very sad,' said the Bishop. 'The reports from Japan read so very hopefully.'

'I think there ought to be some hope if——'

'If what? said the Bishop.

'If all Christians were allowed to dress like the parsons of the Church of England. The Japs have taken to yellow boots and *Pearl Derbies*—oh no, I forgot, that's American—white felt hats. I think it might draw quite well if all Christians wore chokers and shiny black dog-collar coats.'

The Bishop smiled. 'Do the Japanese only play at Christianity then, as they play at European fashions ? '

'Oh no; Christianity is a business with them. It's the cheapest way of learning English. No one can hope to be a waiter at a hotel run in the foreign style, or even a higher railway official, unless he can talk a few words of English. The Japanese are quite as bad as the Chinese in this particular dishonesty to the missionaries. You know that rather blasphemous story about the would - be Chinese convert ? '

'No,' said the Bishop, looking grave.

'May I tell it to you? I disapprove of its irreverence as sincerely as you will, but it really is so illustrative.'

'Subject to this protestation, I think you may.'

'Well, a missionary missed a very promising Chinese convert from his Sunday School. Meeting Ah Ching, he asked him the reason of his absenting himself. " *Me not coming any more,*" said Ah Ching ; " *me savee enough Ing-il-is—me no care about Amelikan man Jesus Ki-list !* " The Chinese, you know, Bishop, always look upon our Saviour as an American, because they cannot understand an American running anything that is not *naytional.*'

'Straws show which way the wind blows,' sighed the Bishop. 'I have heard what you say about Japanese Christianity before ; that even the Chinese, who will hardly listen to a missionary, is a more hopeful subject than the Japanese, who will dabble in anything, only to throw it aside when the next novelty offers itself to his notice; but I am thankful to be able to adduce one instance to the contrary. Did you know that when the religious persecutions were started, soon after the beginning of the present reign in Japan, there were found in villages near Nagasaki a few thousand Christians whose faith had survived the terrible persecutions of the seventeenth century,—when so many thousands were thrown into the sea off Pappenberg,—and the intervening couple of centuries without any communication with Europe?'

'No, it's the first time I have heard anything about it.'

'They were Roman Catholics, of course,' said the Bishop. 'I am afraid they understand Asiatics better than we do. Protestantism is the creed of the robust. My Papuans are much better hands at it. What splendid men the sago-feeders are compared to the rice-feeders!'

Bryn did not understand what he meant exactly, but it sounded all right. She did not know that sago was the staff of life in New Guinea.

While she had been talking to the Bishop about Japan she had forgotten that she was a Penthorne, and had been sunning herself up on the broad inside ledge of the diamond-paned Jacobean window. As she sat up there in graceful *négligé*, aureoled against the light, she seemed to the good Bishop, lately returned from 'the parts of the unfaithful,' not only a very beautiful woman, but a very well-dressed one. Even her Vicarage dresses, in which Bryn was so ashamed of being seen by a 'friend from Japan,' were well cut and well boned, and it was impossible for Bryn to look anything but smart ; she had such a figure, and held herself so royally.

'The transition from the inner man to the outer woman may seem abrupt,' said the Bishop, 'but I must tell you what a pleasure it gives me to be with such a well-dressed woman. My sister has always lived with me, and I have begged her over and over again to dress fashionably ; the girl isn't bad-looking, but she seems unable to understand how immensely a woman's influence for good depends on her dressing well. A man who would laugh at a Salvation Army lass, will copy like a monkey a woman who is a duchess or looks as if she ought to be a duchess. But though I have new dresses out from England constantly for my sister, she always forgets to put them on, and goes about in a blowsy blouse and such a skirt ! In New Guinea it really doesn't matter so much, because it's about the only skirt on an island that would make a very fair continent. But we have been in places where the sight of a well-dressed woman would have policed a pretty big settlement of wild Englishmen, who had known better days. You have no idea of the moral power of dress.'

'James Penthorne hasn't. He won't let me wear any of my own dresses. This is only a disguise I bought for playing the hypocrite in the parish.'

To Bryn the Bishop merely opened his eyes, but to himself he added that James Penthorne did not know the A B C of human nature, even if he were not one of the stumbling-blocks alluded to in the Gospel.

The Bishop—adored by the scores of naval officers, the hundreds of sailors, the thousands of savages, with whom he spent his busy useful life, for his simple piety and humanity, his dauntless courage, his extraordinary strength, activity, and handiness— was so accustomed to utilising everything, beauty, recklessness, what not, for the glory of God, that he could not understand a Pharisee deciding with mental eyes, as narrow and oblique as a Chinaman's, what God should be allowed to use.

The Vicar, when he joined them, said in his deprecatory way, 'I am sorry to have had to leave your lordship so long to my cousin.'

Bryn bolted.

'Don't apologise,' said the Bishop. 'I have learnt a lesson. You know what I told you I had heard about her. I shall never listen to evil of any one again.'

CHAPTER VIII

'I HOPE you will let me have a quiet evening after my journey,' the Bishop had written—'after so many years in the Bush, railway travel takes it out of me.'

Accordingly, the Vicarage party at supper consisted only of the Penthornes, the curate, and Bryn. James, of course, talked at the Bishop, who occupied one side of the table, so as to be equidistant between him and his wife, Bryn and Mr. Lancing sitting opposite him. The Bishop had little idea of the drift of the pious sentiments, the well-turned sentences and ecclesiastical judiciousness which poured forth in a placid, unbroken stream, like the summing-up of a judge in a long equity case.

After supper he invited the Bishop to join him in the pipe, of which he made such a parade, to show that he had a redeeming vice,—he was shrewd enough in some things. The Bishop's tongue was unloosed.

'What a charming woman your cousin is! It is a great pleasure to any one who lives in savage lands, as I do, to have a talk with such an elegant woman.'

'My poor cousin,' said James, with a suspicion of groan in his voice and a half turn of the white in his eyes, 'is so fond of dress, poor girl; she has been brought up in very worldly surroundings.'

'Well,' said the Bishop, 'I must say that I was never so agreeably surprised in any one after what I had heard from my naval friends. She seems to me absolutely unaffected, a high-spirited, morally-courageous sort of woman, with heaps of potential good in her.'

'I think you are mistaken, my lord; I have taken a great deal of pains with her since she has been with us, and so has my dear wife, but at the bottom I fear she is utterly godless, a vain woman, fretting after the pomps of her former life.'

'A little vanity isn't a bad thing,' said the Bishop. 'Tastefully-dressed women have such an influence on young men. I have always thought women helpers could do much better work if they were more attractive; even Sunday School boys are amenable to such influences.'

James grunted; it came unpleasantly into his recollection that his wife had mentioned a marked improvement in the behaviour of the biggest boys at the Tole Sunday Schools since Bryn had accompanied her.

The Bishop glided on, unconscious of the very thin ice over which he was passing. 'I have had many a tilt at my own sister on this subject; I have had boxes and boxes of the most attractive clothes sent out to us in New Guinea, but I am sorry to say that she is hopeless, and that the clothes generally remain in the boxes until they are mildewed, when they are given to native converts.'

'If you were not my spiritual superior, my lord ——'

'Call me Bishop—colonial bishops are not lords, you know.'

'I was going to say, Bishop, that I'm unwilling to think that you attach so much importance to these adventitious aids. I think in these dark days the Church needs to fall back on the simple habits of its Founder.'

'I am sorry to have implied that I cared anything about the worldliness of clothes,' said the Bishop drily; and James, feeling that they had different ideas about the Balm in Gilead, suggested that they should join the ladies.

After the Bishop had said a few words to his hostess she was called out on some parish business; he naturally crossed the room and sat down by Bryn, because he and James had come up to escape each other. In less than five minutes, she said to herself, 'James has been gassing to the Bishop.'

Conversation hung fire a little at first. At last Bryn, angry at what she considered the Bishop's secession, said that she thought all missions were wrong except of course those to Fetish-worshippers and savages who had absolutely no idea of religion at all, and cannibals,—this being by way of a little sop to the Bishop.

'I'm afraid I can't agree with you, Miss Avon. I think the idea of burrowing out the best points in a religion like Buddhism, and finding a common ground in his own religion with Christianity for a native convert to start on, is most fascinating, and I very much regret that my work has never been cast among nations with civilised religions of their own.'

'I think it's absolutely wrong,' said Bryn, 'to try and convert to Christianity nations which have civilised religions of their own efficacious for untold centuries ; to endeavour to replace their ancient faith with various cheap kinds of Christianity. I am referring, of course, to the self-ordained Nonconformists of the small sects,' she added out of courtesy. 'The Japs really are very funny about it : they suggest that all these different kinds of Christians should start by holding a conference and deciding which is the true form of Christianity. Then they might perhaps adopt the successful form of Christianity as a national religion for Japan.'

James waited for the Bishop to smite her like Dathan and Abiram, but seeing him waiting in calm strength to brush away arguments not seriously advanced, he got up angrily and left the room.

'We have heard all these idle stories before, Bryn-

hild, and I have shown you their futility ; it is neither
ladylike nor Christian of you to repeat them to the
Bishop.'

This ebullition inclined the Bishop's heart towards
Bryn again after her somewhat ungracious remarks.

'It pains me to hear you talking in that strain,'
he said ; 'I could not help asking myself sometimes
if there was not a grain of truth in what you were
saying about disturbing a man's faith in a civilised
religion which has guided his nation to happiness for
hundreds of years ; but I thought you were talking
a little flippantly, a little, if I may say so, to show
off, Miss Avon.'

'I was,' said Bryn penitently.

'I can see that your cousin calls up the spirit of
resistance in you,' he said in excuse for her ; 'it is
astonishing how much harm a good man can do.'

Bryn felt inclined to say, 'Talk of the Devil,' for
at that moment she heard her cousin's saintly tread
at the door.

'I've brought you your candle, Bishop. I understood you to say that you wished to retire early so
as to prepare what you are to give us to-morrow.'

Bryn understood her cousin not to wish them to
have another *tête-à-tête*. He could hardly have got
to the sideboard on which the candles were arranged
and back again in shorter time.

'Good-night, Miss Avon,' said the Bishop, in a
tone of fully-restored sympathy.

'I am going to put the lights out, Brynhild,' said
James.

CHAPTER IX

GOOD form in the mind of the Rev. James Penthorne
occupied a place certainly not second to Christianity,
though it stopped dead at a certain point, where his
whine about Christianity began.

And he had given much thought to making the
Church Missionary Society meeting at Dunstanbury-
cum-Tole the record parish meeting of that ancient,
useful and universal Society.

There must be a lunch of course. The Bishop of
New Guinea was staying in the house, and he had
a very important appetite ; and the Bishop of the
Diocese was coming from a distance to be present,
as was the Archdeacon, whom James loved as Ahab
loved Elijah, and various other church dignitaries.
These all wanted feeding ; eminent laymen would
probably have rather fed themselves ; for the Vicarage table had too much of the *prisca virtus* about it.
But it was important that they should meet the brace
of Bishops at lunch, because lunch being at 1.30, and
the meeting at 3, they could hardly skip the meeting
with any decency if they came to the lunch ; and to
the meeting alone they might forget to come.

The preparations were managed with great adroit-
ness. First went out the invitations to meet the
Lord Bishop of the Diocese and the Missionary
Bishop of New Guinea on printed cards. With these
cards went notes explaining to the wives of the
Wiltshire peers and squires that the Bishop of New

Guinea was the celebrated Bishop Morcsby, whose
coolness and heroism had so often been the theme
of the *Times* telegrams about the Cannibal Islands.
When these invitations had all been answered,
notices were sent forth broadcast about the meeting for the Church Missionary Society at 3 o'clock
on the same day, at which the Bishop of New Guinea
would deliver an address.

There was no one whose acceptance gave James
Penthorne a greater thrill of satisfaction than Lord
Romney's. Lord Romney was the richest man in
the county. As the youngest steward of the Jockey
Club he was leader of the sporting set, which in a
grass country is of course *the* set, and he was known
to be well disposed to the Church, though he had
hitherto been indolent about giving it much attendance.

Living near him, and knowing him personally,
James Penthorne had often angled for him, but so
far without success, so he was almost surprised when
he received acceptances from Lord Romney and his
mother. The explanation being that Lord Romney had
accidentally learned Bryn's presence at Dunstanbury
Vicarage from his chaplain, who was also Rector of
Landguard. The Rector, who of course knew that
his noble patron had visited Japan, asked him if he
had met while he was there the beautiful girl, a
Miss Avon, who had recently come to live with the
Vicar of Dunstanbury.

The luncheon offered a favourable opportunity of
renewing her acquaintance. When the Romneys
arrived, fairly early, Bryn was talking to her Bishop
and one or two other people. James, who had not the

slightest inkling of Lord Romney's ever having met Bryn, introduced the young peer to the whole group with an air which showed that the only introduction which he was intended to follow up was that to the Bishop, and himself drew Bryn away to prevent her interfering with the scheme ; so the young lord simply bowed to her and awaited a more favourable opportunity for a talk.   At lunch Bryn was given the Archdeacon of Combe, whom James hated as a drag on hierarchical progress.   In spite of his faults, he was a better churchman than the Archdeacon, a county parson of the old school, who regarded church organisation as a development of the caucus, and being head of one of the great territorial families (by the shipwreck of his brother with all his family) had great power in resisting innovations.   The Archdeacon was a good Christian, and in his plain way had a good deal of shrewdness, and some wit.   James always felt that he was the ship and the Archdeacon the rock, and this did not add to his love for the Venerable Aubrey Long.

He was watching his cousin like a cat ; Bishop Moresby's pleasure in her society had put so much heart into her that she seemed to have entirely forgotten the Vicarage etiquette and deportment, in which he had so strictly been disciplining her for the past six months.   She was laughing and chatting with the Archdeacon like an ordinary leader of society.   (In James's eyes a leader of society could do no wrong if it was not actionable in a divorce court.)

By the constant laugh on his hearty red face the Archdeacon seemed to have been very well amused by Bryn.   And more than once the Bishop of New

Guinea, who was sitting within earshot, had joined in
with his rather brainless laugh.

At last James's opportunity arrived. During a
sudden lull in the general conversation every one
heard his cousin reply to an argument of the Venerable Archdeacon of Combe, 'You're giving yourself
away.'

James grew purple with dignity and rage, real or
assumed.

'Go to your room, Brynhild,' he almost hissed.
'You do not know how to behave either like a lady
or like a Christian.'

Bryn, mortified beyond description, with flaming
cheeks and proud, rebellious head, marched out of
the dining-room.

'You were too hard on her, Mr. Penthorne,' said
the Archdeacon. 'I am sure Miss Avon said nothing
to justify the humiliation of sending a grown-up
young lady to her room, especially before company.'

'You must allow me to know better for once,
my dear Archdeacon,' said the Vicar, with restored
suavity. 'It is a question of discipline, and I have
had great difficulty in disciplining my cousin. She
had the misfortune to be brought up in Japan, you
see, so I have to treat her as a child still. If we
had had the bringing up of her, of course such a
thing as her unladylike and unchristian behaviour to
you would never have happened, so there would have
been no occasion for an act of discipline. I am a
strict disciplinarian, a strict disciplinarian.'

It is not Christian of a bishop to wish to thrash
a man, much less a clergyman, so Bishop Moresby's
feelings have to pass unrecorded.

Bryn went to her room, tore off the Vicarage dress made for her in Bath so impatiently that the buttons and button-holes were decimated, took down her plainly-arranged hair and did it up in the very latest fashion, and then proceeded to array herself with great care as smartly and daringly as her wardrobe permitted. The hat she selected no one less beautiful and aristocratic-looking could have ventured to put on her head, though on her its orchids, imitated at a fabulous expense, were *chic* to the last degree. The dress was a rich, soft Japanese brocade, light as a surah, pure white (she knew she looked best in pure white), except for the glorious old lace with which it was so prodigally and tastefully draped ; and she took special delight in unlacing the thick country boots she had been wearing as the only thing in her possession austere enough for the Rev. James's pharisaical susceptibilities, and slipping her beautiful feet into her most delicate slippers and stockings. Then, fitting on with great care her most particular gloves, and a diamond bangle (the diamond crescent at her throat quite threw the one the Dowager Lady Romney was wearing into the shade), she picked up the costly parasol which matched her dress and rustled leisurely downstairs. The company, she could hear by the rattle of the coffee cups, were in the drawing-room, and she saw by the hall clock that the meeting would begin in a few minutes. There was no time to be lost. Her amiable cousin was talking in his most grandiose way to the Bishop of the diocese and Lord Romney, who was fidgeting with his moustache in his endeavour to look interested. Bryn walked straight up to the peer—Bryn whom he had seen but three-quarters of an hour ago sent out of the room in disgrace, and in the dress almost of a poor relation. And here was the old Bryn, wearing the very dress in which he had seen her last in Japan. (She had kept it for the lace originally, and afterwards because her loss of income compelled her to retrench.)

'Romney,' said Bryn, exactly in the old supercilious way, which he remembered so well at Netheravon, 'I'm sick of this ; take me into the garden.'

He could have killed her as easily as refused her in that dress with its tender memories ; and as he had been afraid that he was not going to have his talk with her at all, he had been too *ennuyé* for words before she came up.

His face positively beamed with pleasure as he offered her his arm, and she swept out through the assembled company with the air of a duchess. Bryn had dealt her blow with particular cruelty and cleverness. Lord Romney's presence at the meeting was to have been the great *coup*. It was such a good example, James said ; and it was for this reason that he had been trying to entangle the Bishop of the diocese and the young peer in a conversation which they could not keep up alone, just as Bryn made her appearance. And now it looked very much as if they were not going to have his lordship, who had simply accepted the invitation to lunch to learn how to see more of Bryn, and had not in any way pledged himself to attend the meeting.

And Bryn took very good care that he did not attend the meeting.

The moment they sat down ;—she had led him to

a most secluded seat, for she felt that that afternoon she must taste the sweets of power to wipe out that humiliation,—she said—

'Lord Romney, I want you to give me a promise.'

'Anything you like.'

'Promise me not to give one sixpence to the collection which they're going to make to-day.'

'Of course, I promise; but shan't I look rather mean?'

Bryn thought a minute. 'Write a letter to Bishop Moresby, if you don't see him before he goes away. Tell him that you didn't care to subscribe to James's collection, but that you would be glad if he would accept the enclosed cheque for the special use of his own diocese. I should like you to pay the compliment to the Bishop, he's such a splendid fellow.'

'Yes, that's fine. I'd like to jockey Penthorne, too, for—you know what. I promise.

'And now, Miss Avon, tell me how long have you been here?' he asked. He was simply devouring her with his eyes; his feelings had certainly not changed.

'Let me see—the best part of a year.'

'And why haven't you let me know? You are almost within the boundaries of Landguard, though the mansion house is five miles off.'

'Frankly, because I am no longer an heiress, but a girl with ever such a little income of her own, who has to make or save money for a living. You know how proud I am. I did not choose to meet you in a subordinate position. I know enough now, since I have been in England, to be aware that if you

were the usual kind of lord, and not yourself, however cordial you might have been in Japan, you
would have turned up your nose at me when you
were back with your own womenkind, even if I were
still the heiress I used to be. And I have my pride
left if I have nothing else, though sometimes I think
that I have lost that too when I put up with the
things I endure at the hands of my cousin.'

'Your cousin is a very Low Churchman, a Plymouth Brother, or a Bible Christian, or something of
that sort, isn't he?'

'He's a beastly Christian,' said the girl viciously.
'He does nothing but "do good" from morning to
night. And he does make people jolly miserable
with it.'

'Where does the good come in?'

She shrugged her shoulders.

'I didn't mean good, I meant right, righteousness
or something.

'He does what he considers his own duty, and
makes everybody else do what he considers theirs.'

'For instance.'

'Oh well, take going to church. I don't mean
myself only. I have to go in every time the door is
open, until Providence inspires him to have it shut;
but other people who might have souls that they
could call their own, and at any rate don't meet
their jailer at every meal . . .'

'Well, how does he make them go? I'm glad
to say he's not my chaplain, you know.'

'I don't believe a creature would go to his dull
church unless he hounded them in. But they'd a
deal rather go to church on Sunday than have

him calling on Monday to know why they hadn't been. It's only the poor people I'm talking about, who don't pay for their pews. Of course a man who takes half-a-dozen sittings shows by that very fact that he would have gone if he possibly could.'

'You're very bitter, Miss Bryn.'

'So would you be if you'd lived with that Pharisee and Sadducee, and saw him making every person and thing around him miserable with his professional unselfishness. And then the hypocrisy of him. He is always in church from the moment the bell begins to ring, walking up and down among his people, giving them a happy Sunday grin.'

'What I want to know is, why do you put up with it, when you know you have but to say the word to be mistress of Landguard? I'm going to break the promise I made to you at Netheravon. It was meant only for Japan. Won't you marry me, Bryn?'

'I can't,' she said quite firmly, but with a pathos in her voice which was new to him. Now that she knew how unique in a globe-trotter this fidelity was, she felt a good deal touched. Besides, she could not help gloating over the picture of what snobby James, whom she had read like an open book to be the greatest toady that ever lived, would think of Landguard being at her feet; but she never gave a thought to accepting it.

'I'm sure you're very unhappy now. I am willing that you should marry me just to make a convenience of me. I don't ask for love all in a hurry. I mean to earn that afterwards. But in the interval it will make me infinitely proud and happy that you are my wife.'

'I could love you quite well enough to marry you. I'm a different woman from what I was when you last saw me. I know the beauty of man's love now, when it has no taint of passion in it. But I cannot marry you.'

'Why?'

'Well, I can trust you with the reason that no one here in England knows but Bell,' she said, looking into his honest blue eyes, and went on without waiting for his assistance. 'You remember Philip Sandys?'

'Yes. A good chap; I liked him best of all the chaps I met out there. There was no nonsense about him. Didn't he marry your sister?'

Bryn nodded, and her eyes grew moist. 'She is dead.'

'Poor little girl.'

There was a pause, and then he exclaimed, 'Ah, I see; it is Mr. Sandys stands between us?'

Bryn blushed. She was never so beautiful as when she blushed.

'I would very nearly give my soul to marry Philip.'

'Why don't you go to Switzerland or somewhere where they do it?' asked his lordship, utterly forgetful of his own interests for the time being.

'Because it is not right,' said Bryn. 'It's against the prayer-book as well as the law.' But she spoke with much less certainty in her voice than when she had used the same arguments to Philip.

'If the law was changed, would you?'

'I suppose that would alter the prayer-book too. The table of forbidden affinities does not rest upon the Bible.'

'I've always voted against the Bill in the House,' said his lordship; 'but I couldn't vote against it again with your trouble in my mind. Tell me one thing, Miss Avon.'

'What is it?'

'I'm very stupid. But what has all this to do with your living over here in this uncomfortable fashion, instead of happily in Japan?'

'It's like this. When my father died——'

'Is Mr. Avon dead too, then?'

Bryn nodded and went on—'He left his affairs in such a critical state that there was nothing for me to do but to go and live with my sister and her husband, who was fortunately well off. When Mary died I lived on with my brother-in-law so happily till somebody spread a report that—— I can't tell you, Lord Romney.'

She was overcome with shame.

'Do marry me,' he pleaded; 'it is more than ever necessary.'

He looked up and saw that Bryn's eyes were streaming with tears.

'I can't; I love Philip, body, and soul too, I think. I am over here because if I was in Japan I could not restrain myself from marrying him. I could never marry any one else. I thought that, if I gave myself up to a life of good works with my clergyman cousin and his wife, I might in time be able to forget Philip. But he was so good compared to all these good people. Christians are so uncharitable—I mean professional Christians, of course —that I am beginning to doubt the efficacy of works which are dragged down by such a faith.'

She was getting a little beyond Lord Romney's depth. He could understand that she would have liked to marry Philip, if it had not been wrong, and that she dared not stay in Japan lest she should be tempted into marrying him. But when she tried to hint that the calculating hypocrisy of James Penthorne made her doubt the value of the religion he expounded on questions of right and wrong, his lordship became fogged. He had never been ill enough to think much about religion.

'Mr. Sandys would have to be very careful about his will,' he sagely remarked. 'The children would have nothing if he died intestate.'

Then seeing by Bryn's scarlet cheeks that he had said the wrong thing, and wishing to see as much as he could of the girl he had lost his heart to, while she was his neighbour, he said, 'I'll get my mother to call on you, if you will let me.'

As Bryn intended to assert her independence belligerently, this was very desirable. So she said; 'Do. You can let your mother know that I shan't be here long, and that I have positively refused to marry you, and then perhaps she won't mind so much.'

'My mother and I never differ,' he said, by his change of tone evidently pained or offended. 'If either desires a thing very much the other gives in. If either objects very much the other gives in. It is a question of whether the desire or the objection is the more earnest. One or other gives in absolutely.'

Bryn liked his change of manner ; he had perhaps been too deferential with her.

'Well, then, if your mother objects mind you give in,' pleaded Bryn frankly.

'My mother will not object; where my heart is concerned she has only one wish.'

Bryn and he rambled round the gardens talking of Japan, till a footman came in with the air of a discoverer on his face. When the servant approached them with his 'Her ladyship says every one is gone, my lord. Shall you soon be ready?' Lord Romney inquired if Bryn would like to come and be introduced to his mother there and then.

When the footman had retired Bryn gave one of her smiles. 'I think I'd rather give Lady Romney the option of calling,' she replied, as they stepped into a maze with high hedges of clipped box, which was their shortest way to the house.

He looked so pained that she added in a soft, grave voice not usual with her, 'It's better.'

With a sudden impulse he took her in his arms. 'May I take a kiss, Bryn?'

'You don't deserve one,' she said, without attempting to extricate herself; 'you ought to have taken it, without asking, as part of the proposal.'

Their lips met lightly two or three times.

'I wanted a kiss from some one I liked, badly,' she said simply, 'or you would have lost it by your timidity. I was so upset by what happened at lunch.'

CHAPTER X

THE guests had all gone, except the Bishop of New Guinea, who was in the study counting the spoils and discussing the proceedings with Mr. Penthorne over a cup of tea.

Bell was having tea upstairs in her own little sitting-room, when Bryn walked in, still blushing a little.

' I had no conception how beautiful you were till this afternoon,' said Bell. ' I wish you could see yourself in the glass now.'

Bryn thought she would rather not. Bell resumed, ' But how could you, Bryn ? '

' How could I what ? '

' Go and dress yourself up like a duchess, and stalk all through those big-wigs and address a man you had never seen till an hour or two before so familiarly.'

' Oh, set your mind at rest about that, Bell. I have known Romney nearly two years, and he has asked me to marry him three times.'

' Well, he certainly ought to know you pretty well,' said Bell, unable to repress a smile ; and she added, ' Why didn't you say anything about this when I took you over Landguard Manor ? '

' I should never have gone at all if I had known it was his before we got there. You remember my asking the footman if Lord Romney was at home when you mentioned his name at the door ? '

'Yes, quite well. I remember thinking it so very funny—not quite good form.'

'Well, if he had been at home I should have run away at full speed, leaving you to deal with the mystification of the footman. I wasn't going to be patronised by Lord Romney in my altered position, after spurning his offers of marriage in the days of my vanity. But as he was safe away in London, I thought it would be rather fun to see all the nice things he had offered me with his hand.'

'Did I introduce you to him again?'

'James did, with a lot of other people, and we just bowed.'

'Before we sat down to lunch had you been talking a lot to him or said anything about having a walk together in the afternoon?'

'I had never opened my lips to him; I was particularly anxious not to. I was meeting him under such different circumstances. We were *the* people in Japan, you know. I simply dreaded explanations.'

'Well, how could you risk being snubbed before all those people?'

'There wasn't much chance of that. For one thing, I believed that Romney was a gentleman, if ever I had met one; for another, don't you know, Bell, if an old lover is still in love with you by the way he looks at you?'

Isabel Penthorne sighed and grew younger.

Presently she began again, 'I'm glad the Bishop of New Guinea is here still to give us a little respite before—before———'

'Before hell begins,' suggested Bryn grimly.

'Well, perhaps that was what I meant,' sighed Mrs. Penthorne, 'though James would almost turn you out of the house if he heard you. I think he'll feel inclined to as it is. Mad won't be the word for it when he comes in. He'll almost devour you.'

Bryn snorted—from amusement or defiance?

'Of course the meeting went off all right. But you had taken away his trump card. It is so seldom that anybody can get Lord Romney to a meeting. If he had not behaved so badly to you at lunch, I should have been wild with you myself. I haven't much except parochial triumphs to live for,' she said bitterly. 'But James was such a brute to you that I was glad to see you hit him back. But I tremble to think what he'll say when he comes in.'

'I'm sure I don't care,' said Bryn, kicking a slipper off savagely. 'I've no use for James.'

Bell picked it up admiringly.

'I never saw such a beautiful thing in my life; but James will think it is only fit for the scarlet woman.'

CHAPTER XI

'ISABEL,' called James, almost in his pulpit voice 'come and say good-bye to the Bishop.'

Good taste, of course, prevented the Bishop from asking for the only person in the household whom he particularly wished to see. Since the Vicar's unprovoked attack on her at lunch, he desired a

further conversation with her more than ever. But
he determined to call upon her on a more auspicious
occasion ; she had dropped a hint about leaving the
Penthornes soon.

When he had been duly God-sped, the Vicar
asked—

'Where is Brynhild ? '

'In the morning room. Shall I come with you,
James ? ' asked Bell, summoning up her courage, for
she was afraid that he was going to smite Bryn hip
and thigh.

'No,' he said severely. 'I think what I have to
say to her, I had better say alone.'

'Very well, James,' said Bell meekly—he had
long since squeezed all the resisting power out of her
conscience with his oppressive Christianity.

He marched into the morning room and scanned
Bryn from her haughty head to her haughty feet.
She had been very particular not to abate a jot or
tittle of her rebellious finery.

She stood up by the mantelpiece kicking the
fender defiantly, and watched him taking in every
detail—the fine white straw, so marvellously white,
of her hat, and the daring orchids with which it was
dashed up on one side to show her dazzling fairness
and the superb colour of her hair—the dress-brocade,
the like of which he had never seen, so simple but so
sumptuously elegant (he paid such assiduous attention to dowagers that he knew rare lace when he
saw it)—her slender, high-bred hands, one ungloved,
with three glorious rings flashing on the second
finger—the other, in the delicate buff suede, which
fitted it to such perfection, and was still confined

with the diamond hoop at the wrist, holding upside down, with careless grace, the sumptuous parasol.

The beautiful face wore a look of contemptuous indifference.

James Penthorne was thunderstruck. He had no conception that his cousin was so beautiful. Ever since she had been with them she had been industriously toning down her charms, partly in deference to his prejudices, and partly because she was conscious herself that her Yokohama royalty was unsuitable for parish use.

James Penthorne was in the best set in the county, in the on-sufferance way in which parsons are admitted, and had, therefore, seen plenty of women, lovely, high-bred, dressed in the height of fashion ; but somehow he felt that he had never seen a beautiful woman before. A new spirit entered that swept and garnished house—the Rev. James Penthorne's earthly tenement.

Why should he reject as common and unclean in the religious sense this goodly thing, this exquisite cousin—which the good God had let down before him ? Surely the vision of St. Peter was intended to include this. He did not consider the vision of St. Anthony just then. It had not biblical authority like the other.

Fortunately he had not committed himself since he entered the room, so he went up to the girl with a lie on his lips—a multifold lie :—

'Brynhild, I came to say that I was very sorry for what I did at lunch to-day ; only I was thinking about what the Archdeacon might think. I think so much of him.'

A JAPANESE MARRIAGE

After all he had got off with half a lie less than he expected, because, with regard to the Archdeacon, it was only a lie to Bryn. It was no good trying to deceive heaven as to his sentiments towards his spiritual superior.

Bryn was very much mollified. It was the first time she had seen James Penthorne exhibit a spark of humanity, but she said, quite civilly—

'I don't think any gentleman has any business to speak to a lady like that.'

'I know it. I can only say again I am sorry. Will you be friends?' he said, advancing and taking her right hand.'

'Very well.'

All might have been patched up, and Bryn gone on living at Dunstanbury indefinitely, if the fates had not been kind to their favourite—Philip—who had with that one exception treated them with such tact.

The caressing warmth and sybarite delicacy of that little gloved hand maddened James Penthorne, and in an evil moment he kissed his cousin.

Bryn's soul revolted, but it flashed through her mind that he was her cousin—her only blood relation in the world—and that it was hard to repulse him, when she had, only an hour before, submitted to Lord Romney. How strange it was that in this one afternoon she should have been kissed by the only two men who had ever kissed her except her father and Philip! That glove, so cunningly fitted, so delicate, had sent fire through his veins, but it was nothing to the unresponded kiss. The reaction from twenty years of priestly cant swept over him like a tidal wave.

354

CHAPTER XII

IT was about sunset, and a beautiful day in early summer. Philip was walking in his garden on the Bluff, which he often visited now. He found that the garden with the gentle jealousy of nature was gradually changing from the garden Bryn had known. And it had been the hobby of his leisure hours to try and restore it to the exact *status quo*.

If the weather was suitable he always took the baby Bryn with him. The child, like her mother, had the great absorbing love for Philip, such as a dog has for the owner who will make a friend of him, and loved nothing better than to be carried round by her father when he was directing the Japanese gardeners, or to play round when he was gardening himself.

His *rôle* in gardening was principally destructive, removing effects which had not been there in his sister-in-law's time. In that soft, well-watered climate, vegetable intruders grow up like beanstalks. If he had wished to make any constructive alterations he would have left it to his gardeners. In the bringing up and training of plants he knew that the Japanese have no equals. Flowers are intelligent beings in their hands.

Just now he was standing by the little lily-pond in which the first lotus was opening its great white crown. The *amah* was away having her tea, and Mary Brynhild, who was always called by her aunt's pet name for the pleasure it gave him in using the word, was peeping through the gray stone balustrade at the lazy antics of a tortoise, which was trying to establish itself on one of the broad lily-pads. This balustrade, ancient and mossy, had been one of Phil's purchases while bargain-hunting with his sister-in-law at Kamakura. It was in the garden of a poor Japanese, who had established himself in one of the many ruined monasteries of the Hojo capital, and though it enclosed a tortoise pond nearly twenty feet square, its owner by prescription considered himself liberally paid for it—including taking it down, trucking the long ten miles to Yokohama, and re-erecting it—by a five-dollar note, worth about fifteen shillings English.

The delighted vendor, moreover, as soon as Philip's pond was ready, brought some of the lotus roots which had grown in the original pond as a *buonamano*, with which the courtly Oriental down to the very lowest likes to conclude a transaction of any importance. Philip's return to him was an old hat —size does not signify to a Japanese. The money value of the plants he gave to the little boy who brought them from Kamakura, and planted them with the certainty of an experienced gardener.

It was a lovely old balustrade, with the straight, flat, elegant shafts, shaped like slender beams, which the Japanese substitute for the sausage-shaped balustrades (of plaster) used for London villa door-steps.

Philip was leaning over it to-day with special pride, because this was the first time that the trans-planted lotus had flowered, and because some one, now so far away, had been so enthusiastic in the laying out of this lily-pond.

'Look, Bryn,' he called excitedly, 'the lotus is out at last.' Of course he knew that his little two-year-old daughter would not understand; only sometimes he could not help addressing a remark to her that was intended for the other Bryn.

'And I am here to see it. It is an omen.'

When that long-missed music fell upon his ear, his heart gave a wild bound. Then he felt deadly sick and almost fainted — all in a fraction of a minute.

There was the real Bryn, beautiful, smiling, more superb than ever in the latest London fashion.

'I have come back to you, Phil, for ever, and you must take a kiss very quickly, because I want you to have the first, and I want to devour that dear delightful baby, playing like any other little Jap round the *Kame-ido* (tortoise-well). You see I haven't forgotten my native——'

That sentence was never finished. Bryn was quite breathless when she stooped to pick up the baby, who, *more Japonico*, received her attentions without the least alarm or embarrassment.

'Now, Bryn,' said Philip, sitting down on the flat rim of the balustrade, on which, regardless of her wonderful frock, she had seated herself to play with her namesake, 'give me part of your attention.'

She happened to notice the stain made by the moss on the delicate tint of her glove as she gave him one hand. She made a little *moue*, but laughed it away.

'What does it matter? They'll all get damp

spots in a week in dear old Japan. What is it,
Phil?'

'How did you drop down from heaven?

'I'm Miss Jones of London, who came off the P.
and O. steamer twenty minutes or half an hour ago
—who has left all her keys with little Ichi-da, the
head of the Yokohama Customs, who was in love
with her before she went away, so as to come straight
home without wasting a single precious minute.'

'It's a wonder you found me here.'

'Explain, Mr. Mystery. Do you spend all night
at the office now?'

He had not mentioned it in his letters, and had
pledged his friends not to. He did not answer now.
The *amah* came out just at that moment, and for
once forgot the ceremonious etiquette of Japanese
servants. With a cry of 'Bryn San' she scuffed
back into the house to break the good news to Otori-
san and Taro.

Perhaps, too, she wanted to receive her mistress
on the threshold. For when Phil and Bryn, leading
the toddling little Bryn, reached the house a few
seconds later, there were Taro and Otori-san and
the *amah* in a row on the gravel outside the front
door, bowing and rubbing their knees together, and
drawing in their breath like the *mousmees* in a tea-
house, with gladness shining out of their brown faces.

Bryn greeted them in Japanese with the full
etiquette of a mistress receiving the congratulations
of her servants on some auspicious occasion, and
then, telling the *amah* to take the baby, passed with
Philip through the dining-room and drawing-room
into his sanctum. As she passed through the rooms

her quick eye noted the withered flowers in the vases, the very vases she had filled the day before she went, the very vases standing as it seemed in the very places. Looking more carefully she saw that the ink-bottles were dry and Philip's writing-table bare.

She flew up to her bedroom. Philip followed her as far as the door, which led from her boudoir into her bedroom.

The tiniest trifle was yet on her dressing-table as she was wont to arrange it. She flung the wardrobe open. Every dress she had not taken with her was hanging in its place. She came into the boudoir ; the afternoon tea-service was on its little table, washed and spick, just waiting for the teapot. And then she felt certain of the truth, and buried a weeping face against his shoulder, crying, ' God forgive me, Philip! It would have been better that what they said should have been true than this !'

' The loveliest thing in the world,' he said, ' is waking up from a bad dream, and knowing that it was only a dream.'

' It was only a dream,' said Bryn, breaking from her tears into one of her incomparable smiles, ' and I won't give you any more dreams.' And then, so as not to break down afresh, she put into playful words the question—

' You've never been home since I left, you bad boy ?'

' I hadn't the heart, Bryn. We've been living over the *godown* ever since the morning you left. I wanted this house to be just as you remembered it. And do you know, Bryn, it's only because it's the hardest thing in the world to make gardens stay as they are in these sub-tropical places that I'm up here now. Otherwise Miss Jones of London would have come and found only a house, not a home, at 70A Bluff—and why Miss Jones of London?'

'For the same reason that I never said a word about coming in my letters. I wanted to step into your life, not to have crimson baize spread over everything for the princess's or prodigal's return. You follow? I just planned to come in exactly as I came, for you to turn round and find me there. If you were to look in the *riksha* I left a little way up the road, you'd find a loose China silk wrapper and a very thick veil. I couldn't resist the temptation to come ashore incog. None of the officers knew me; for it was a through boat which had never been to Japan before, and there was not a soul on board who belonged to Japan; they were, every one of them, globe-trotters to whom Miss Jones of London was Miss Jones.'

Then her eyes fell on the tea-things again. She rang the bell.

'What are you ringing for, Bryn?'

'I'm going to give you tea.'

'But it's half-past six.'

'I can't help that. I simply must give you tea as I used to.'

'Well, I don't mind even spoiling my dinner for such an occasion.'

The door opened and Otori-san entered with tea quite ready. With Japanese intuition she had anticipated what Bryn would do.

'I'll let you off with one cup, Phil. I'm going

to drink two or three; but I can take mine very hot, and nothing spoils my dinners.'

'Baby San go home now?' asked the *amah*, who had come to the door with that young lady just behind Otori-san. 'Soon Baby San's bedtime.'

'Home!' said Bryn magnificently, 'this is Baby San's home.'

Then there was a conspiracy in Japanese, which resulted in a shake-down of carefully-aired clothes being made for Baby San, till it was dark enough for Taro to bring up the cradle and its belongings unobserved. It also resulted in the bedding being aired for Philip's and Bryn's bedrooms. Mr. Ichi-da had already received instructions that Bryn's belongings from the ship were not to come up until after nightfall.

Bryn was so delighted to get back to Japan that her old love of a joke was uppermost in her mind, in spite of the short pathetic outburst when she found that the house had never been a home since she left.

'Otori-san, can you give us dinner?'

Otori-san's face fell. '*Yoroshi*,' she said doubtfully; '*dekimas*' (can do), very doubtfully.

The Japanese dislike saying *No*, and you have to infer the negative from the negative tone of the voice. Even the Napoleonic genius of a Japanese servant quailed before the prospect of improvising dinner with no *batterie-de-cuisine*—no sauces, no butter, no dripping, no household stores of any description. The wedded life of Otori-san and Taro was strictly *à la Japonais* in its victualling.

'Bryn,' said Philip, 'you'll have to share a bachelor's dinner at the *godown*.'

A JAPANESE MARRIAGE

'That's all right,' she replied. 'I've had some mighty bad dinners since I saw you last. Silver plate and broken victuals, and not too much of that. But, Phil, I'm like old Spong, I'm going to make conditions, or I won't dine at the *godown*.'

'All right, Bryn ; give us the conditions,' said Phil, laughing.

'Well, somehow or other, by hook or by crook, you must get Punch and Bob and Mr. Dacres here to breakfast to-morrow morning.'

'Here, in this house ? '

'Yes.'

'But how are we to manage about the breakfast ?'

'You have Kano still with you ?'

'How can you ask ? '

'Oh, then, it's quite simple. Kano will manage, if the whole Japanese population of Yokohama has to sit up all night. And now, Phil, I know you're pining for dinner, though you haven't complained because you're so glad to see me again. But we're not going down together, or some one might see us, and smell a rat, and spoil the joke. You go down first, and I'll start a minute later, and come in by the back door in Water Street.'

When she got there Bryn opened the door and passed in. Though she was veiled and her figure was concealed in the ill-fitting yellow wrapper, not for an instant did she deceive the sharp Japanese eyes of the servants. One and all fell into the attitude of salute, murmuring ' *Ohayo*, Bryn San.' Asiatics notice gait and a score of small points which are lost on the average European.

The interview with Kano was quite affecting.

Bryn was glad she had a big order to give him. He saw no difficulty about the breakfast; he would have it ready at 70A, by 9 A.M. Before they sat down to dinner Philip had written three notes, addressed respectively R. Mathdine, Esq., 117 Bluff; C. Dacres, Esq., 117 Bluff; and F. C. Spong, Esq., Consulate of Siam, Bund, to ask them to breakfast with him to-morrow morning at 9 A.M., at his own house, 70A Bluff, and not to expect him that night at the Club, because he had some special business.

The next day being Sunday, there was nothing so very extraordinary in his sudden invitation to breakfast, or his having the breakfast at 70A, which he had not used for a year past. It was natural to breakfast on a summer Sunday morning where there was a garden to loaf about and smoke in afterwards.

Only Bob Mathdine said to himself—perhaps a brain wave was washing faintly up against his mind—'I believe he has heard something of Bryn, and wants to talk it over,' a suspicion he did not communicate to his stable companion.

After dinner Phil told Kano to send up something to drink and smoke at once to 70A, and his night things later on, and to have some one handy to unfasten Bryn's hold-luggage, besides getting up the things for breakfast and what not. You can issue orders wholesale in the East, where servants also are wholesale.

As soon as it was dark he and Bryn went home. The nine o'clock bugling on the ships, the twinkling of the *riksha*-lanterns along the Bund, did not appeal to her as they would have appealed to him after a long absence in England, for she had lived far away back on the Bluff ever since she could remember.

Still they sounded deliciously quaint and restful to her. She wanted to be in the old familiar study at 70A sitting on the arm of Philip's chair, resting her golden head against his cheek, talking or not as the spirit might move her; thence, as the night wore on, with very faint remonstrance, to be drawn down to insatiable lips.

It was late before Bryn, full of unquestioning happiness, climbed up to her old familiar bed after all these stormy nights on sea and land—climbed up slowly, pausing twice to call out more good-nights.

Otori-san was there, with all the boxes Bryn had asked for in the room duly opened, and ready to pull out anything that could be required. And she and Taro were quite ready to resume single life, and their former *rôles* of lady's-maid and *riksha*-boy.

'Japanee marriage no matter much,' said Otori-san.

CHAPTER XIII

THE three friends arrived before nine on the following morning. The invitation had been sufficiently without explanation to pique their curiosity, and make each anxious 'not to get left,' as they would have phrased it.

Kano, who had been taken into confidence, had

given his fellow-servants instructions not to let the cat out, and ushered them into the drawing-room on their arrival, because nothing had been disturbed there. Punctually at nine he threw open the folding-doors and showed Philip in his familiar attitude of rubbing the mantelpiece with the small of his back, and—rinsing the tea-cups out with hot water for the opportunity of drooping her eyes,—Bryn.

As they came into the room she raised them with a half-saucy, half-amused smile, and said, 'Good-morning, Punch; good-morning, Bob; good-morning, Mr. Dacres,' as if she had never been a day away.

For a moment they were staggered, then Bob Mathdine called out, 'No, you don't get off so easily as that, Bryn,' and, rushing forward, nearly wrung her hand off.

'Oh, Bob, stop, and I'll kiss you,' said Bryn; 'you're wringing my hand off.'

'All right,' he said, preparing to take her at her word.

'No, not that way, your forehead.'

'Cheek, Bryn; forehead doesn't count.'

'Well, I don't mind the cheek, as it is the first and last I shall ever give you, and there are so many people present to see that you behave yourself. You'll promise not to try and take more than I give you?'

'I promise.'

She kissed him fairly—in a frank way in which he read his *congé* as a lover.

'Am I going to have one too?' asked Mr. Spong.

Bryn gave him a look which made him say hastily—' I didn't mean to be cheeky, Miss Bryn,' and then she shook hands heartily, as she did with Mr. Dacres.

CHAPTER XIV

ABOUT 10.30 the three friends said they must be going to get ready for church.   In Mr. Spong's case, at any rate, it was obviously an excuse, for he had never been inside a church since he came to Japan, except for a wedding—some one else's.

The genuineness of the declaration was not questioned, whatever doubts Phil and Bryn may have entertained.

' Going to church, Bryn ? ' he asked, as soon as the others had said good-bye.

' No,' she said shortly.

' Why, you used never to miss ; and I have never missed since you were away.   I thought you'd like me to go.'

' I'm glad that you went for my sake, Phil ; but do something else for my sake in the future.'

' Why, Bryn ? ' he asked rather anxiously.

' Oh, because religion's a failure.'

' How do you mean ? '

' Well, you know what I gave up for religion, all that I valued in the world—your love and companionship ? '

He answered her with a look.

'I went to England intending to devote myself
to the works of religion. I found the service cruelly,
brutally hard. My own cousin, my mother's sister's
child, began by praying at me as if I was Jezebel,
because I was not dressed as sinfully—or I suppose I
ought to say Christianly—as his wife, good little
soul that she afterwards turned out to be. Though
I was very hard-up then, as you know, I had new
clothes made in Bath to please him, black and navy
blue ; I had them made plainly enough for a
Quakeress, but because they fitted and had a little
style he raved on. He bullied me if I did not go to
church every morning, and Wednesday, Friday and
Sunday evening, and teach in the Sunday School as
well. I tried to do it all, and tried to do it cheerfully, as a duty.

'Then he fell foul of my vocabulary and my conversation, said I used language not fit for a lady, and
had ideas not fit for a Christian. I meekly improved
myself, and, in obedience to the behests of Christianity, I altered the style of my hair and my walk.
I submitted to being half starved ; that was easy,
because having denied myself the glass of wine at
meals which had become a second nature to me, I
could hardly swallow my food.

'The climax was when he sent me to my room
like a child from a luncheon of nearly twenty people,
including a bishop or two, and several of the higher
clergy, beside the local county big-wigs. Because I
was enjoying myself and had forgotten the snuffling
cant he was instilling into me, I was laughing and
talking naturally. In my excitement I told an
Archdeacon with whom I was talking "not to give

himself away." The Archdeacon didn't seem to
mind, but James overheard it and ordered me to
my room.

'Well, I went; it was his house, and he had the
right to order me out of the dining-room if he wanted
to, but I should not have gone to my room had not
a bright idea struck me—Lord Romney was there.
You remember him, as nice a man as I ever met.
His place, Landguard Manor, is the principal seat in
the county; so of course his presence was a great
catch for the missionary meeting which was to follow
the luncheon. Now Romney, as you know, once
proposed to me—as a matter of fact he has done it
three times—he is very much in love with me, and
though I had never seen him since he left Japan
until that day, and had not exchanged a single word
with him, I felt confident of my power over him.
So I put on the very smartest clothes I possessed,
my handsomest rings, my diamond hoop bracelet,
and that lovely diamond star brooch, far handsomer
than the one my Lord's mother, the Dowager, was
wearing—James regarded jewellery as open profligacy
in a clergyman's family—and rustled downstairs. I
found the company in the drawing-room, walked
through them with great deliberation, straight up to
my Lord, who was being buttonholed to the Bishop
of the diocese by James. "*Romney*," I said, "*I'm
sick of this; take me into the garden.*" And he at
once offered me his arm and off we went, not five
minutes before the meeting began. He was fright-
fully indignant at the way in which I had been
treated, and proposed to me again, as the shortest
way of putting a stop to it. I couldn't resist letting

him propose; it was so lovely after having been snubbed by James for all those months to have the richest lord in the county proposing to me. But I told him that you had my heart, and my soul too, I was afraid, that the only reason I was over in England was that it was wrong to marry you, that I knew I couldn't keep from it if I stayed in Japan, and that my religious scruples were rapidly being overthrown as I saw more and more of the office-life of religion.'

'Oh, Bryn,' said Philip, taking both her hands in his, and regarding her with such eyes, 'how can I show you my gratitude for your thinking of me at such a moment?'

'By listening to what I have to say to the end,' she replied, not shrinking from his gaze, but withdrawing her hands. She needed hands as well as tongue to express what was coming.

'And now, Phil,' she went on, coming up to him coaxingly, 'I want your forgiveness. As he was saying good-bye, Lord Romney drew me to him and begged that he might steal a kiss, and, after my humiliation at lunch and his goodness to me, I wanted a pick-me-up so badly that I let him—the first kiss I yielded to any man except you and my father. Don't scold me, Phil, I told him he deserved to lose it for not taking it without asking. He had just proposed, you know. Are you cross, Phil?'

'How could I scold, dear, when you like me well enough to confess and be scolded?'

'I should think I did. But you have not heard the worst. When he had gone, I went upstairs and had tea with Bell, my cousin, in her boudoir—they have heaps of rooms at the Vicarage. James was in his study with the Colonial Bishop counting out the plunder of the meeting.'

'What did Mrs. Penthorne think of her husband's conduct to you at lunch?'

'She was as disgusted as she dared to be. He had reduced her very nearly to the level of the penny-in-the-slot machine—so disgusted that she forgave me for spoiling their grand *coup* in the parochial meeting line by taking away Lord Romney. But she was in terror of what James would say when the C. B. was off his hands. Presently we heard James in his church-notice voice calling her down to say good-bye to the Bishop. And then I heard him striding upstairs to me.'

'Did you quake in your shoes?'

'Not I, my monkey was up. The little woman was frightened for my sake, and for once summoned up her courage to say that she was coming too. But James squelched her. He came in looking as black as thunder, and I prepared for a pitched battle. We eyed each other for about two minutes, and I kicked the fender to show him what sinfully lovely slippers I had on. He made us observe all sorts of sumptuary laws on that subject. Suddenly with a big effort he told a big, big lie. He said he had come to say that he was very sorry for his behaviour at lunch—that he only did it for the Archdeacon, and so on. And he simply loathes the Archdeacon!'

'What did you say?'

'I told him that no gentleman had any right to treat a lady as he had treated me. He was quite nice about it—he confessed that it was so, and said

that all he could say was that he was sorry, would
I forgive him? I suppose I looked specially pro-
voking;—What is it about a scornful woman that
charms men so? Anyhow, I was so affected by
James's confessing himself in the wrong for the first
time in his great life—it was such a tribute to my
charms—that I forgave him and gave him my hand.
I had a glove on. It was certainly a particularly
nice glove, a most delicate suede, the most clingingly
fitted glove I ever had. He told Bell, and I think
he was telling the truth, that the subtle velvetiness
and clingingness of this glove woke the passion in
him. At all events he kissed me. Can you forgive
me, Phil, twice in one afternoon?'

'Oh, I can forgive you that one quite easily.'

'You may; it made me feel quite sick. But I
didn't see how I could stop him—my only blood
relation, when I had let Lord Romney—how I
hated myself then for letting Romney, especially as
James had just made the *amende honorable* for his
behaviour at lunch. So in a fatal moment—fatal
to us both—I just let him. I hate to tell you what
followed — the coarse embraces, the kisses he
showered on my face, my throat, my gloved hand,
my skirts, my ankles, the very slippers he would
have flung on the fire the day before had I ventured
to wear them. At last something went into his eye
in my struggles, and I escaped.'

The beast!' said Philip; 'oh, if I had him here!'

'Don't be too hard on him, Phil,' said Bryn, with
a pretty shy smile; 'if I'm not mistaken, he's the
best friend you ever had.'

'That dirty hypocrite my friend!'

'Well, that depends.'

'Depends on what?'

'If you still wish to marry me, Phil,' she said, standing before him with a blushing tenderness which no one had ever seen on Bryn Avon's face since she was a little child.

.   .   .   .   .   .

When at last she was able to free herself, she said—

'You didn't wait to hear why he was your best friend.'

'I think I understand,' he replied, 'but you tell me too.'

'Well, James Penthorne shook my faith in our Church's interpretation of Church laws. He was so very good, I may say so offensively good, the apple of his Bishop's eye, the mirror of orthodoxy. To me coming from Japan—Japan, as you, a mere stranger in the land, taught me to understand it—the land which, nearer than all others, has the peace of God; the gentle land, where voices are never raised save by the white Christian ; where all time—a minute, an hour, a day,—is but an unconsidered atom of eternity ; where life is so restful, so full of thankfulness for the beauty of scenes one sees and the beauty of air one feels, that it is almost a religion ; where oneself and one's Japanese servants and the Japanese one deals with are all members of one smiling family. To me, living in an English religious household was just hell. Yes, life itself is a religion in Japan if one is content to live like a flower in a garden. I often feel that a garden is the ideal republic, where rivals have not even the liberty ·

of chess-men, but are limited to the impalpable movements of their own growth, and where the only superiority is superior vitality. But I am wandering. The Church laws, as interpreted by James— and he appeared to be regarded as the most infallible interpreter in the diocese—were often so revolting to my feelings, not to say my common-sense, that a conviction gradually grew upon me that their interpretation of our beautiful religion must be hopelessly warped. Still I could not deny that there was an atmosphere of self-denial. There were so many others like myself giving up what they valued more than anything else in the world because—not the Bible,—but the Prayer-Book, said it was wrong. So I struggled on despairingly, waiting for more light. And the light came out of darkness.

'When the system which he had been expounding for twenty years could not prevent James, our pattern and ensample, who had just left his Bishop, and his wife, from insulting his own cousin in his own house, the earthquake came, and the whole edifice, reared so high on sand, toppled down.

'Of course I decided there and then to leave his house the very next day. As my fury cooled, I took long counsel with myself, reflecting that I had to begin life afresh. I did not go down to the cheerless thing they called supper. Bell sent me some to my room. I had told her as much as I could of what had happened, and, in spite of her entreaties, that I was going. I did not tell how soon; indeed, I had not then made up my mind.

'But as I sat still in the costume which I put on to madden James and command Romney, I saw myself in the cheval glass, just as I had seen myself when last I wore that dress in the old Netheravon days. And I said to myself, "I am a better woman than I was in those days." Why? Because of this professional religious life I have been practising so assiduously this last year? It did not seem so. Besides, I should never have tried it but for one thing, the humanising influence your gentleness had exercised upon me. That, then, was religion—or, at any rate, the rule of life—for all of us, whether we confess it or no, believe in a God—so diversely interpreted.

'Then side by side came into my head the text, "I will arise and go to my Father, and will say unto Him, Father, I have sinned against heaven and before Thee, and am no more worthy to be called Thy son," and the saying "that the devil can quote to serve his own ends." And then I said to myself, "There is only one solid and ultimate fact in the world, and that is Philip's goodness. I will go back to Philip, and if Philip thinks he ought to marry me he shall, and if he thinks I ought to live with him as his sister-in-law, as I used to, I'll just do it. He has been my good genius."

'All that night I packed, and the next morning, before any one was about, I locked my boxes ready for forwarding, and slipped out of the house with only a handbag, leaving a letter for Bell enclosing a cheque for a month's board and lodging. I had my very nicest travelling clothes on, because I was going to fulfil my promise to you of going to your father if I was in trouble.

'When I got to Latchford Towers in the afternoon, I was received like a prodigal daughter ; and I arrived rather like one, carrying my own little bag, for there was no trap at the station. It was strange arriving on foot all the way from Japan!

' "Who shall I say?" said the footman, eyeing me with considerable surprise.

' "Miss Avon."

' "Who do you want to see?" he asked objectingly. He evidently thought by the bag that I meant to sell or steal something.

' "Anybody."

' He went away very unsatisfied with himself for not having shut the door in my face before he left the house at my mercy.

' And then your father came running to the door with a Liverpool evening paper in his hand—he had just come out from the office by the train running the other way—crying "Bryn."

' "Yes, Bryn," I said ; and the footman made me such a handsome apology afterwards.

' "I'll call the girls," your father said.

' "No, please, Mr. Sandys, let me talk to you a little first." And then I told him, very sketchily, what had happened. Having made sure that I was welcome, before I let your father call the girls, I dashed off a note to Bell telling her where I was, and asking her to forward my boxes.

' I got the sweetest little note by return of post, saying that the boxes were on their way, and returning my cheque, which they could not think of accepting. James had torn the signature off to make it valueless, and written across it, "Please destroy this. J. P." Bell overwhelmed me with tender messages from herself, and said that James didn't attempt to palliate his conduct, but that he was very penitent and awfully nice to her, and that he hoped and she hoped that I would try and forgive him.   And I wrote back that I would forgive him if he was nice enough to her, and that she would be the best judge whether I had forgiven him or not.

'The part I liked best about her letter was that it forwarded one from you, one of your own sweet self-effacing letters (except the sad little postscript that you still prayed day and night whenever your thoughts were one moment free, that God might put it into my heart to come back to you), and full of tender solicitudes for me.'   .

'Why were you so glad, little sister?'

'Please don't call me that, Phil.   I love you a different way now, and that word makes the old barriers spring up again——Oh, I was telling you it was such a relief when that four hundred pounds came, quite unexpectedly too, for it both relieved me of the necessity of asking your father to lend me enough money for the passage out, and it gave me three hundred to buy some presents for you and a regular trousseau for myself.   I did so want to have a lot of pretty things to come before you in, dear. For I wanted you to be very much in love with me when I came back, so much in love that I shouldn't care whether I did right or wrong in coming back to you.   And you can scold me as much as you like or send me to the Consulate as a pauper; but I don't believe I have five dollars left of the four hundred pounds.   I just spent every halfpenny that I could spare, because——'

'Because why?'

'Because I'm afraid of England without you, Phil. I don't ever want to go back there till you can go with me.'

'That's a bargain, Bryn. But all you've told me about England as yet is the nasty part, unless I except your quarrel with James Penthorne——'

'Ugh,' she shuddered.

'Now tell me about the nice parts. You saw something of my people?'

'I spent a week in your old home, Philip—only a week, because I was dying to get back to you, and I had to spend a month in London to get a——I can call it a trousseau now. Your father and sisters went with me. It was the height of the season. They took a flat in some mansions looking right over the Park, and we had a most heavenly time. We had horses and carriages galore—Romney's. When I left Dunstanbury so suddenly I had of course to write and tell him not to let his mother call. I just told him vaguely that James had made love to me, and that I was going to stay with your people before going back to Japan; and he wrote me the sweetest letter, begging me to let him know if it was him I was really avoiding. If it was, he promised faithfully not to approach me again—he would be going away to London for the meeting of the House; if it was really not his fault that I was going, he asked me to let him know of my movements till I left England.

'I wrote back, of course, that it had nothing to do with him, and that I should only be too delighted to see him again whenever occasion offered; and a week later I wrote to tell him that I was to spend the rest of my time in London.

'Now I am only human, Phil, horribly human; and I did like having a handsome young lord dangling about after me—in London, especially when we had done with the proposal business, and I had not that bogey hanging over my head if I made myself nice to him.   So when we got to London I asked him to a *tête-à-tête*, and said if he understood once for all that I couldn't marry him, I would see as much of him as ever he liked, because I had your sisters to chaperone me.

He promised, and then he hummed and hawed a little, and finally jerked out that Lady Romney wasn't in London, so that his horses and carriages were at our disposal if we would accept them; one of his grooms would call at nine o'clock every morning for orders.

'And what did you say, Bryn?'

'I said, "Make it eight o'clock.   I shall have six weeks to rest in on board ship, and I mean to make the most of London."

'Well, Romney was just like a tame dog, he took us everywhere himself, except when we told him we were busy—races, up the river, cricket matches, theatre parties, even shopping.   But the time I enjoyed most of all, Phil, was the week I spent at your old home, plaguing them with questions as to what you did when a boy, and examining the things in the dressing-room you used as a study.   All your Oxford things are there.   I *would* sleep in your bedroom, though they wanted to put me in a regular suite—to show me what they can do in English country houses; but I said I thought it much more fun sleeping in your room to see the way the light struck in of a morning, and how much you could hear of the birds, and try and picture you as a boy.'

'They're not boys at Oxford, Bryn.'

'Oh, I beg pardon, men. I forgot to say that Bell came and saw me in London before I started ; and so did James.'

'Had she forgiven him ? '

'Oh dear, yes. Bell was a little brick about it. She was calling him Jim when they called, and she never ventured to do that when I was with them ; I daresay it was rather a relief to her to find that he was human. Perhaps he made the discovery that she was a woman—and a very human little woman she was. He told me all about it one night when we had been to a concert—he drew the line at theatres. There were six of us, so I let him take me home in a hansom, while the others went in the carriage. I thought the poor wretch would like a *tête-a-tête*, so as to have a chance of setting himself straight. Romney raised his eyebrows to know if he should interfere ; I signalled back that it was my wish. I had had time to get sorry for him. I hadn't given him credit for being manly enough to speak about it in the way he did. I was quite glad that I had given him the chance.'

'It was pretty plucky of you.'

'If you only have one relation in the world you may just as well think well of him ; he said Bell had been a pet about it, and that they were most awfully happy now.'

'Well, it certainly does take a very ill wind to blow nobody any good.'

CHAPTER XV

HEARING that Bryn had returned, and was keeping house for Phil again, the Bishop called. After he had taken tea, and recurred more than once to his satisfaction at seeing Bryn back again at 70A, Philip took the opportunity of her having left the room to fetch her sister's baby, to ask the Bishop if he would himself marry them. He felt, of course, that he was asking for an honour, but Bryn and the Bishop were old friends. And he was utterly dumbfounded when the Bishop rejoined, 'Impossible; I could never agree to your marriage with your deceased wife's sister.'

'I know,' said Philip, 'that there is a table tacked on to the very end of the Prayer-Book by King James I., or some other wiseacre, directly in the face of scriptural precedent, to the effect that a man may not marry his wife's sister, and I know that the law of England does not recognise the offspring as legitimate. But on the one hand, Bryn and I are willing to risk public opinion upon the status of our children—which is the only penalty the law attaches; and on the other hand, we did not think that you would consider it necessary to insist upon such a jot and tittle of the rubric — out here *in partibus infidelium !* '

'My dear Sandys,' said the Bishop, 'there is nothing in the world which would give me more satisfaction than to see you married to Miss Avon. It is so conspicuously in the earthly fitness of things. But I have no option in the matter. It is laid down plainly in clause 17 of the Table of Affinities that a man may not marry his wife's sister.'

'It says nothing about a deceased wife's sister?' said Philip, catching at a straw.

'The Prayer-Book does not contemplate bigamy,' said the Bishop rather testily.

'Nor do I,' said Philip, laughing; and the Bishop joined in the laugh, which restored the *entente cordiale*.

'This settlement of English in Japan, of course, in the eyes of the Church as in the eyes of the law, is simply a little piece of England separated by the sea—though there happen to be ten or twelve thousand miles of separating water. Even if I were to marry you, the Consul would declare the marriage illegal.'

'But if we jump on board a China merchant's ship and run down to Australia, there is more than one colony in which the marriage would be perfectly legal.'

'Even there,' said the Bishop, 'the Church does not recognise such marriages.'

'But, my dear Bishop,' said Philip, 'consider the facts of the case—my comparative youth and the remarkable beauty of my sister-in-law. Do you mean to say that—putting all consideration of anything happening in a moment of passion out of the question—it is better for her to live with me, running the risk of such imputations as were cast on her before, than to be married fairly and squarely to me?'

'Referring to the last,' said the Bishop, 'I do certainly, and if you have any doubts as to your ability for continence, it is your duty to separate once more.'

'O God!' groaned Philip.

'Besides,' said the Bishop kindly, 'you told me yourself only a year ago, when you invoked my interference, that your sister-in-law had conscientious scruples.'

'So she had, my lord—but circumstances, in which I had no finger, led her to reconsider these scruples.'

'That is very sad—may I ask what they were?'

Philip was dying to tell the worthy Prelate; it would have been such a practical homily, but he thought of Bryn, and his lips were sealed.

'Then you cannot do it?' was all he said.

'I am afraid not,' replied the Bishop with genuine sorrow, 'and I must tell you that I cannot consent to any of my clergy performing this marriage. Far from sharing your view about what the Church should do *in partibus*, I think that we should take special precautions against relaxing in any way.'

Philip did not answer; he was sitting at the table with his head buried in his hands. Once more the cup was dashed from his lips. How could Bryn go on living with him indefinitely without charges like that, which had driven her into exile, being levelled at her by enemies from time to time?

The Bishop passed out softly; seeing him without Philip, Bryn said good-bye to him hurriedly, and flew to her brother-in-law. She found him in despair. He told her what had happened.

'What are we to do, Bryn?' he groaned. 'Of course we could run down to Australia, whenever I can spare a long enough holiday from business. There would probably be some conditions about residence—very possibly for as much as six months, when we got there—and even then the clergy, and perhaps our Consul here, would not recognise it. We have to look things right in the face, dear; are you prepared to live on with me as we did in the good old days, before slander stole like a serpent into our paradise—running the risk of rumours, and steadily living them down?'

Bryn said nothing.

'Of course,' he continued, when she did not reply, 'we could have Mrs. Plumtree or some one of the kind to chaperone us. That might help.'

Still Bryn said nothing, and Philip was sick with anxiety. 'I don't mind for myself, Bryn,' he said tenderly, 'but you, dear—oh, the Church!' and he ground his teeth.

'Phil,' said Bryn deliberately, and his heart thumped against his ribs as he heard the first sound of her voice. 'There is only one thing to be done.' As he raised his head she was frightened at the tension of his anxiety, and, dreading for his heart, flung her arms round his neck, and sinking on her knees, drew his face to hers.

'I will never leave you,' she said quickly. 'Be assured of this, Phil.'

The look which had frightened her left his face, and he gently raised her to her feet

'There is only one thing to be done,' she repeated, taking his hands in hers, as if she desired their magnetism, and looking him steadily in the eyes.

He waited for her to proceed.

'The only way to escape calumny,' she said, 'is to live together openly as man and wife.'

'Without marriage?'

'Yes. If neither the Bishop nor Consul will marry us.'

'But, Bryn,' he said, turning scarlet at the word, 'people will simply say that you are my mistress.'

'Let them,' she said impatiently: 'I shall know that I am your wife in my conscience, and,' she continued, 'they can call me what they like. Provided that I satisfy you and my own conscience, I do not care a finger's snap for the rest of the world.'

CHAPTER XVI

BOTH the Bishop and the Consul wrote the kindest letters, expressing their genuine regret that their office precluded them from performing such a marriage. The Consul added a postscript, hoping that they would not take such a step without the maturest consideration, and the Bishop called more than once to prevent it by personal entreaty. But he found Bryn even more adamantine than a year before.

'My dear Bishop,' she said, 'I am a daughter of

the Church. It is for you to consider whether you would rather waive a point and marry us, or see us living in a marriage of consent.'

Other friends tried to find a *via media* by getting the ceremony performed by a Nonconformist clergyman. There are all sorts and conditions of them in Japan, and there was little doubt of finding a complacent one—such as he might be. Philip, in his anxiety to save Bryn's good name as he thought, would have clutched at it, but Bryn would not hear of it.

'We don't believe in their teaching,' she said, 'and I should not regard a marriage performed by a chance—perhaps self-ordained—minister of a chance creed as one whit more binding, more sanctified, or more respectable, than a marriage of consent.'

When once Philip had told her with his lips what her own heart told her, that he would take her for better or worse, Church or no Church, law or no law, she had neither doubt nor qualm.

Invitations were issued announcing that the wedding would take place that day week. The Bishop received an invitation like any other friend, with a gentle little note from Bryn to the effect that she hoped that he would change his mind at the last moment and marry them.

With the other invitations a printed letter was sent, setting forth the circumstances of the case, and the probability that the marriage ceremony would consist of no more than a declaration by bride and bridegroom before those assembled, of their intention to live together as man and wife.

Mighty was the discussion that arose. Club bachelors like the three friends of course would go to the wedding. Old friends of Latimer Avon's, many of them fathers of families, seeing that nothing could deter his daughter from taking the law into her own hands, judged that they would be truer to his memory by lending their weight to the ceremony than by denouncing it, and brought their wives and daughters. Americans, as a rule, were charmed with the novelty, and having in some States, such as the highly representative State of New York, absolute freedom in choosing ways of declaring themselves married, saw nothing very irregular. Mrs. Prince, who had no respect for anything except spirit, as well as Mrs. Amory, was active in winning American support. And American support, headed as it was by Minister, Admiral, and Consul, with their respective households, counted for more than half the battle, with English opinion divided. The absent were chiefly the uninvited, such as the Phelpses and the Sparlings.

The wedding was an impressive one. The beautiful bride, anxious of course to accentuate the wedding character of the ceremony, was in full bridal array, and the house was a blaze of white flowers, conspicuous among them the lilium auratum, with its memories of that drive from Yokosuka for bride and bridegroom. How to commence the ceremony might have been a difficulty, but for the zeal of the American minister, who, regardless of the fact that he was the representative of a sister Power, did not see any question of delicacy arise in his taking a prominent part in proceedings regarded as entirely irregular by the representatives of the Power to which the parties concerned belonged.

Arresting the attention of the meeting with the ease of a practised orator, he made a little speech so felicitous as to strip this novel marriage of the least appearance of irregularity.

As the applause which greeted his speech died away, Philip led Bryn forward by the hand, and they said together—

'I, Philip Sandys, and I, Brynhild Avon, call upon you all to witness, before God and man, that we intend to live henceforward as man and wife, as strictly one as if we had been married with the rites of our Church.   And at this last hour, if any one of its clergy is present, and ready to perform those rites, we will be joined by him.'

No clergyman of course was present.   This would apparently have completed the ceremony, for Philip took up the ring, which had lain on a table conspicuous to everybody.   But the American Minister once more stood up, and taking an English prayer-book from his pocket, with the place found, read—

'Philip Sandys, wilt thou have this woman to thy wedded wife, to live together after God's ordinance in the holy estate of matrimony?   Wilt thou love her, honour, and keep her in sickness and in health; and, forsaking all other, keep thee only unto her, so long as ye both shall live?'

And Philip said firmly, 'I will.'

'What did you say your full name was, my dear?' whispered the strange Minister to Bryn.

'Brynhild,' said Mr. Mathdine hushingly.

'Brynhild?   B.R.Y.N.H.I.L.D.?'

'Yes' (very hushingly).

'Brynhild Avon, wilt thou have this man to thy

387

wedded husband, to live together after God's ordinance in the holy estate of matrimony? Wilt thou
obey him, and serve him, love, honour, and keep him
in sickness and in health; and, forsaking all other,
keep thee only unto him, so long as ye both shall
live?'

And Bryn, with a face full of happiness and
blushes, answered in the clear voice which was one
of her charms, 'I will.'

Then came a slight hitch, for he read on—

'Who giveth this woman to be married to this
man?'

There was a chilling pause. Both Mr. Spong and
Mr. Mathdine were rising to their feet, when Bryn
said simply—

'I give myself.'

'I can't make this next part out,' said the American Minister to Philip in an audible whisper; 'what
am I to do?'

'Leave it to us, thanks, we can do the rest.'

With these words he took Bryn's right hand in
his, and began to repeat in an audible voice—

'I, Philip Sandys, take thee, Brynhild Avon, to
my wedded wife, to have and to hold from this day
forward, for better for worse, for richer for poorer, in
sickness and in health, to love and to cherish, till
death us do part, according to God's holy ordinance;
and thereto I plight thee my troth.'

As soon as he repeated the first vow the American Minister 'caught on' again, to use his own
expression, and read the prayer for him to repeat,
and, understanding now what the rubric meant, as
soon as they had loosed hands, and Bryn had taken

Philip's right hand in hers, read out for her to repeat—

' I, Brynhild Avon, take thee, Philip Sandys, to my wedded husband, to have and to hold from this day forward, for better for worse, for richer for poorer, in sickness and in health, to love, cherish, and obey, till death us do part, according to God's holy ordinance ; and thereto I give thee my troth.'

Rather a painful thrill ran through the assemblage as Bryn, in following him, after a moment's hesitation, omitted the words ' *according to God's holy ordinance.*'

It was noted also by such of those present as belonged to the Church of England, that both she and Philip, contrary to the usual custom, repeated their surnames as well as their Christian names.

And then Philip, omitting the earlier ceremonies, simply slipped the ring over Bryn's ' fourth ' finger, saying—

' With this ring I thee wed, and with my body I thee worship, and with all my worldly goods I thee endow. In the name of the Father, and of the Son, and of the Holy Ghost. Amen.'

And the American Minister, laying the prayer-book on the table with a thud, said, in a manful voice, and with the look in his eyes once more which had been there when he crossed the Potomac with his Virginians, while Southern hopes were high—

' Those whom God hath joined together let no man put asunder.' And the room rang with English and American cheers.

. . . . . .

This was the marrying of Bryn Avon.

CHAPTER XVII

BRYN'S courage had carried them to port. It was useless to throw stones at a proceeding which so many of the principal inhabitants of the settlement had acknowledged by their attendance, and which had been celebrated in a way by a man holding such a responsible position as Minister of the United States.

As a matter of fact the clergy were almost the only people who looked askance at the marriage, and they of course were compelled to. Any chance they might have had of emphasising their disapproval was destroyed by the fact of Mr. and Mrs. Sandys being too incensed with the part they had taken to go to church. Until they tried to attend it, they could not be excluded from the communion.

The turn affairs had taken was a great relief to Philip in writing to his father. Nobody guessed that the American Minister's interference was as great a surprise to the bride and bridegroom as to themselves. The newspapers gave a good complexion to affairs for divers motives. In the first place, for all her airs, Bryn had always been the pride of the port ; and since she had been under Philip's influence she had been more conciliatory. To say anything unpleasant about beautiful Bryn almost the moment she had returned to her native shores would have gone against the grain.

In the second place, it was plain business to con-

sider Philip's feelings as one of the largest advertisers,
even if he had not been a man whom nobody disliked. And in the third place, there was the entire
American community to deal with. Americans are
proverbially touchy where the action of an American
representative is in question. Fourthly, the Nonconformists might be trusted to enjoy the discom-
fiture of the Church. And lastly, there was just as
much copy to be made out of trumpeting the wedding
as by attacking it. Therefore the newspapers came
out with such headings as—

'*Fashionable Wedding in Yokohama—Marriage
of a Leading Merchant to the Daughter of one of the
Oldest Residents—The American Minister performs
the Ceremony.*'

To a fine old English gentleman like his father it
might not have been easy to explain that he and
Bryn had married themselves because the Church
would not marry them, though possibly in his heart
of hearts Mr. Sandys senior had no great respect for
American ambassadors as amateur clergymen.

Fortunately the papers (Philip was careful to send
his father a copy of each) did not bring out the
fact that the American Minister out of his official
surroundings was only, strictly speaking, a private
individual.

And fortunately his father and sisters had known
Bryn, and could forgive his taking such a social
liberty as marrying his deceased wife's sister.

Philip, it must be owned, was not entirely candid
in his letters, for while he was explicit about the
refusal of the Church and the British Consul, he left
them to build up any pretty little theory they chose

about the way in which the American Minister came in.

It was curious for them to revisit as man and wife the places they had visited as brother and sister. Europeans might have commented on it; the Japs did not trouble themselves about it. They liked Philip and they adored 'Bryn San,' and accepted thankfully the happiness of having them back.

'Phil,' said Bryn the wife, ' I shall pray to have our lives prolonged a year beyond their natural term to make up for the year I threw away.

' I can hardly believe the good fortune,' she continued, 'licensed and encouraged to see as much of each other as we can, and not even separated in the long night.'

They spent their honeymoon at Nikko, at her earnest request.

'Take me to Nikko, Phil. The first time you corrected me coming back from Chiusenji was the turning-point of my life; it was the first set-back I had ever had. Up to that I had never considered any one's good opinion but my own ; but from that time forward I was determined to have yours—the man's who had dared to withhold it—as well. I soon found that there was only one way of getting it—by being really nice. Besides, there was another thing. When we first met at Netheravon, and I was sizing you up in the hurried, supercilious way which was my habit then, I thought I read in your eyes that you were willing to be my slave as some other men were in those days (and now a hundred times over, Bryn the gentle !), and then somehow or other you slipped away and became Mary's.'

'It was a genuine love-match. I never contemplated the possibility of having you as wife.' He noticed the slip he had made even before the pained look came into her face—'as you are now,' he added. 'I was content to feel that I was one of the family— to look upon your beauty as a brother.'

'Foolish Philip! I would have married you, if you had been free to ask me, the day you married Mary. I was sick with jealousy the day you married— miserably home-sick when I kissed you on the steamer just before she started. But after I had been an inmate of your home, basked in your happy, gentle nature, revelled in the awakening of my mind, I was beginning, when the breath of slander blasted us, to feel what perfect bliss it was to look forward to going through life together as brother and sister. You would never have married any one else, would you, Phil dear?' said the young wife, with a sudden, impulsive caress. 'No—I know I need not ask, for I have a heartache whenever I think of going back into that desolate house with the flowers withered where I had left them. . . . But, Phil, do you know, I'm almost glad now that they did say that—that we were slandered,—because if it hadn't been for that, we should have been brother and sister still, and——'

'And what, little woman?'

'Being brother and sister isn't quite the same thing as being a wife——'

CHAPTER XVIII

WITH the consent either of his fellow members or of the Japanese magnificoes, to whom the premises belong (he did not himself know which—some one about the Legation must have known), Her Britannic Majesty's Minister Plenipotentiary to Japan was giving a garden party at the Rokumei-Kwan, the Club of foreign and Japanese swells in Tokyo.

Mrs. Prince, whose husband was now the senior American officer on the station, was talking to the new American Minister, whom a change of administration at Washington had sent to Tokyo. Years had not changed her habit of talking to amuse herself, and her sub-acid definitions of the various personages present had, as the Minister told his wife on their way home (in the huge Legation barouche, with its Japanese footmen in amber silk liveries lozenged with the stars and stripes), given him an insight into the people of this place right down to the marrow in their bones.

'Did you happen to take note of that lovely woman with the sweet little niece and the two little goldilocks babes, who was talking to me just now?' Mrs. Prince asked him.

'Well, yes,' he said; 'seemed to me pretty nearly the only man or woman in the whole show that wasn't a misfit somehow, according to your showing.'

She did not seem at all offended (Americans contrive to say things to each other without comment, which would separate two families for a generation in the old world), but remarked, ' Well, I guess there's less wrong with her than any one in Japan anyway. Did you note anything about her?'

' Well, I noted that she was as lovely a woman as I ever reckoned to see.'

' You didn't notice anything more particularly?'

' Now, as I come to think of it, there was a kind of hunted look came into her eyes—just when first you spoke to her—that was all.'

' That was it. You don't know what it means. It means that she cannot escape from the knowledge that some day or other some one will tell the two younger ones, those little God's own children with their fair innocent heads——'

' Tell them what?'

' That their father and mother never were married.'

' You don't say,' blowing his nose violently. ' But weren't they? Does the British Minister know the kind of folks he has here?'

' Every one in Japan knows it before they have been here a week.'

' The English——' began the Minister, who owed his appointment to his control of the Irish vote in the State of ——

' No. It isn't the English this time,' replied Mrs. Prince, who knew his record and was accustomed to the playful habit her political countrymen have of relapsing into hustings speeches at some chance word in general society. ' Yet I suppose you might say it was. It is the English Bishop anyway, and the English law is in the same basket; but I mean that it has nothing to do with the Marquis of Salisbury, who is responsible for the sins of the universe, according to the *Boston Pilot.*'

'What did they do?' said the Minister, who was rather tangled in Mrs. Prince's lengthy sentence.

'Oh well, don't you see, she was his sister-in-law. And the English law and prayer-book won't let a man marry his deceased wife's sister. Only they do; but these didn't. Japan's a little place; and the Bishop roped in the three or four episcopal clergy and wouldn't celebrate the marriage. Most any of the other clergy might have done it. But that wouldn't do for Mrs. Sandys. We all call her Mrs. Sandys. She went to the Bishop—you must mind he was an old friend of her family—and said, with more of the old gentleman than you would expect from such a 'lovely' woman—but what a limb she was in those days (not then I don't mean, she'd had her peck of troubles before that, but when she was Bryn Avon of Netheravon. I've seen some American girls in my time, but for tossing her head she could have given any one of them points)—"You say that if you went through the form of marrying me to Mr. Sandys, I should still not be his wife before God, or the law, or any right-thinking man or woman."

'"I must adhere to that way of thinking," said the Bishop primly but quite kindly; he is uncommonly like the rest of us.

'And then she told him that she would live with Mr. Sandys, as his wife, without any ceremony beyond a declaration before her friends, until such time as he should see fit to unite them.'

'And did she?'

'Bryn Avon would have done; but you see I
loved the girl for her spirit—she's about the only
thing I ever did love, except the Commodore and my
children—for all that she spoke to me once as I never
let any other woman speak to me without war to the
end of our lives. And Daff Amory loved her—loved
her better than I did—and Colonel Fairfax, who was
here before you, loved Daff Amory, and couldn't say
no to her. No; I don't mean that there was anything between them—thank God a man can still
love a woman without the eternal sex question
coming in, in America. Well, Daff and I made him
come to the wedding, as they called it, because we
guessed that the British Minister wouldn't find himself able to countenance so irregular a proceeding.
I'm not sure but that he would have had them married
at the American Consulate; but anyway wild horses
wouldn't have dragged Bryn Avon there. She had
made up her mind to be married at her church, or to
marry herself. She sent invitations to the Bishop
and all the parsons of the Church of England, with
the rest of us, to come to the house in which she was
staying with her brother-in-law on a certain day. If
any one of them came and was willing to marry
her, so much the better; if not, they would declare
themselves married before their friends, and live as
husband and wife from that time forward.

'Colonel Fairfax never thought but that some
parson would have been found to do it, and not
being very well up in the English service, he borrowed
a prayer-book and brought it along. Mr. Sandys
was kind of nervous—small wonder—he kept saying
to me, " I wish some clergyman would come"; but of

course none came ; so, knowing what an orator Colonel Fairfax was, I persuaded him that it would break the ice if he (the Colonel) explained in a few words what exactly was going to happen. Of course the Colonel didn't mind. What American, accustomed to public speaking, ever did mind making the speech of the day ?—and that's how it began.'

She went on describing the scene with melodramatic attention to detail.

' And weren't that a good enough wedding for any man and woman ? ' said the new representative of the United States.

' The English law doesn't seem to think so.'

' The English law is mighty particular. Compare that marriage with one I saw just before I came across. We were running from Tacoma to Vancouver in an American coastwise steamer to catch the C.P.R. ' packet ' to Japan. My wife wouldn't cross the Pacific in an American ship ; she had a kind of idea that a British ship was safer for a stormy ocean. And I don't know but what she was right. They haven't so many masters on British ships. You mind that the ship we were on, then, was an American vessel, not a British ; we weren't going on a British ship till we got to Vancouver.

' Well, no sooner had we steamed away from the wharf at Seattle, our last port of call on the American side, than a man and a very handsome young lady —not perhaps what we call a lady when we mean what we say—came to the captain and asked him to marry them.

' It seemed mighty queer that they must be married just in this three or four hours of their lives while they were crossing Puget Sound, when they might have had their choice of a couple of mayors and two or three dozen assorted clergy at Seattle and Tacoma ; but he just said, " All right, by and by ; I'll let you know when I'm ready," and off they went.

' " Likely going back by the next boat," he remarked, shooting the quid out of his cheek all the way from his cabin door to over the ship's side.

' " Do much marrying ? " I asked.

' " Much as I can," he said. " Twenty dollars a time."

' " Always get the twenty dollars ? I didn't hear that ' groom ' allude to it."

' " You bet. These kind of marriages don't want any kind of talking about."

' The captain had got a new quid ready, and the subject dropped. In fact he became very busy with his charts and his instruments — mighty busy for a captain.

' So I took up one of Mr. Kipling's books, *pirayted* by some publisher of religious literature, and waited for developments. Presently my captain called his boy and pointed out the two conspirators. " Go and tell those folks that if they are here in five minutes exactly I'll marry them ; but if they're a second late, by God, I won't." They were on hand a full minute before time. " Clasp your right hands," says he, " and wait." They did ; and exactly at the fiftieth second of the fifth minute he says, " You wish to marry each other ? " " We do." " Then you're married."

' " Shortest on record," I observed, as the man

handed him a big gold twenty-dollar piece, such as they use considerable on the Pacific coast.

' " Come in my cabin," says he.   I went.   " You're going to Japan ? "—I nodded—" and won't give me away this side of the pond ? "

' " No."

' " Well, I'll just let on to you why I made them come out at that particular minute.   I saw you smelt something."

' " Well, yes ? "

' " Why, just at that minute I couldn't have told you for the life of me whether we were in British or American waters, and my two officers would swear either way through a two-inch board, according to the court we came before.   For celebrating marriages I choose the 49th parallel, which is the border, as close as constant practice enables me to calculate it ; but we don't let on, or there'd be so many in the business.   The officers make their dollar apiece every time, and have never yet had to do a solitary swear for it."

' So far so good, Mrs. Prince.   But just as we were leaving the steamer, my captain comes to me with a very long face—" Boodled this time ; the man was a Roman Catholic priest and the woman his sister's daughter."   So you see that Mrs. ——'

' Sandys.'

' Mrs. Sandys had a pretty good wedding as weddings go in our country.'

' The English are so pig-headed,' said Mrs. Prince.

' But tell me, is it all right ? ' he asked, jerking his head towards Bryn.   ' Do people visit them, as the English say, here ? '

' They are the most popular and respected people in the settlement. There is nothing anybody would not do for Mrs. Sandys. Only there is one thing which makes me almost cry about it.'

' What's wrong ? ' said the Minister.

' She's lost her old spirit,' said the Commodore's wife. ' Right up to the day of her marriage she was so defiant ; but after she was married and folks made up their minds to recognise it as a marriage, and there was an all-in competition to show how nice they could be, she just gave in, and she's been so south-wind-and-sun-gentle ever since, that every other woman in the settlement seems a regular fury.'

' That must have been one of the marriages made in heaven,' said the Minister. ' Are they happy ? '

' Happy ! there never were two people so devoted to each other. When they're together, every man, woman, and child in Japan might throw mud at them without them caring a continental. She's ever so young now, five or six and twenty, I daresay, and they've just gone back to live at her father's old place, Netheravon. Philip Sandys had made such lots of money out of his father-in-law's business, which he took over when it didn't seem worth a cent. Anybody else would have wound it up, only he didn't want to throw the clerks out of employ.'

' Well, as James Whitcomb Riley said, " I 'spect the Lord just sat round and felt good the day He made that man." Have they fixed it up with their church yet ? '

' That's it ; they're waiting for the House of Lords to abolish the Deceased Wife's Sister.'

EDINBURGH: PRINTED BY NEILL AND COMPANY.

BELL'S COLONIAL EDITIONS OF STANDARD BOOKS.

When we were Strolling Players in the East.

By LOUISE JORDAN MILN.

WITH ILLUSTRATIONS.

PRICE 7s. 6d.

CONTENTS.

My First Glimpse of the Orient—Andrew—Our Day Out—My First 'Rickshaw Ride—In the Burra Bazaar—A Christmas Dinner on a Roof—Oriental Obsequies—A Hindoo Burning Ghât—Oriental Nuptials—A Hindoo Marriage—King Theebaw's State Barge—Burmese Burials—Burmese Bridals—A Jaunt in a House Boat through the Home of the Wild Rose—An Opium Den in Shanghai—Memories of Hong Kong—A Glimpse of Canton—Chinese Prisoners—The Chinese New Year—Chinese Coffins—Chinese Espousals—Chinese Shoes—Japanese Touch—Four Women that I knew in Tokio—Tom Street—A Japanese Funeral—Japanese Wedlock—Bamboo—On the Himalayas—My Ayah—Sambo—How we kept House on the Hills—The Parsi Towers of Silence—A Parsi Wedding—At Subathu, where the Bagpipes and the Lepers hide—In the Officers' Mess—At the Mouth of the Khyber Pass—An Impromptu Party in the Punjab—Salaam !

SOME OPINIONS OF THE PRESS.

" A series of personal sketches and reminiscences of life in the nearer and further East; lively, enthusiastic, shrewd in observation, and always kindly in appreciation."—*Times.*

" Liveliness, in truth, is the chief note of this very readable and entertaining volume. Mrs Miln has a sense of humour, writes straight from the heart, and is delightfully frank. We have found her book genuinely entertaining, and can recommend it heartily. It is exceptionally well illustrated."—*Globe.*

" A book of travel of real novelty as well as of genuine attraction."—*Spectator.*

" Brightly written, clever, and delightful."—*Athenæum.*

" A book upon which there need be no hesitation in bestowing the highest praise."—*Glasgow Herald.*

LONDON: GEORGE BELL AND SONS,
AND BOMBAY.

BELL'S INDIAN AND COLONIAL LIBRARY.

"TRILBY'S FOREBEARS."

No. 65.

THE NEW

ILLUSTRATED EDITION

OF

DU MAURIER'S

TRILBY,

WITH UPWARDS OF ONE HUNDRED AND TWENTY ILLUSTRATIONS
BY THE AUTHOR.

LONDON: GEORGE BELL & SONS,
AND BOMBAY.

BELL'S INDIAN AND COLONIAL LIBRARY.

No. 65.

TRILBY

BY

GEORGE DU MAURIER.

ILLUSTRATED EDITION.

"THREE MUSKETEERS OF THE BRUSH."

LONDON: GEORGE BELL & SONS, AND BOMBAY.

BELL'S COLONIAL EDITIONS OF STANDARD BOOKS.

Works by Sir Robert S. Ball,
D.Sc., LL.D., F.R.S.

LOWNDEAN PROFESSOR OF ASTRONOMY IN THE UNIVERSITY OF CAMBRIDGE.

Now ready. Demy 8vo.

IN THE HIGH HEAVENS.

ILLUSTRATED.

PRICE 5s.

Nearly Ready.

IN STARRY REALMS.

ILLUSTRATED. · *9*

GREAT ASTRONOMERS.

[*In the Press.*

LONDON : GEORGE BELL AND SONS,

AND BOMBAY.

BELL'S

INDIAN & COLONIAL LIBRARY.

Issued for Circulation in India and the Colonies only.

ALEXANDER (Mrs.). A Ward in Chancery.

ALEXANDER (Mrs.). A Choice of Evils.

ALLEN (GRANT). Science in Arcady.

ANSTEY (F.). Under the Rose. With Illustrations by BERNARD PARTRIDGE.

APPLETON (GEORGE). The Co-Respondent.

BARRINGTON (Mrs. RUSSELL). Helen's Ordeal.

BENSON (E. F.). The Rubicon. By the Author of 'Dodo.'

BJÖRNSON (BJÖRNSTJERNE). Arne, and the Fisher Lassie. Translated by W. H. Low, M.A.

BROUGHTON (RHODA) and BISLAND (ELIZABETH). A Widower Indeed.

CALVERLEY (C. S.). Verses and Fly-Leaves.

CAMERON (Mrs. LOVETT). A Bad Lot.

COLERIDGE (S. T.). Table-Talk and Omniana.

DICKENS (CHARLES). Pickwick Papers. With Eight Illustrations by 'Phiz.'

DICKENS (CHARLES). A Tale of Two Cities. With I
  trations.

DICKENS (CHARLES). David Copperfield.

DOYLE (CONAN). The White Company.

DU MAURIER (G.). Trilby. With Illustrations by
  Author.

EBERS (GEORG). An Indian Princess. Translated
  E. S. Buchheim.

EMERSON (R. W.). Essays and Lectures.

EMERSON (R. W.). English Traits and Nature.

FENN (G. MANVILLE). The Star-Gazers.

FOSTER (JOHN). The Evils of Popular Ignorance, &c.

FRANCIS (M. E.). A Daughter of the Soil.

GIFT (Theo.). An Island Princess.

GISSING (GEORGE). Denzil Quarrier.

GISSING (GEORGE). The Emancipated.

GISSING (GEORGE). In the Year of Jubilee.

GISSING (GEORGE). Eve's Ransom.

HAGGARD (Lieut.-Col. ANDREW). Tempest-Torn.

HARDY (THOMAS). Tess of the D'Urbervilles.

HARRADEN (BEATRICE). Ships that Pass in the Nig

HAWTHORNE (NATHANIEL). Transformation. (
  Marble Faun).

HOOPER (GEORGE). Waterloo: The Downfall of
  First Napoleon. With Maps and Plans.

HUNGERFORD (Mrs.). Peter's Wife.

HUNGERFORD (Mrs.). A Tug of War.

HUNT (VIOLET). The Maiden's Progress.

JÓKAI (MAURUS). Eyes Like the Sea. Translated by R. NISBET BAIN.

JÓKAI (MAURUS). 'Midst the the Wild Carpathians. Translated by R. NISBET BAIN.

KEARY (C. F.). The Two Lancrofts.

KENNARD (MRS. E.). The Catch of the County.

MALLOCK (W. H.). A Human Document.

MEADE (MRS. L. T.). A Life for a Love.

MEADE (L. T.) and HALIFAX (CLIFFORD). Stories from the Diary of a Doctor.

MEREDITH (GEORGE). Richard Feverel.

MEREDITH (GEORGE). Evan Harrington.

MEREDITH (GEORGE). The Egoist.

MEREDITH (GEORGE). Diana of the Crossways.

MEREDITH (GEORGE). One of Our Conquerors.

MEREDITH (GEORGE). The Adventures of Harry Richmond.

MEREDITH (GEORGE). Lord Ormont and his Aminta.

MERRIMAN (HENRY SETON). With Edged Tools.

MIDDLETON (COLIN). Without Respect of Persons.

MIGNET (F. A.). History of the French Revolution, from 1789 to 1814. Translated from the French.

MUDDOCK (J. E.). The Star of Fortune.

A NEW NOTE.

OLIPHANT (MRS.). The Prodigals.

PARKER (GILBERT). The Translation of a Savage.

PARKER (GILBERT) and others.   The March of the Whi
   Guard, and other Stories.   Illustrated.

PATERSON (ARTHUR).   A Man of his Word.

PHILLPOTTS (EDEN).   In Sugar-Cane Land.

PHILLPOTTS (EDEN).   Some Every-Day Folks.

POUSHKIN (A.).   Prose Tales.   Translated by T. KEANE

SIX THOUSAND TONS OF GOLD.

STINDE (JULIUS).   The Buchholz Family.   Translated |
   L. DORA SCHMITZ.

THACKERAY (W. M.).   The Newcomes.

THACKERAY (W. M.).   Vanity Fair.

VANDAM (ALBERT D.).   The Mystery of the Patrici:
   Club.

WARDEN (FLORENCE).   A Perfect Fool.

WARDEN (FLORENCE).   Kitty's Engagement.

WESTALL (WILLIAM).   For Honour and Life.

WILKINS (MARY E.).   Pembroke.

WINTER (JOHN STRANGE).   A Born Soldier.

WINTER (JOHN STRANGE).   A Blameless Woman.

ALPHABETICAL LIST OF BOOKS

CONTAINED IN

BOHN'S LIBRARIES.

748 Vols., Small Post 8vo. cloth. Price £160.

Complete Detailed Catalogue will be sent on application.

Addison's Works. 6 vols. 3s. 6d. each.

Aeschylus. Verse Trans. by Anna Swanwick. 5s.

—— Prose Trans. by T. A. Buckley. 3s. 6d.

Agassiz & Gould's Comparative Physiology. 5s.

Alfieri's Tragedies. Trans. by Bowring. 2 vols. 3s. 6d. each.

Alford's Queen's English. 1s. & 1s. 6d.

Allen's Battles of the British Navy. 2 vols. 5s. each.

Ammianus Marcellinus. Trans. by C. D. Yonge. 7s. 6d.

Andersen's Danish Tales. Trans. by Caroline Peachey. 5s.

Antoninus (Marcus Aurelius). Trans. by George Long. 3s. 6d.

Apollonius Rhodius. The Argonautica. Trans. by E. P. Coleridge. 5s.

Apuleius, The Works of. 5s.

Ariosto's Orlando Furioso. Trans. by W. S. Rose. 2 vols. 5s. each.

Aristophanes. Trans. by W. J. Hickie. 2 vols. 5s. each.

Aristotle's Works. 5 vols, 5s. each; 2 vols, 3s. 6d. each.

Arrian. Trans. by E. J. Chinnock. 5s.

Ascham's Scholemaster. (J. E. B. Mayor.) 1s.

Bacon's Essays and Historical Works, 3s. 6d.; Essays, 1s. and 1s. 6d.; Novum Organum, and Advancement of Learning, 5s.

Ballads and Songs of the Peasantry. By Robert Bell. 3s. 6d.

Bass's Lexicon to the Greek Test. 2s.

Bax's Manual of the History of Philosophy. 5s.

Beaumont & Fletcher. Leigh Hunt's Selections. 3s. 6d.

Bechstein's Cage and Chamber Birds. 5s.

Beckmann's History of Inventions. 2 vols. 3s. 6d. each.

Bede's Ecclesiastical History and the A. S. Chronicle. 5s.

Bell (Sir C.) On the Hand. 5s.

—— Anatomy of Expression. 5s.

Bentley's Phalaris. 5s.

Björnson's Arne and the Fisher Lassie. Trans. by W. H. Low. 3s. 6d.

Blair's Chronological Tables. 10s. Index of Dates. 2 vols. 5s. each.

Bleek's Introduction to the Old Testament. 2 vols. 5s. each.

Boethius' Consolation of Philosophy, &c. 5s.

Bohn's Dictionary of Poetical Quotations. 6s.

Bond's Handy-book for Verifying Dates, &c. 5s.

Bonomi's Nineveh. 5s.

Boswell's Life of Johnson. (Napier). 6 vols. 3s. 6d. each.

—— (Croker.) 5 vols. 20s.

Brand's Popular Antiquities. 3 vols. 5s. each.

Bremer's Works. Trans. by Mary Howitt. 4 vols. 3s. 6d. each.

Bridgewater Treatises. 9 vols. Various prices.

Brink (B. Ten). Early English Literature. 2 vols. 3s. 6d. each.

—— Six Lectures on Shakespeare 3s. 6d.

Browne's (Sir Thomas) Works. 3 vols. 3*s.* 6*d.* each.

Buchanan's Dictionary of Scientific Terms. 6*s.*

Buckland's Geology and Mineralogy. 2 vols. 15*s.*

Burke's Works and Speeches. 8 vols. 3*s.* 6*d.* each. The Sublime and Beautiful. 1*s.* & 1*s.* 6*d.* Reflections on the French Revolution. 1*s.*

—— Life, by Sir James Prior. 3*s.* 6*d.*

Burney's Evelina. 3*s.* 6*d.* Cecilia 2 vols. 3*s.* 6*d.* each.

Burn's Handbook to the Ruins of Old Rome.

Burns' Life by Lockhart. Revised by W. Scott Douglas. 3*s.* 6*d.*

Butler's Analogy of Religion, and Sermons. 3*s.* 6*d.*

Butler's Hudibras. 5*s.*; or 2 vols.,5*s.*ea.

Caesar. Trans. by W. A. M'Devitte. 5*s.*

Camoens' Lusiad. Mickle's Translation, revised. 3*s.* 6*d.*

Carafas (The) of Maddaloni. By Alfred de Reumont. 3*s.* 6*d.*

Carpenter's Mechanical Philosophy 5*s.* Vegetable Physiology. 6*s.* Animal Physiology. 6*s.*

Carrel's Counter Revolution under Charles II. and James II. 3*s.* 6*d.*

Cattermole's Evenings at Haddon Hall. 5*s.*

Catullus and Tibullus. Trans. by W. K. Kelly. 5*s.*

Cellini's Memoirs. (Roscoe.) 3*s.* 6*d.*

Cervantes' Exemplary Novels. Trans. by W. K. Kelly. 3*s.* 6*d.*

—— Don Quixote. Motteux's Trans. revised. 2 vols. 3*s.* 6*d.* each.

—— Galatea. Trans. by G. W. J. Gyll. 3*s.* 6*d.*

Chalmers On Man. 5*s.*

Channing's The Perfect Life. 1*s.* and 1*s.* 6*d.*

Chaucer's Works. Bell's Edition, revised by Skeat. 4 vols. 3*s.* 6*d.* ea.

Chess Congress of 1862 By J. Löwenthal. 5*s.*

Chevreul on Colour. 5*s.* and 7*s.* 6*d.*

Chillingworth's The Religion of Protestants. 3*s.* 6*d.*

China : Pictorial, Descriptive, and Historical. 5*s.*

Chronicles of the Crusades. 5*s.*

Cicero's Works. 7 vols. 5*s.* ea 1 vol., 3*s.* 6*d.*

—— Friendship and Old Age. 1*s.* a 1*s.* 6*d.*

Clark's Heraldry. (Planché.) 5*s.* a 15*s.*

Classic Tales. 3*s.* 6*d.*

Coleridge's Prose Works. (Ash 6 vols. 3*s.* 6*d.* each.

Comte's Philosophy of the Scienc (G. H. Lewes.) 5*s.*

—— Positive Philosophy (Harriet Ma neau). 3 vols. 5*s.* each. [*In the pr*

Condé's History of the Arabs in Spa 3 vols. 3*s.* 6*d.* each.

Cooper's Biographical Dictiona 2 vols. 5*s.* each.

Cowper's Works. (Southey.) 8 v 3*s.* 6*d.* each.

Coxe's House of Austria. 4 vols. 3*s.* each. Memoirs of Marlborou 3 vols. 3*s.* 6*d.* each. Atlas Marlborough's Campaigns. 10*s.*

Craik's Pursuit of Knowledge. 5*s.*

Craven's Young Sportsman's Manu 5*s.*

Cruikshank's Punch and Judy. Three Courses and a Dessert. 5*s*

Cunningham's Lives of British Paint 3 vols. 3*s.* 6*d.* each.

Dante. Trans. by Rev. H. F. Ca 3*s.* 6*d.* Inferno. Separate, 1*s.* 1*s.* 6*d.* Purgatorio. 1*s.* and 1*s.* Paradiso. 1*s.* and 1*s.* 6*d.*

—— Trans. by I. C. Wright. (Fl man's Illustrations.) 5*s.*

—— Inferno. Italian Text and Tra by Dr. Carlyle. 5*s.*

—— Purgatorio. Italian Text a Trans. by W. S. Dugdale. 5*s.*

De Commines' Memoirs. Trans. A. R. Scoble. 2 vols. 3*s.* 6*d.* ea

Defoe's Novels and Miscel. Wor 6 vols. 3*s.* 6*d.* each. Robins Crusoe (Vol. VII). 3*s.* 6*d.* or The Plague in London. 1*s.* a 1*s.* 6*d.*

Delolme on the Constitution of E land. 3*s.* 6*d.*

Demmins' Arms and Armour. Tra by C. C. Black. 7*s.* 6*d.*

Demosthenes' Orations. Trans. by C. Rann Kennedy. 4 vols. 5s., and 1 vol. 3s. 6d.

Demosthenes' Orations On the Crown. 1s. and 1s. 6d.

De Stael's Corinne. Trans. by Emily Baldwin and Paulina Driver. 3s. 6d.

Devey's Logic. 5s.

Dictionary of Greek and Latin Quotations. 5s.
—— of Poetical Quotations (Bohn). 6s.
—— of Scientific Terms. (Buchanan.) 6s.
—— of Biography. (Cooper.) 2 vols. 5s. each.
—— of Noted Names of Fiction. (Wheeler.) 5s.
—— of Obsolete and Provincial English (Wright.) 2 vols. 5s. each.

Didron's Christian Iconography. 2 vols. 5s. each.

Diogenes Laertius. Trans. by C. D. Yonge. 5s.

Dobree's Adversaria. (Wagner). 2 vols. 5s. each.

Dodd's Epigrammatists. 6s.

Donaldson's Theatre of the Greeks. 5s.

Draper's History of the Intellectual Development of Europe. 2 vols. 5s. each.

Dunlop's History of Fiction. 2 vols. 5s. each.

Dyer's History of Pompeii. 7s. 6d.
—— The City of Rome. 5s.

Dyer's British Popular Customs. 5s.

Early Travels in Palestine. (Wright.) 5s.

Eaton's Waterloo Days. 1s. and 1s. 6d.

Eber's Egyptian Princess. Trans. by E. S. Buchheim. 3s. 6d.

Edgeworth's Stories for Children. 3s. 6d.

Ellis' Specimens of Early English Metrical Romances. (Halliwell.) 5s.

Elze's Life of Shakespeare. Trans. by J. Dora Schmitz. 5s.

Evelyn's Diary and Correspondence. (Bray.) 4 vols. 5s. each.

Fairholt's Costume in England. (Dillon.) 2 vols. 5s. each.

Fielding's Joseph Andrews. 3s. 6d. Tom Jones. 2 vols. 3s. 6d. each. Amelia. 5s.

Flaxman's Lectures on Sculpture. 6s.

Florence of Worcester's Chronicle. Trans. by T. Forester. 5s.

Foster's Works. 10 vols. 3s. 6d. each.

Franklin's Autobiography. 1s.

Gesta Romanorum. Trans. by Swan & Hooper. 5s.

Gibbon's Decline and Fall. 7 vols. 3s. 6d. each.

Gilbart's Banking. 2 vols. 5s. each.

Gil Blas. Trans. by Smollett. 6s.

Giraldus Cambrensis. 5s.

Goethe's Works and Correspondence, including Autobiography and Annals, Faust, Elective affinities, Werther, Wilhelm Meister, Poems and Ballads, Dramas, Reinecke Fox, Tour in Italy and Miscellaneous Travels, Early and Miscellaneous Letters, Correspondence with Eckermann and Soret, Zelter and Schiller, &c. &c. By various translators. 16 vols. 3s. 6d. each.
—— Faust. Text with Hayward's Translation. (Buchheim.) 5s.
—— Faust. Part I. Trans. by Anna Swanwick. 1s. and 1s. 6d.
—— Boyhood. (Part I. of the Autobiography.) Trans. by J. Oxenford. 1s. and 1s. 6d.
—— Reinecke Fox. Trans. by A. Rogers. 1s. and 1s. 6d.

Goldsmith's Works. (Gibbs.) 5 vols. 3s. 6d. each.
—— Plays. 1s. and 1s. 6d. Vicar of Wakefield. 1s. and 1s. 6d.

Greek Testament. 5*s*.

Greene, Marlowe, and Ben Jonson's Poems. (Robert Bell.) 3*s*. 6*d*.

Gregory's Evidences of the Christian Religion. 3*s*. 6*d*.

Grimm's Gammer Grethel. Trans. by E. Taylor. 3*s*. 6*d*.
—— German Tales. Trans. by Mrs. Hunt. 2 vols. 3*s*. 6*d*. each.

Grossi's Marco Visconti. 3*s*. 6*d*.

Guizot's Origin of Representative Government in Europe. Trans. by A. R. Scoble. 3*s*. 6*d*.
—— The English Revolution of 1640. Trans. by W. Hazlitt. 3*s*. 6*d*.
—— History of Civilisation. Trans. by W. Hazlitt. 3 vols. 3*s*. 6*d*. each.

Hall (Robert). Miscellaneous Works. 3*s*. 6*d*.

Handbooks of Athletic Sports. 8 vols. 3*s*. 6*d*. each.

Handbook of Card and Table Games. 2 vols. 3*s*. 6*d*. each.
—— of Proverbs. By H. G. Bohn. 5*s*.
—— of Foreign Proverbs. 5*s*.

Hardwick's History of the Thirty-nine Articles. 5*s*.

Harvey's Circulation of the Blood. (Bowie.) 1*s*. and 1*s*. 6*d*.

Hauff's Tales. Trans. by S. Mendel. 3*s*. 6*d*.
—— The Caravan and Sheik of Alexandria. 1*s*. and 1*s*. 6*d*.

Hawthorne's Novels and Tales. 4 vols. 3*s*. 6*d*. each.

Hazlitt's Lectures and Essays. 7 vols. 3*s*. 6*d*. each.

Heaton's History of Painting. (Cosmo Monkhouse.) 5*s*.

Hegel's Philosophy of History. Trans. by J. Sibree. 5*s*.

Heine's Poems. Trans. by E. A. Bowring. 3*s*. 6*d*.
—— Travel Pictures. Trans. by Francis Storr. 3*s*. 6*d*.

Helps (Sir Arthur). Life of Thomas Brassey. 1*s*. and 1*s*. 6*d*.

Henderson's Historical Documents of the Middle Ages. 5*s*.

Henfrey's English Coins. (Keary.) 6*s*.

Henry (Matthew) On the Psalms. 5*s*.

Henry of Huntingdon's History. Trans. by T. Forester. 5*s*.

Herodotus. Trans. by H. F. Cary. 3*s*. 6*d*.
—— Wheeler's Analysis and Summary of. 5*s*. Turner's Notes on. . 5*s*.

Hesiod, Callimachus and Theognis. Trans. by Rev. J. Banks. 5*s*.

Hoffmann's Tales. The Serapion Brethren. Trans. by Lieut.-Colonel Ewing. 2 vols. 3*s*. 6*d*.

Hogg's Experimental and Natural Philosophy. 5*s*.

Holbein's Dance of Death and Bible Cuts. 5*s*.

Homer. Trans. by T. A. Buckley. 2 vols. 5*s*. each.
—— Pope's Translation. With Flaxman's Illustrations. 2 vols. 5*s*. each.
—— Cowper's Translation. 2 vols. 3*s*. 6*d*. each.

Hooper's Waterloo. 3*s*. 6*d*.

Horace. Smart's Translation, revised, by Buckley. 3*s*. 6*d*.

Hugo's Dramatic Works. Trans. by Mrs. Crosland and F. L. Slous. 3*s*. 6*d*.
—— Hernani. Trans. by Mrs. Crosland. 1*s*.
—— Poems. Trans. by various writers. Collected by J. H. L. Williams. 3*s*. 6*d*.

Humboldt's Cosmos. Trans. by Otté, Paul, and Dallas. 4 vols. 3*s*. 6*d*. each, and 1 vol. 5*s*.
—— Personal Narrative of his Travels. Trans. by T. Ross. 3 vols. 5*s*. each.
—— Views of Nature. Trans. by Otté and Bohn. 5*s*.

Humphreys' Coin Collector's Manual. 2 vols. 5*s*. each.

Hungary, History of. 3*s*. 6*d*.

Hunt's Poetry of Science. 5*s*.

Hutchinson's Memoirs. 3*s*. 6*d*.

India before the Sepoy Mutiny. 5*s*.

Ingulph's Chronicles. 5*s*.

Irving (Washington). Complete Works. 15 vols. 3*s*. 6*d*. each; or in 18 vols. 1*s*. each, and 2 vols. 1*s*. 6*d*. each.
—— Life and Letters. By Pierre E. Irving. 2 vols. 3*s*. 6*d*. each.

Isocrates. Trans. by J. H. Freese. Vol. I. 5*s*.

James' Life of Richard Cœur de Lion. 2 vols. 3*s*. 6*d*. each.
—— Life and Times of Louis XIV. 2 vols. 3*s*. 6*d*. each.

Jameson (Mrs.) Shakespeare's Heroines. 3s. 6d.

Jesse (E.) Anecdotes of Dogs. 5s.

Jesse (J. H.) Memoirs of the Court of England under the Stuarts. 3 vols. 5s. each.

—— Memoirs of the Pretenders. 5s.

Johnson's Lives of the Poets. (Napier). 3 vols. 3s. 6d. each.

Josephus. Whiston's Translation, revised by Rev. A. R. Shilleto. 5 vols. 3s. 6d. each.

Joyce's Scientific Dialogues. 5s.

Jukes-Browne's Handbook of Physical Geology. 7s. 6d. Handbook of Historical Geology. 6s. The Building of the British Isles. 7s. 6d.

Julian the Emperor. Trans by Rev. C. W. King. 5s.

Junius's Letters. Woodfall's Edition, revised. 2 vols. 3s. 6d. each.

Justin, Cornelius Nepos, and Eutropius. Trans. by Rev. J. S. Watson. 5s.

Juvenal, Persius, Sulpicia, and Lucilius. Trans. by L. Evans. 5s.

Kant's Critique of Pure Reason. Trans. by J. M. D. Meiklejohn. 5s.

—— Prolegomena, &c. Trans. by E. Belfort Bax. 5s.

Keightley's Fairy Mythology. 5s. Classical Mythology. Revised by Dr. L. Schmitz. 5s.

Kidd On Man. 3s. 6d.

Kirby On Animals. 2 vols. 5s. each.

Knight's Knowledge is Power. 5s.

La Fontaine's Fables. Trans. by E. Wright. 3s. 6d.

Lamartine's History of the Girondists. Trans. by H. T. Ryde. 3 vols. 3s. 6d. each.

—— Restoration of the Monarchy in France. Trans. by Capt. Rafter. 4 vols. 3s. 6d. each.

—— French Revolution of 1848. 3s. 6d.

Lamb's Essays of Elia and Eliana. 3s. 6d., or in 3 vols. 1s. each.

—— Memorials and Letters. Talfourd's Edition, revised by W. C. Hazlitt. 2 vols. 3s. 6d. each.

—— Specimens of the English Dramatic Poets of the Time of Elizabeth. 3s. 6d.

Lanzi's History of Painting in Italy. Trans. by T. Roscoe. 3 vols. 3s. 6d. each.

Lappenberg's England under the Anglo-Saxon Kings. Trans. by B. Thorpe. 2 vols. 3s. 6d. each.

Lectures on Painting. By Barry, Opie and Fuseli. 5s.

Leonardo da Vinci's Treatise on Painting. Trans. by J. F. Rigaud. 5s.

Lepsius' Letters from Egypt, &c. Trans. by L. and J. B. Horner. 5s.

Lessing's Dramatic Works. Trans. by Ernest Bell. 2 vols. 3s. 6d. each. Nathan the Wise and Minna von Barnhelm. 1s. and 1s. 6d. Laokoon, Dramatic Notes, &c. Trans. by E. C. Beasley and Helen Zimmern. 3s. 6d. Laokoon separate. 1s. or 1s. 6d.

Lilly's Introduction to Astrology. (Zadkiel.) 5s.

Livy. Trans. by Dr. Spillan and others. 4 vols. 5s. each.

Locke's Philosophical Works. (J. A. St. John). 2 vols. 3s. 6d. each.

—— Life. By Lord King. 3s. 6d.

Lodge's Portraits. 8 vols. 5s. each.

Longfellow's Poetical and Prose Works. 2 vols. 5s. each.

Loudon's Natural History. 5s.

Lowndes' Bibliographer's Manual. 6 vols. 5s. each.

Lucan's Pharsalia. Trans. by H. T. Riley. 5s.

Lucian's Dialogues. Trans. by H. Williams. 5s.

Lucretius. Trans. by Rev. J. S. Watson. 5s.

Luther's Table Talk. Trans. by W. Hazlitt. 3s. 6d.

—— Autobiography. (Michelet). Trans. by W. Hazlitt. 3s. 6d.

Machiavelli's History of Florence, &c. Trans. 3s. 6d.

Mallet's Northern Antiquities. 5s.

Mantell's Geological Excursions through the Isle of Wight, &c. 5s. Petrifactions and their Teachings. 6s. Wonders of Geology. 2 vols. 7s. 6d. each.

Manzoni's The Betrothed. 5s.

Marco Polo's Travels. Marsden's Edition, revised by T. Wright. 5s.

Martial's Epigrams. Trans. 7s. 6d.

Martineau's History of England, 1800–15. 3s. 6d.

—— History of the Peace, 1816–46. 4 vols. 3s. 6d. each.

Matthew Paris. Trans. by Dr. Giles. 3 vols. 5s. each.

Matthew of Westminster. Trans. by C. D. Yonge. 2 vols. 5s. each.

Maxwell's Victories of Wellington. 5s.

Menzel's History of Germany. Trans. by Mrs. Horrocks. 3 vols. 3s. 6d. ea.

Michael Angelo and Raffaelle. By Duppa and Q. de Quincy. 5s.

Michelet's French Revolution. Trans. by C. Cocks. 3s. 6d.

Mignet's French Revolution. 3s. 6d.

Mill (John Stuart). Selected Essays. *[In the press.*

Miller's Philosophy of History. 4 vols. 3s. 6d. each.

Milton's Poetical Works. (J. Montgomery.) 2 vols. 3s. 6d. each.

—— Prose Works. (J. A. St. John.) 5 vols. 3s. 6d. each.

Mitford's Our Village. 2 vols. 3s. 6d. each.

Molière's Dramatic Works. Trans. by C. H. Wall. 3 vols. 3s. 6d. each.

—— The Miser, Tartuffe, The Shopkeeper turned Gentleman. 1s. & 1s. 6d.

Montagu's (Lady M. W.) Letters and Works. (Wharncliffe and Moy Thomas.) 2 vols. 5s. each.

Montaigne's Essays. Cotton's Trans. revised by W. C. Hazlitt. 3 vols. 3s. 6d. each.

Montesquieu's Spirit of Laws. Nugent's Trans. revised by J. V. Prichard. 2 vols. 3s. 6d. each.

Morphy's Games of Chess. (Löwenthal.) 5s.

Motley's Dutch Republic. Illustrated. 3 vols. 3s. 6d. each. *[In the press.*

Mudie's British Birds. (Martin.) 2 vols. 5s. each.

Naval and Military Heroes of Great Britain, 6s.

Neander's History of the Christian Religion and Church. 10 vols. Life of Christ. 1 vol. Planting and Training of the Church by the Apostles. 2 vols. History of Christian Dogma.

2 vols. Memorials of Christian Life in the Early and Middle Ages. 16 vols. 3s. 6d. each.

Nicolini's History of the Jesuits. 5s.

North's Lives of the Norths. (Jessopp.) 3 vols. 3s. 6d. each.

Nugent's Memorials of Hampden. 5s.

Ockley's History of the Saracens. 3s. 6d.

Ordericus Vitalis. Trans. by T. Forester. 4 vols. 5s. each.

Ovid. Trans. by H. T. Riley. 3 vols. 5s. each.

Pascal's Thoughts. Trans. by C. Kegan Paul. 3s. 6d.

Pauli's Life of Alfred the Great, &c. 5s.

—— Life of Cromwell. 1s. and 1s. 6d.

Pausanias' Description of Greece. Trans. by Rev. A. R. Shilleto. 2 vols. 5s. each.

Pearson on the Creed. (Walford.) 5s.

Pepys' Diary. (Braybrooke.) 4 vols. 5s. each.

Percy's Reliques of Ancient English Poetry. (Prichard.) 2 vols. 3s. 6d. ea.

Petrarch's Sonnets. 5s.

Pettigrew's Chronicles of the Tombs. 5s.

Philo-Judæus. Trans. by C. D. Yonge. 4 vols. 5s. each.

Pickering's Races of Man. 5s.

Pindar. Trans. by D. W. Turner. 5s.

Planché's History of British Costume. 5s.

Plato. Trans. by H. Cary, G. Burges, and H. Davis. 6 vols. 5s. each.

—— Apology, Crito, Phædo, Protagoras. 1s. and 1s. 6d.

—— Day's Analysis and Index to the Dialogues. 5s.

Plautus. Trans. by H. T. Riley. 2 vols. 5s. each.

—— Trinummus, Menæchmi, Aulularia, Captivi. 1s. and 1s. 6d.

Pliny's Natural History. Trans. by Dr. Bostock and H. T. Riley. 6 vols. 5s. each.

Pliny the Younger, Letters of. Melmoth's trans. revised by Rev. F. C. T. Bosanquet. 5s.

Plotinus : Select Works. Trans. by Thomas Taylor. 5s. *[In the press.*

Plutarch's Lives. Trans. by Stewart and Long. 4 vols. 3s. 6d. each.
—— Moralia. Trans. by Rev. C. W. King and Rev. A. R. Shilleto. 2 vols. 5s. each.

Poetry of America. (W. J. Linton.) 3s. 6d.

Political Cyclopædia. 4 vols. 3s. 6d. ea.

Polyglot of Foreign Proverbs. 5s.

Pope's Poetical Works. (Carruthers.) 2 vols. 5s. each.
—— Homer. (J. S. Watson.) 2 vols. 5s. each.
—— Life and Letters. (Carruthers.) 5s.

Pottery and Porcelain. (H. G. Bohn.) 5s. and 10s. 6d.

Propertius. Trans. by Rev. P. J. F. Gantillon. 3s. 6d.

Prout (Father.) Reliques. 5s.

Quintilian's Institutes of Oratory. Trans. by Rev. J. S. Watson. 2 vols. 5s. each.

Racine's Tragedies. Trans. by R. B. Boswell. 2 vols. 3s. 6d. each.

Ranke's History of the Popes. Trans. by E. Foster. 3 vols. 3s. 6d. each.
—— Latin and Teutonic Nations. Trans. by P. A. Ashworth. 3s. 6d.
—— History of Servia. Trans. by Mrs. Kerr. 3s. 6d.

Rennie's Insect Architecture. (J. G. Wood.) 5s.

Reynold's Discourses and Essays. (Beechy.) 2 vols. 3s. 6d. each.

Ricardo's Political Economy. (Gonner.) 5s.

Richter's Levana. 3s. 6d.
—— Flower Fruit and Thorn Pieces. Trans. by Lieut.-Col. Ewing. 3s. 6d.

Roger de Hovenden's Annals. Trans. by Dr. Giles. 2 vols. 5s. each.

Roger of Wendover. Trans. by Dr. Giles. 2 vols. 5s. each.

Roget's Animal and Vegetable Physiology. 2 vols. 6s. each.

Rome in the Nineteenth Century. (C. A. Eaton.) 2 vols. 5s each.

Roscoe's Leo X. 2 vols. 3s. 6d. each.
—— Lorenzo de Medici. 3s. 6d.

Russia, History of. By W. K. Kelly. 2 vols. 3s. 6d. each.

Sallust, Florus, and Velleius Paterculus. Trans. by Rev. J. S. Watson. 5s.

Schiller's Works. Including History of the Thirty Years' War, Revolt of the Netherlands, Wallenstein, William Tell, Don Carlos, Mary Stuart, Maid of Orleans, Bride of Messina, Robbers, Fiesco, Love and Intrigue, Demetrius, Ghost-Seer, Sport of Divinity, Poems, Aesthetical and Philosophical Essays, &c. By various translators. 7 vols. 3s. 6d. each.
—— Mary Stuart and The Maid of Orleans. Trans. by J. Mellish and Anna Swanwick. 1s. and 1s. 6d.

Schlegel (F.). Lectures and Miscellaneous Works. 5 vols. 3s. 6d. each.
—— (A. W.). Lectures on Dramatic Art and Literature. 3s. 6d.

Schopenhauer's Essays. Selected and Trans. by E. Belfort Bax. 5s.
—— On the Fourfold Root of the Principle of Sufficient Reason and on the Will in Nature. Trans. by Mdme. Hillebrand. 5s.

Schouw's Earth, Plants, and Man. Trans. by A. Henfrey. 5s.

Schumann's Early Letters. Trans. by May Herbert. 3s. 6d.
—— Reissmann's Life of. Trans. by A. L. Alger. 3s. 6d.

Seneca on Benefits. Trans. by Aubrey Stewart. 3s. 6d.
—— Minor Essays and On Clemency. Trans. by Aubrey Stewart. 5s.

Sharpe's History of Egypt. 2 vols. 5s. each.

Sheridan's Dramatic Works. 3s. 6d.
—— Plays. 1s. and 1s. 6d.

Sismondi's Literature of the South of Europe. Trans. by T. Roscoe. 2 vols. 3s. 6d. each.

Six Old English Chronicles. 5s.

Smith (Archdeacon). Synonyms and Antonyms. 5s.

Smith (Adam). Wealth of Nations. (Belfort Bax.) 2 vols. 3s. 6d. each.
—— Theory of Moral Sentiments. 3s. 6d.

Smith (Pye). Geology and Scripture. 5s.

Smollett's Novels. With Cruikshank's Illustrations. 4 vols. 3s. 6d each.

Smyth's Lectures on Modern History. 2 vols. 3s. 6d. each.

Socrates' Ecclesiastical History. 5s.

Sophocles. Trans. by E. P. Coleridge, B.A. 5s.

Southey's Life of Nelson. 5s.

—— Life of Wesley. 5s.

—— Life & Letters. (John Dennis) 3s. 6d.

Sozomen's Ecclesiastical History. 5s.

Spinoza's Chief Works. Trans. by R. H. M. Elwes. 2 vols. 5s. each.

Stanley's Dutch and Flemish Painters, 5s.

Starling's Noble Deeds of Women. 5s.

Staunton's Chess Players' Handbook. 5s. Chess Praxis. 5s. Chess Players' Companion. 5s. Chess Tournament of 1851. 5s.

Stöckhardt's Experimental Chemistry. (Heaton.) 5s.

Strabo's Geography. Trans. by Falconer and Hamilton. 3 vols. 5s. each.

Strickland's Queens of England. 6 vols. 5s. each. Mary Queen of Scots. 2 vols. 5s. each. Tudor and Stuart Princesses. 5s.

Stuart & Revett's Antiquities of Athens. 5s.

Suetonius' Lives of the Caesars and of the Grammarians. Thomson's trans. revised by T. Forester. 5s.

Sully's Memoirs. Mrs. Lennox's trans. revised. 4 vols. 3s. 6d. each.

Tacitus. The Oxford trans. revised. 2 vols. 5s. each.

Tales of the Genii. Trans. by Sir. Charles Morell. 5s.

Tasso's Jerusalem Delivered. Trans. by J. H. Wiffen. 5s.

Taylor's Holy Living and Holy Dying. 3s. 6d.

Terence and Phædrus. Trans. by H. T. Riley. 5s.

Theocritus, Bion, Moschus, and Tyrtæus. Trans. by Rev. J. Banks. 5s.

Theodoret and Evagrius. 5s.

Thierry's Norman Conquest. Trans. by W. Hazlitt. 2 vols. 3s. 6d. each.

Thucydides. Trans by Rev. H. Dale. 2 vols. 3s. 6d. each.

—— Wheeler's Analysis and Summary of. 5s.

Trevelyan's Ladies in Parliament. 1s. and 1s. 6d.

Ulrici's Shakespeare's Dramatic Art. Trans. by L. Dora Schmitz. 2 vols. 3s. 6d. each.

Uncle Tom's Cabin. 3s. 6d.

Ure's Cotton Manufacture of Great Britain. 2 vols. 5s. each.

—— Philosophy of Manufacture. 7s. 6d.

Vasari's Lives of the Painters. Trans. by Mrs. Foster. 6 vols. 3s. 6d. each.

Virgil. Trans. by A. Hamilton Bryce, LL.D. 3s. 6d.

Voltaire's Tales. Trans. by R. B. Boswell. 3s. 6d.

Walton's Angler. 5s.

—— Lives. (A. H. Bullen.) 5s.

Waterloo Days. By C. A. Eaton. 1s. and 1s. 6d.

Wellington, Life of. By 'An Old Soldier.' 5s.

Werner's Templars in Cyprus. Trans. by E. A. M. Lewis. 3s. 6d.

Westropp's Handbook of Archæology. 5s.

Wheatley. On the Book of Common Prayer. 3s. 6d.

Wheeler's Dictionary of Noted Names of Fiction. 5s.

White's Natural History of Selborne. 5s.

Wieseler's Synopsis of the Gospels. 5s.

William of Malmesbury's Chronicle. 5s.

Wright's Dictionary of Obsolete and Provincial English. 2 vols. 5s. each.

Xenophon. Trans. by Rev. J. S. Watson and Rev. H. Dale. 3 vols. 5s. ea.

Young's Travels in France, 1787–89. (M. Betham-Edwards.) 3s. 6d.

—— Tour in Ireland, 1776–9. (A. W. Hutton.) 2 vols. 3s. 6d. each.

Yule-Tide Stories. (B. Thorpe.) 5s.

BELL'S ENGLISH CLASSICS.

A New Series. Edited for Use in Schools. With Introductions and Notes. Crown 8vo.

BROWNING'S STRAFFORD. Edited by E. H. Hickey. With Introduction by S. R. Gardiner, LL.D. 2s. 6d.

BURKE'S LETTERS ON A REGICIDE PEACE. I. and II. Edited by H. G. Keene, M.A., C.I.E. 3s. Sewed, 2s.

BYRON'S CHILDE HAROLD. Edited by H. G. Keene, M.A., C.I.E., Author of a ' Manual of French Literature,' &c. 3s. 6d. Also Cantos I. and II. separately. Sewed, 1s. 9d.

BYRON'S SIEGE OF CORINTH. Edited by P. Hordern, late Director of Public Instruction in Burma. 1s. 6d. Sewed, 1s.

CHAUCER, SELECTIONS FROM. Edited by J. B. Bilderbeck, M.A., Professor of English Literature, Presidency College, Madras. [*Preparing.*

DE QUINCEY'S REVOLT OF THE TARTARS and THE ENGLISH MAIL COACH. Edited by C. M. Barrow, M.A., Principal of Victoria College, Palghât, and Mark Hunter, B.A.

DE QUINCEY'S OPIUM EATER. Edited by Mark Hunter, B.A.
[*In the press.*

GOLDSMITH'S SHE STOOPS TO CONQUER and THE GOOD-NATURED MAN. Edited by K. Deighton. Each, 2s. cloth. Sewed, 1s. 6d. Or together. Sewed 2s. 6d.

IRVING'S SKETCH-BOOK. Edited by R. G. Oxenham, M.A. Sewed, 1s. 6d.

JOHNSON'S LIFE OF ADDISON. Edited by F. Ryland, M.A., Author of 'The Students' Handbook of Psychology,' &c. 2s. 6d.

JOHNSON'S LIFE OF SWIFT. Edited by F. Ryland, M.A. 2s.

JOHNSON'S LIFE OF POPE. Edited by F. Ryland, M.A. 2s. 6d.

JOHNSON'S LIFE OF MILTON. Edited by F. Ryland, M.A. 2s.

JOHNSON'S LIFE OF DRYDEN. Edited by F. Ryland, M.A. 2s. 6d.
LIVES OF MILTON AND DRYDEN. Together. Sewed, 2s. 6d.
LIVES OF POPE AND SWIFT. Together. Sewed, 2s. 6d.

LAMB'S ESSAYS. Selected and Edited by K. Deighton, late Principal of Agra College. 3s. Sewed, 2s.

LONGFELLOW'S EVANGELINE. Edited by M. T. Quinn, M.A.
[*Preparing.*

MACAULAY'S LAYS OF ANCIENT ROME. Edited by P. Hordern. 2s. 6d. Sewed, 1s. 9d.

MACAULAY'S ESSAY ON CLIVE. Edited by C. M. Barrow, M.A. A New and Revised Edition. 2s. ; sewed, 1s. 6d.

MASSINGER'S A NEW WAY TO PAY OLD DEBTS. Edited by K. Deighton. 3s. Sewed, 2s.

MILTON'S PARADISE REGAINED. Edited by K. Deighton. 2s. 6d. Sewed, 1s. 9d.

MILTON'S PARADISE LOST. Books III. and IV. Edited by R. G. Oxenham, M.A., Principal of Elphinstone College, Bombay. Sewed 1s. 6d., cloth 2s. or Books III. and IV. separately 10d. each.

POPE, SELECTIONS FROM. Containing Essays on Criticism, Rape of the Lock, Temple of Fame, Windsor Forest. Edited by K. Deighton. 2s. 6d. Sewed, 1s. 9d.

SHAKESPEARE'S JULIUS CÆSAR. Edited by T. Duff Barnett, B.A. Lond. 2s. (The Notes, &c., separately, paper, 1s.)

SHAKESPEARE'S THE TEMPEST. Edited by T. Duff Barnett, B.A. Lond. 2s. (The Notes, &c., separately, paper, 1s.)

SHAKESPEARE'S MERCHANT OF VENICE. Edited by T. Duff Barnett, B.A. Lond. 2s. (The Notes, &c., separately, paper, 1s.)

THE ALL-ENGLAND SERIES.

HANDBOOKS OF ATHLETIC GAMES.

The only Series issued at a moderate price, by Writers who are in the first rank in their respective departments.

'The best and most reliable brief descriptions of athletic sports and games yet published.'
Morning Post.

Small 8vo, cloth, Illustrated. Price 1s. each.

Cricket. By the Hon. and Rev. E. LYTTELTON.

Lawn Tennis. By H. W. W. WILBERFORCE. With a Chapter for Ladies, by Mrs. HILLYARD.

Tennis and Rackets and Fives. By JULIAN MARSHALL, Major J. SPENS, and Rev. J. A. ARNAN TAIT.

Golf. By W. T. LINSKILL.

Rowing and Sculling. By W. B. WOODGATE.

Sailing. By E. F. KNIGHT. Double vol. 2s.

Swimming. By MARTIN and J. RACSTER COBBETT.

Canoeing. By J. D. HAYWARD, M.D. Double vol. 2s.

Camping Out. By A. A. MAC-DONELL, M.A. Double vol. 2s.

Mountaineering. By CLAUDE WILSON, M.D. With Illustrations by Ellis Carr. Double vol. 2s.

Athletics. By H. H. GRIFFIN.

Riding. A Handbook to Practical Horsemanship. By W. A. KERR, V.C. Double vol. 2s.

Riding for Ladies. By W. A. KERR, V.C.

Dancing. By EDWARD SCOTT. Double vol. 2s.

Cycling. By H. H. GRIFFIN, L.A.C., N.C.U., C.T.C. With a Chapter for Ladies, by Miss L. C. DAVIDSON.

Boxing. By R. G. ALLANSON-WINN. With Prefatory Note by Bat Mullins.

Wrestling. By WALTER ARMSTRONG ('Cross-buttocker').

Fencing. By H. A. COLMORE DUNN.

Broadsword and Singlestick. By R. G. ALLANSON-WINN and C. PHILLIPPS-WOLLEY.

Gymnastics. By A. F. JENKIN. Double vol. 2s.

Indian Clubs. By A. F. JENKIN and G. T. B. COBBETT.

Football—Rugby Game. By HARRY VASSAL.

Football—Association Game. By C. W. ALCOCK.

Hockey. By F. S. CRESWELL. (In Paper Cover, 6d.)

Skating. By DOUGLAS ADAMS. With a Chapter for Ladies, by Miss L. CHEETHAM, and a Chapter on Speed Skating, by a Fen Skater. Double vol. 2s.

Baseball. By NEWTON CRANE.

Rounders, Bowls, Quoits, Curling, Skittles, &c. By J. M. WALKER and C. C. MOTT.

THE CLUB SERIES OF CARD AND TABLE GAMES.

Small 8vo, cloth, Illustrated. Price 1s. each.

Whist. By Dr. WM. POLE, F.R.S.

Solo Whist. By ROBERT F. GREEN.

Billiards. By Major-Gen. A. W. DRAYSON, F.R.A.S. With a Preface by W. J. PEALL.

Chess. By ROBERT F. GREEN.

Chess Openings. By ISIDOR GUNSBERG.

The Two-Move Chess Problem. By B. G. LAWS.

Draughts and Backgammon. By 'BERKELEY.'

Reversi and Go Bang. By 'BERKELEY.'

Dominoes and Solitaire. By 'BERKELEY.'

Bézique and Cribbage. By 'BERKELEY.'

Écarté and Euchre. By 'BERKELEY.'

Piquet and Rubicon Piquet. By 'BERKELEY.'

Skat. By LOUIS DIEHL.

Round Games. By BAXTER-WRAY.

Card Tricks and Puzzles. By 'BERKELEY' and T. B. ROWLAND.

THE ALDINE EDITION

OF THE

BRITISH POETS.

'This excellent edition of the English classics, with their complete texts and scholarly introductions, are something very different from the cheap volumes of extracts which are just now so much too common.'—*St. James's Gazette.*

'An excellent series. Small, handy, and complete.'—*Saturday Review.*

New Editions, fcap. 8vo. 2s. 6d. each net.

Akenside. Edited by Rev. A. Dyce.

Beattie. Edited by Rev. A. Dyce.

***Blake.** Edited by W. M. Rossetti.

***Burns.** Edited by G. A. Aitken. 3 vols.

Butler. Edited by R. B. Johnson. 2 vols.

Campbell. Edited by his son-in-law, the Rev. A. W. Hill. With Memoir by W. Allingham.

Chatterton. Edited by the Rev. W. W. Skeat, M.A. 2 vols.

Chaucer. Edited by Dr. R. Morris, with Memoir by Sir H. Nicolas. 6 vols.

Churchill. Edited by Jas. Hannay. 2 vols.

***Coleridge.** Edited by T. Ashe, B.A. 2 vols.

Collins. Edited by W. Moy Thomas.

Cowper. Edited by John Bruce, F.S.A. 3 vols.

Dryden. Edited by the Rev. R. Hooper, M.A. 5 vols.

Falconer. Edited by the Rev. J. Mitford.

Goldsmith. Edited by Austin Dobson.

***Gray.** Edited by J. Bradshaw, LL.D.

Herbert. Edited by the Rev. A. B. Grosart.

***Herrick.** Edited by George Saintsbury. 2 vols.

***Keats.** Edited by the late Lord Houghton.

Kirke White. Edited by J. Potter Briscoe. [*Preparing.*

Milton. Edited by Dr. Bradshaw. 3 vols.

Parnell. Edited by G. A. Aitken.

Pope. Edited by G. R. Dennis. With Memoir by John Dennis. 3 vols.

Prior. Edited by R. B. Johnson. 2 vols.

Raleigh and Wotton. With Selections from the Writings of other COURTLY POETS from 1540 to 1650. Edited by Ven. Archdeacon Hannah, D.C.L.

Rogers. Edited by Edward Bell, M.A.

Scott. Edited by John Dennis. 5 vols.

Shakespeare's Poems. Edited by Rev. A. Dyce.

Shelley. Edited by H. Buxton Forman. 5 vols.

Spenser. Edited by J. Payne Collier, 5 vols.

Surrey. Edited by J. Yeowell.

Swift. Edited by the Rev. J. Mitford. 3 vols.

Thomson. Edited by the Rev. D. C. Tovey. 2 vols. [*Preparing.*

Vaughan. Sacred Poems and Pious Ejaculations. Edited by the Rev. H. Lyte.

Wordsworth. Edited by Prof. Dowden. 7 vols.

Wyatt. Edited by J. Yeowell.

Young. Edited by the Rev. J. Mitford. 2 vols.

* These volumes may also be had bound in Irish linen, with design in gold on side and back by Gleeson White, and gilt top, 3s. 6d. each net.

www.ingramcontent.com/pod-product-compliance
Lightning Source LLC
Chambersburg PA
CBHW032307280326
41932CB00009B/729